THE ARTS, ARTISTS
AND THINKERS

Dancing or writing poetry can be a religious activity, even a religion in itself. Art can be a law to itself. How is it compatible with a whole view of life? How can it be explained positively or religiously? What is the place of the Arts in human life? These were the questions put to those who took part in this symposium held at Downside in 1957.

Artists with Christian beliefs were invited to say how their art fitted in to their vision of life. Historians were invited to place the discussion historically. Critics, a neurologist and a psycho-therapist were invited to give their assessment of artistic achievement and activity. Philosophers and theologians were invited to give an insight into this material. This book includes all the papers read, and one not read, at the meeting which occupied a week. They are introduced by the editor who sometimes adds a note about the discussions. This is the second symposium in a series of which the first was entitled *The Springs of Morality*.

The Springs of Morality (Papers of the first symposium in this series). *Pub. by Burns Oates.*

Also by John M. Todd

John Wesley and the Catholic Church. *Pub. by Hodder and Stoughton*

Catholicism and the Ecumenical Movement.

The Arts, Artists and Thinkers

AN INQUIRY INTO THE PLACE OF
THE ARTS IN HUMAN LIFE

A SYMPOSIUM EDITED BY JOHN M. TODD

LONGMANS, GREEN AND CO
LONDON · NEW YORK · TORONTO

LONGMANS, GREEN AND CO LTD
6 & 7 CLIFFORD STREET LONDON W1
THIBAULT HOUSE THIBAULT SQUARE CAPE TOWN
605–611 LONSDALE STREET MELBOURNE C1

LONGMANS, GREEN AND CO INC
55 FIFTH AVENUE NEW YORK 3

LONGMANS, GREEN AND CO
20 CRANFIELD ROAD TORONTO 16

ORIENT LONGMANS PRIVATE LTD
CALCUTTA BOMBAY MADRAS
DELHI HYDERABAD DACCA

First Published 1958

Made and printed in Great Britain by
William Clowes and Sons, Limited, London and Beccles

Contents

INTRODUCTORY

PART I

HISTORIANS LOOKING AT THE ARTS

PART II

THE WITNESS OF THE ARTISTS

v

Part III

CRITICIZING THE ARTS

Part IV

PHILOSOPHIZING ABOUT THE ARTS

Plates

between pages 144 and 145

Editor's Note

THIS volume is formally introduced in its first chapter. My task is to thank all those who have collaborated with me in assembling the materials and making the symposium possible.

First, I must thank the Abbot and Monks of Downside Abbey who so kindly welcomed us and our meetings. Secondly, I must thank all the contributors for bearing so patiently with my requests. I must thank them also for their choice of the illustrations. Lastly, I must thank the other members of the sponsoring committee for their co-operation and advice. Together we planned the symposium itself; it is a joint achievement, and I am only the editorial executive, though for this editorial work I am alone answerable.

The reader is asked to treat the notes on the discussions, printed after some of the papers, with a certain tolerance. These selections from the discussions have been included to provide some idea of the exchanges between the authors and to point the nature of the volume as work in progress.

For the record, the committee for whom I have acted as secretary and editor is composed as follows: R. F. Trevett (Chairman), John Coulson, Hugh Dinwiddy, Eric John, Dom Sebastian Moore, Dom Ralph Russell, Roger Sharrock, Lancelot Sheppard, and myself. The present volume, as will be clear from Chapter 1, is the second in a series of communications.

J. M. T.

ACKNOWLEDGEMENTS

We are indebted to the following for permission to quote copyright material:

Messrs. Faber & Faber Ltd. and Messrs. Harcourt, Brace & Co., New York, for extracts from *Four Quartets* and *Family Reunion* both by T. S. Eliot; *The Observer* for an extract from an article on 'Superman', which appeared in the 3rd March 1957 issue of that paper; Harvard University Press for an extract from *Composer's World* by Paul Hindemith; Messrs. Routledge & Kegan Paul Ltd. for extracts from *Theory of Beauty* and *Aesthetics and Criticism* both by Harold Osborne; Messrs. Sheed & Ward Ltd. and Messrs. Sheed & Ward Inc. for an extract from *The Confessions of St. Augustine* translated by F. J. Sheed, Copyright 1943, Sheed & Ward Inc., New York.

INTRODUCTORY

1. The Symposium

REGINALD F. TREVETT

THIS book is the record of the second Symposium held at Down-side. Readers of its predecessor *The Springs of Morality* will remember that in the introductory chapter it was explained that the gathering from which the book had issued was itself the result of the activity of a small group of Christians in the West Country. This group has continued to meet regularly and the present volume, like the former, contains the papers read during a Symposium at which, once again, a larger number of men and women met to communicate to one another their experiences and thoughts, this time upon the arts and their place in human life.

The subject of the arts was chosen because it presents a series of baffling problems and impinges directly and sometimes tragically upon the lives of all of us. Most people feel reasonably certain that they know what morality is and what it involves by way of conduct both personal and social. Few people on the other hand, at least if pressed, would be willing to state any firm convictions concerning art in general—if there is such a thing—or the arts in particular. Ethics may still offer food for thought to the philosopher or theologian, but 'the man in the street' has his idea of right and wrong even if he is hard put to it at times to say whether any given action is one or the other. The problems of art, however, are as mysterious to the general public as to the thinker. True, modern education has apparently taught us all to consider ourselves able to sit in judgment upon individual works of art, although our criterion may be no more than that implied in the well-worn *boutade*: 'I may know nothing about art, but I

I

know what I like.' This superficial attitude to a fundamental human activity clearly will not do. The matter of man the artist needs looking into.

The first question that faced us in this task was that of deciding what end we should attempt to pursue. So much has been said and written about art, particularly in the last two or three centuries that the whole terrain seemed to bristle with a hundred contradictory theories. On the other hand, whereas the great thinkers of the past had devoted much of their thought to metaphysics, ethics and other disciplines of the mind, the amount of attention devoted to what we may term a philosophy of art was in comparison very small. We could not hope, obviously enough, to make up for this deficiency, if deficiency it is, in the course of a few days of discussion. All that we could attempt to do was to investigate some of the questions and suggest in what direction the answers might possibly lie. It is therefore essential for the reader to grasp at the start that this could not and does not pretend to be an authoritative book. It is simply an inquiry into a vital matter and—we hope—an honest inquiry.

Our second problem was that of method. Rightly or wrongly, we decided on the following course. The opening section of the inquiry would consist of a summary survey of a few of the historical conditions under which the arts have flourished. We had perforce to limit and to limit severely this excursion into the past. Its purpose was merely to set the rest of the argument in some sort of perspective. When this had been achieved, however sketchily, we could pass on to our next section. Here, it was felt, we should call in those who are engaged in the practice of one or other of the arts. We would ask them to describe as clearly as they could their experiences in either the creation or the creative interpretation of works of art. We hoped thus to be able to obtain some light on the mysterious process by which such works are generated. We were well enough aware of the fact that the artist's normal means of expression is the technique of his own art and that to ask him to translate into linguistic terms an experience which must be in many ways as mysterious to him as to us, was to set him a task for which he might well feel ill-equipped. Yet this was to be a symposium. Those who were to hear the paper read were also to discuss it with the reader and with one another. Between us, any defects due to the artist's change of medium might thus be remedied.

Our artist contributors will, we hope, forgive us if we say that, in one sense, their experience was intended to be the raw material of the whole inquiry. From that experience we would pass to our third section. We would attempt to appraise the arts of which each of our artists was an exponent. This would lead us to a more general consideration of language, music, the dance, and the visual arts. It would also raise the question of the physiology and psychology of perception and emotion, both of which are of obvious relevance. Once we had begun to tie together the ends of the inquiry in this way and in however rough and ready a fashion, we could approach our final stage of inquiry and ask the logical, metaphysical and theological questions to which the rest of the argument would have led us.

It is obvious that any Christian thinker will owe much to the past; likely enough he will be indebted amongst others to St. Thomas Aquinas. One could note, in this volume, that the position taken up by the artists is almost without exception in line with St. Thomas's own common sense; they describe themselves as craftsmen making things, or, to use language nearer to St. Thomas, artefacts. It could be noted that amongst our philosophers and theologians, one criticizes the aesthetic theories of philosophers commonly referred to as neo-scholastics, whilst another finds his inspiration in the Dominican mysticism which was in some sense a fruit of St. Thomas's thought. But to attempt to add all this up to some kind of party line or a priori assumption would be an error. The organizers of the symposium had no axes to grind. This is not to lay claim to some uncommitted god-like detachment, but simply to say that the symposium was an inquiry undertaken by a group of people whose attachment to each other has nothing at all to do with divisions in the schools.

Different readers will naturally look for different things in a

book of this kind and upon this subject. It is no business of ours
to tell them what they ought to think and how they should use
what they are reading. Yet, in order that they may be thoroughly
conversant with the evolution of the symposium in which they
are being asked to play a part—*post factum* though it has to be—we
shall conclude this opening chapter with a list of the questions
which were always at the back of our minds and which, each in
its turn, came to the forefront of our discussion.

Are we raising any new questions? Are we discovering any
possible answers to old ones? Are we making a thorough and
honest survey of the ground? Have we thrown any light on what
is meant by (a) the useful, (b) the beautiful, (c) their distinctions
—if any—in theory and in practice? Are we any nearer to discovering the origin and purpose or direction of a work of art? Are
we yet able to define aesthetic pleasure in such a way as to
distinguish it from other forms of pleasure? Has neurology or
psychology anything to say which is relevant to this last question?
Have our artists in fact told us anything we did not already know
or helped us to throw a little light upon the mysteries with which
we are confronted? How far have they and we been impeded by
the inevitable limitations of language or by the emotional overtones
of the words we have been using? How far can a work of art have
a 'meaning'? Is 'Art' an umbrella word or has it a true general
sense that can be applied to any form of art? Is a philosophy of art
possible? if not, why not? if so, what is its basis and how can we
formulate it? Can a work of art be unintelligible? And finally,
what is the place of the artist's creative act in the process of
cosmic creation? What is his relation, as an artist, to the creative
act of God?

As we have already said, we have not been so rash as to provide
glib answers to these questions. We would ask the reader to
imitate us at least in this.

2. The Freedom of the Imagination

ALAN PRYCE-JONES

Mr. Alan Pryce-Jones, Editor of The Times Literary Supplement, *opened the symposium with this paper on the freedom of the imagination, introducing us to our central topic, the place of the arts in human life.*

It is a large subject which I am going to discuss in these pages, and one, moreover, upon which most people feel very strongly. Briefly, I want to talk about the desirability of allowing total freedom to the imagination as it is displayed in the arts; or, if some check upon total freedom seems necessary, to discuss what check there should be, and where a line ought to be drawn between what is permissible and what is not.

The subject is not made easier by the fact that, whatever we may think of it, the imagination *is* free: that is to say, there is no possible means of checking it at its moment of creation. Later, perhaps, we can show different degrees of severity to the product of the imagination; but while the creative faculty is at work it can only be its own censor. So we shall have to consider, however cursorily, the nature of the creative temperament, and the extent to which that can be made the excuse for different elements of personal imperfection.

I confess that my first thought, when I began to think of these matters at all, was that all checks, in principle, were bad. A man decides to write, to paint, to build, to compose music. Very well, then: let him show what he has to offer. And let no one else presume to tell him that he ought to have tackled his subject differently. *Ought*: that is the important word. For obviously the critic can legitimately point out to him where, in the light of his own intentions, he has succeeded or failed. But to say that he ought to do one thing rather than another; to invoke a moral imperative of some kind: that at first seemed to me quite outside the critic's province.

On reflection, I am not so sure. And I am not thinking chiefly of such matters as literature which may corrupt by obscenity or suggestion, or objects similarly undesirable, or propaganda aimed at troubling the peace of the state. There will always be custodians of decency who will jump to the defence of the supposed inno-cent: indeed, they will probably jump with rather too much alacrity. What deserves much closer examination are those uses of the imagination which require freedom of another kind: freedom to experiment, freedom to break with all accepted conventions, even freedom to be absurd.

Take, for instance, the question of architecture. I have come at random on an article in that incomparable reference-book, *Der Grosse Herder*: a short article copiously illustrated, on modern church-building. It shows a good many churches which would cause surprise to the builders of Chartres or Cologne, and it put me in mind of one or two unconventional churches I had seen myself in the last few years—especially Niemeyer's church at Pampulha in Brazil, and Matisse's Dominican chapel in Vence, and the plans for a new cathedral at Coventry.

What do people really think of these surprising buildings? We know what the bishop thought in Brazil, for he refused to con-secrate the church at all. But how about the ordinary worshipper or visitor? Is he stimulated? Does he feel that the human spirit is undergoing a stage of renewal, that the architect has had the courage to be true to himself; has turned his back on stale copies of past masterpieces; has thought out afresh the idea 'church', and clothed it in an appropriately new material conception?

I rather doubt that he does any of these things. Most people are frightened by the unfamiliar, and it could be argued that the last place to awaken unnecessary fright in should be a church. I very well remember—to press this point—my own reaction on going to Matisse's chapel in Vence. There were a good many cars in front of the door, and several autocars as well. Inside, the visitors were jammed into a narrow entrance, and once within the precincts kept moving by harassed nuns. It is hardly fair to blame the visitors upon Matisse, yet they were the kind of visitor which seems inseparable from such places: rather fat men in linen trousers, with a camera slung over the shoulder, girls carrying a towel or a picnic basket—for it was a hot day, and the Mediterranean lies just below Vence—and very cross children. They had to be reminded that they must not take photographs, nor chatter, nor linger; and since they had come entirely from curiosity, and therefore were hoping for the building to be as odd as possible, they became rather surly by the time they reached the fresh air again.

Well, you might say that in time the crowds will dwindle away, and the building turn to its proper conventual purpose. Or you might wonder whether the design of the chapel possesses that quality of conviction, of repose, which will establish it among the successful buildings of the twentieth century. Personally, I find it far more like a bathroom than a church; it seems to me a place without a spirit of place: a mere collection of tiles and glass. But surely any such objection must arise because it is not a very good modern building. There can be nothing wrong with the attempt to build churches in a contemporary style. And then at once further doubts assail us. Perhaps it *is* a mistake to try to make a link between Christian action and some kinds of modern architecture or decoration; perhaps they are really too different in kind to be brought together even by a Matisse or a Niemeyer.

It cannot be the oddness which shocks. After all, some very strange buildings have been designed in the past, which have now passed into the ordinary currency of architecture: the work of Gaudí in Barcelona, or—earlier still—the designs of Ledoux in eighteenth-century France. We may smile indulgently but we accept these curiosities, whereas when Gropius or Le Corbusier puts up a building we use entirely different standards of appreciation. I believe it is because we have very little affection for our own time, and so we conceive its buildings almost exclusively in terms of function. The Gothic and the classical we can love, because we have long-standing associations with them. The absolutely contemporary, however, we associate with power-stations and factories, towering blocks of offices and railway termini. Now, none of these buildings is expected to have a heart of its own, none of them is expected to do more than organize efficiency. Perhaps, then, we have already here one limiting factor in the freedom of the imagination. Perhaps it is a mistake to build a church in an idiom which might equally well serve for a bus-station.

I don't want to think this, for the practical deductions from such a conclusion are not encouraging. What: here we are in 1957, in the world of this very moment, and we cannot stimulate the architect's imagination so that it can turn with equal ease to all the needs of the moment, whether they be office-buildings or cathedrals? So we are to have one province of art stuck in the past, are we, and to use quite different sets of visual response for sacred and for secular constructions?

No, that cannot be right. It may be useful to guide the artist to some extent, but it cannot possibly be wise to hamper him with a purely artificial caprice of convention. And this brings us, I think, a little closer to the centre of our subject. I am thinking of that word 'convention'. For there is an enemy there of which any creator, in any art, has to be anxiously aware.

It is assumed, isn't it, that the imagination cannot be other than free? On the other hand, with a great many people, that freedom is immediately bartered for a convention. I remember, for instance, near relations of my own, now dead: clever, literate people, but brought up in the unadventurous atmosphere of a large country-house in England some sixty or seventy years ago. They went into politics or into the army, they even wrote books. But always they saw things as they had been taught to see them, as their father had seen them, that is. And so I very well remember their puzzled distress, in later life, when they came up against phenomena like the pictures of Picasso or the music of Stravinsky. The conventions were not being observed, and they could not imagine pictures being painted or music composed except in the convention with which they were familiar. Music meant something German—preferably by Schumann or Mendelssohn; painting meant something Dutch in one mood and Italian in another. It would never have occurred to them to think out an expression of the arts for themselves, just as the verses they sometimes scribbled for their own amusement were carefully modelled on Shelley and Tennyson. The arts, in fact, were like physical exercise. There was one approved way of carrying them on, and it could be learned by practice and imitation. One does not invent a fresh way of swimming or holding a golf-club; similarly, one does not invent a new way of writing poetry, they might have reasoned.

Now, if the imagination is to be effectively free, it must dispense at once with this idea of a necessary convention. That is why I should be very reluctant to see any kind of check imposed on mere novelty. It is not the fact of novelty which can possibly be wrong, but the inapposite kind of novelty chosen by an inexpert artist. If we look, therefore, at a great deal of the new art produced in this century, and if we don't like it, we must be careful to state the reasons for our dislike sensibly. Otherwise we shall find ourselves implying that the great poets of the nineteenth century in England, let us say, fixed the art of poetry once for all, or that the school of Paris has set an absolute standard of painting.

For the imagination to profit by its freedom it must cultivate a quality which I can only call tact—a quality better defined by its absence than by its presence. The greatest practitioners of the imagination possess it by instinct. A Goethe, a Stendhal, a Keats— to take three very different writers working on very different scales—had that kind of tact. They could stop their imagination flying off after some fancy. Mozart among musicians, Degas among painters, spring to my mind—not because they are in any way alike, but because they both possessed that quality of tact with which to check an exuberant imagination. It means that no new subject, no new treatment, will be dismissed because it is new; but that the artist will know infallibly just how far he can go in imposing his vision on other people. Even outrage can benefit by this quality of tact. Picasso, say, is often out to shock; in his art he tries to bring off something like a scream, a shout of defiance or protest. If you notice, he sometimes succeeds and sometimes fails—just because, for all his dazzling skill, he has not a reliably sure tact in stating his case. In the same way, the surrealists generally failed to make any very deep impression. Their imagination proliferated without bearing either fruit or flower; it was too free to keep its strength.

These considerations impose another, and a more important, check on the imagination. For they mean that the imagination must learn not only tact but also discrimination. Creative people have to learn by experience that there are certain things which are just not worth the trouble of creating, even if they have not been done before. I spoke of the architect Ledoux. Now Ledoux designed a building which was perfectly spherical, like a ball, and another which was pyramidal. I need not say that they remained designs only. Plans of the same quite useless kind, however, are still being drawn up in all the arts all the time.

There is a poet in New York who adds a comma after every single word, regardless of sense or syntax. There are painters who merely drop paint from a height on to canvas, leaving it to form its own patterns. There is nothing wrong in such pastimes, of course, but it can do no harm to point out that they are a deplorable waste of time—just as a great number of the experiments which made the 1920s so exciting a decade in the arts have turned out to be a waste of time.

At this point, I suppose, it is apposite to mention James Joyce, and perhaps in the same breath Ezra Pound, as obvious examples of what can be done in prose and in verse by allowing the imagination an unchecked rein. A great quantity has been written about both of them; they have been decried as evil, as mad, as decadent. They have been exalted as saints of art, as illuminati, as liberators of the word, as innovators who have pushed back the frontiers of communication for the delight of their readers. I wonder, though, if they are any of those things. Is Joyce really much more than a very complicated, very private, very carefully constructed joke—a joke which—like all good jokes—runs over into poetry and ribaldry from time to time? And is Pound, at least when he is writing verse, much more than an amusingly industrious taker of notes: lyrical notes some of them, but some of them, too, indecipherably wrapped in shorthand? And does it really justify a lifetime to offer no more than that? You see, I do not believe that more than a handful of people have ever really *read* either Joyce or Pound. Read in them, yes: the same passages are always being quoted with a foreseeable approval or irritation. But for a book to be hermetic—truly hermetic—is a contradiction in terms. And once the imagination is locked away among its own secrets, as it is in such books as *Finnegans Wake* and Pound's *Cantos*, it evaporates. Nobody, I believe, will ever struggle with the real difficulties of writers such as these except in a spirit of puzzle-solving which is quite alien to the spirit of literature.

It looks, then, as if the imagination, by asserting its freedom too strongly, is in danger of gaining nothing by it. Nothing is so quickly perceived, in any form of art, as the absence of a sense of direction. And to be totally free is to invite that absence, unless freedom is canalized in a vocation freely chosen. In that sense, perhaps Joyce's experiments were worth attempting—for Joyce; and Pound's—for Pound. But I wonder if a more balanced view might not be to consider both as monuments of misplaced industry. For is it really worth spending years raising the status of the pun (Joyce's ultimate achievement) or gluing together in eighty or ninety cantos fragments from the literature of the whole world? And can we be sure that what they have done is what in fact they tried to do, and not something quite different?

A much more exciting result is achieved, I think, when the imagination is fired by something outside itself—something to which it chooses to be ancillary. The most obvious case, perhaps, is Shakespeare's: when we remember that Shakespeare was a practical commercial dramatist who happened to possess, as well as the trick of writing plays, a vaulting imagination which could be used to make his plays immortal. Not that his imagination was utterly free. Its use was conditioned by the difficult political situation of the time, by the needs of the theatre, by a very human respect for his audience. One never feels that Shakespeare is saying to us, 'You are to take what I give you and like it.' No, he wins us to his side, he harnesses his imagination to the effect he wishes us to undergo. And I believe you will generally find, in any of the arts, that the more strictly the imagination is controlled, with an end in view, the more powerful are its operations. I cannot for instance conceive that a highly imaginative painter like El Greco felt himself perfectly free to indulge his imagination as the whim took him. Must not his calculated distortions of the human frame have been as carefully designed to meet a special need of vision as the shaped columns of the Parthenon? And in the music of Berlioz—an imaginative man if ever there was one—do we not always feel that he is using his imagination to capture a music which already exists ideally? He is not, that is to say, seeing how far he can go in the pursuit of possible effects: it is he who controls the imagination, not it him.

So that it comes to look as if the imagination, whether free or not, must be considered as a means rather than an end. That is, it must not be encouraged to get above itself, to delight in its own perfectibility at the expense of other elements of personality. It must be kept in focus as one part, and no more, of the creative temperament.

That temperament says, in effect, 'I require to make a house, or a book, or a picture, or a symphony.' In order to do any of these things it will need much more than imagination, and to begin with there can be no harm in letting the imagination soar away as high as it can reach. That will leave room for the organizing faculties to get to work, and for some relation to be established between supply and demand. Then the imagination has to be hauled back, like a balloon on its string. It has to take the concrete problem in hand, and compose a plan for the organizing faculties to carry out. In fact, whether it likes it or not, it already finds itself far from free.

Here I think there are two considerations to remember. There is the freedom of the imagination as it affects the creator, and there is the freedom of the imagination as it affects the rest of the world. It has not taken much thought to discover that so far as the creative temperament goes the imagination is never free for long, unless it is to dissolve into a dream. Creation is a practical process, and one which is never for long devoted to producing what nobody wants. Naturally the imagination is free to invent gibberish in place of poetry, to build houses which can't stand up, or to compose symphonies equally unbearable to eye and ear. But it won't go on doing so for any length of time. However reluctantly, it will give up its freedom in order to help make something for which there is a clear demand.

Now, it is at this point that the practical question of freedom arises. For naturally some of the clear demands made by the world are going to be unacceptable. For example, a great many people demand very bad books; they like hideous pictures better than good ones, and saccharine music rather than a masterpiece. In fact, very few people indeed have any feeling for quality in anything. At one level, the response of the imagination is clear. There is no point in giving people fresh versions of Pascal and Dante if what they want is a good murder story or a sentimental ballad. But then there is a more sinister level. Suppose the public—or a part of it—wants to be gratified by suggestions of cruelty, lust, whatever evil you like to name. How is the imagination at this point to be saved from itself?

Of course, here and there in the world, there are various kinds of censorship, and these, to English people, are always thought very shocking. I myself have never quite been able to see why. After all, when I was a small child my parents used to put books which they thought too morbidly exciting or frightening, on top of a wardrobe out of my reach. A censorship does no more than hide certain things out of our reach all through life. And I am not so sure that the result is very different from what happened in my childhood. I know that I nearly always managed to get the books down sooner or later, and probably thus managed to read quite a lot which otherwise I should never have known of. In the same way, the banning of a book turns us all into naughty children. We climb on chairs as soon as we are alone in order to taste an experience of which we might easily have remained for ever in ignorance. It is not one of the most sensible aspects of human activity.

Yet I do not complain of some kind of censorship—and I notice that most people, however sternly libertarian in their views, keep one or two categories apart in their minds, as being censorable. Naturally, they say, we cannot let such-and-such a book get into the hands of the young. Or, we cannot possibly allow the kind of bookshop to exist which deals in pornography under the counter. To go one step farther and define the terms used does not seem to be illiberal. Who are the young? What is pornography? Admittedly, neither question is very easy to answer, and admittedly any answer will lead to confusions of feeling. For instance, Shakespeare is a disgusting writer—in parts. And if we do not feel disgust, it is generally because we have lost the key to his jokes—or can only interpret them through an elaborate apparatus of learned notes which most readers will never take the trouble to look up. As for the young—some of the youngest people in mind that I know are (regrettably) of my own age. They have simply never grown up. And with all the corruption which exists in the world—the straightforward corruption which exists in daily life—it would seem odd to me, and possibly almost commendable, if they confined their excesses to reading, or looking at pictures.

The fact of the matter is that every imagination, if it functions at all, is naturally rebellious. It may not be up to anything harmful; but in any case it will not gladly admit the necessity of a check. Yet society, and indeed ordinary good sense, requires that some kind of check be imposed. In order to work, however, it must be voluntarily assumed. I can see no evidence that outside authority is ever strong enough to make its chosen checks fully operative. What happens in practice is that the thing checked is kept away from those who would in any case have no interest in it, and kept apart only for those who are most certain to be harmed.

What must be done, therefore, is to introduce certain changes into the relationship between the artist and society—changes which I can perhaps best suggest by going to a book written some years ago by Sir Kenneth Clark. It is called *The Gothic Revival*. He is discussing the work of the Camden Society—the university ecclesiological society which played an essential part in reviving the decorated style in English civil and religious building a little more than a century ago.

First, he talks of the theory which lay behind so much of this building, the theory that 'Good men build good buildings'; he quotes a passage to display the connexion between an artist's religion and his work.

His whole conduct of life [Sir Kenneth goes on] was no less important, not only 'the deeply religious habits' of the builders of old, but also 'the Hours, the cloister, the discipline, the obedience, resulted in their matchless works; while the worldliness, vanity, dissipation and patronage of our own architects issue in unvarying hopeless failure'. . . . Here, is the Ethical Fallacy in full sail; on a sea so accommodating a Symbolical Fallacy could be launched without risk.

For the Romantic movement which began at the end of the eighteenth century had taken away all fixed standards by which a work of art could be judged. I go on quoting:

The sensible old Johnsonian criticism was long ago discredited, and as Grecians retired before Goths in the battle of the styles, the magic light of authority faded from Vitruvius. Vitruvius had provided the world with the simplest of critical weapons—a set of rules; and when these lost their power the critic was forced to rely on his individual judgment, an exhausting and risky state of affairs. By 1840 the world was looking for a new set of rules, for some new authority to spare it the discomforts of thought. . . . [From a] babel of uncertain sound one voice rose, clear and firm—the voice of the Camden Society. The fact that they usually spoke of questions only accidentally concerned with architecture did not matter. They spoke confidently and they provided a set of definite rules: accept their values and it was once more possible to use the precious word *correct*.

It is at this point that the freedom of the imagination is likely to be imperilled. For of course there is no such thing as *correctness* in matters of imagination. Precious the word may be, and consoling—anyway to mediocre talents—it certainly is as well. But what we have to do nowadays is to give the imagination a more flexible guide. We have to teach it to look for the appropriate.

This may not seem a very ambitious thought, yet I believe it touches the heart of this question of freedom. How far is any work of art appropriate to its purpose? If it is, well and good. If it is not, its secondary virtues will not be strong enough to save it.

I spoke just now of Ezra Pound's *Cantos*. They are written, we know, by a man whose head is packed with learning—even if some of it is misleading—by a poet who has proved his high gifts elsewhere, by a planner perfectly capable of designing a long poem. Why, then, is it so hard to feel a sustained enthusiasm for these volumes? Simply, I believe, because Pound has not been able to balance his imagination by a corrective sense of what is appropriate and what is not. For one thing, his poem is exceedingly hard to read. I can imagine him saying, 'Why should it not be? Why should my imagination make things easy for yours? Why won't you do some hard work as well as I do?' Yet somehow I doubt very much if that is the way to write an epic, or a poetic commentary, or whatever you may define the *Cantos* to be. And again, smaller improprieties keep creeping in: breaks in the argument, harshnesses of opinion, ugly fancies—all cutting into what, in conception, is one of the outstanding long poems of our century. So much so that I wonder whether posterity may not totally neglect these cantos simply on grounds of unreadability. And if they do, it will be because Pound has let his imagination run too free. He has not checked it by any guiding concept of what is appropriate to his purpose and what is not.

This opens up another big set of questions. What exactly are the appropriate purposes for the imaginative nowadays? The questions have to be asked in our context, because clearly the freedom of the imagination is to be put.

There is the question of pleasure, for instance. Is that to be the governing factor in a writer's decisions: the pleasure, I mean, which he gives to others? Once upon a time it would have been so. I don't imagine that Dickens or Balzac or Wordsworth or Hugo set anything high above pleasure—even if the pleasure they had in view was that of communication. It is only in the last century, at most, that the purposes of writing have become so complicated. The agonies of a Mallarmé or (to a lesser extent) of a T. S. Eliot are quite new factors in art—just as the austerities of abstract painting or the mathematical music of Schönberg are new. Pleasure, in all this, has somehow flown out of the window; it has become slightly disreputable, whereas in all great periods of creation it has been, not the gratifying only of the imagination, but also the justifying element of attempting to create anything at all.

But in this puritanical age we distrust pleasure. It suggests triviality. And it is not hard to see why. For if we indulge our imagination too wilfully we shall allow no time for a faculty which has become, whether we like it or not, almost as important as the imagination: I mean, the faculty of criticism. New ideas are being hurled at us all the time. We are beset with possibilities, not only of good, but of extreme evil. Outrageous philosophies contend against established systems; and if we do not use our critical gifts we shall be the prey of every fancy which is put forward if only it be persuasive enough.

This means that the imagination has to submit to a certain limitation. It cannot risk displacing ordinary good sense while there is so little good sense at large in the world. I conceive, for instance, the imagination to be rather like the life of an old-fashioned country house—a large country house. It is a life which does not have to worry overmuch about money. There are departments in that life which are all admirably staffed and run. The inhabitants are good-mannered, if a trifle eccentric when they feel like it. The past joins neatly to the present, the future stretches ahead untroubled. But nowadays, of course, there is no such house intact. Troops have been billeted in it; the staff is reluctant or perhaps there is no staff. The inhabitants spend their

2

time thinking up new ways of paying their taxes, and their manners, in the anxiety of making both ends meet, have often become abominable. Scarcely the place, you will say, in which to sit and plan an epic poem or a complicated novel like *War and Peace*. Rather, a place in which to repress the imagination. However, it will not be repressed for long. Only, to be effective, it may have to seek new forms. A great many people, for instance, are wondering whether novels will not die away, whether stories will not in future be told on radio and television, and in films. Poetry, too, and the better sort of painting have reached a paradoxical state. The poet, for one, is not free to use his imagination in recreating the classical sonnet or the ode, and the painter is not free to see form as it was seen by Goya or Manet or Turner. Otherwise he will find that all he has made is a pastiche. For some reason or other, the imagination has become very much more personal than it used to be. It is not free to be anything else.

This brings us to the chief point I want to make: which is that all these questions about imagination and its freedom really come back to a very personal matter indeed. It is people we are discussing, not an abstract idea, and so, for the imagination to be given the right component of freedom, people—whether creators or absorbers—will have to assume a more exact sense of their responsibilities than it is usual to find among them.

Lest you fear that I am about to break into a sermon, let me quote a little from an intelligent and almost forgotten book, *The Gay Science*, by E. S. Dallas—a book almost a century old, the theme of which is an approach to a scientific theory of criticism:

Nobody tells us [he says] what the imagination really is, and how it happens that being, as some say, nothing at all, it plays an all-powerful part in human life. Driven to our own resources, we must see if we cannot give a clearer account of this wonder-working energy, and above all, cannot reconcile the philosophical analysis which reduces imagination to a shadow with the popular belief which gives it the empire of the mind. I propose this theory that the imagination or fantasy is not a special faculty but that it is a special function. It is a name given to the automatic action of the mind or any of its faculties to what may not unfitly be called the Hidden Soul. . . . For the most part this automatic action takes place unawares; and when we come to analyse the movement of thought we find that to be quite sure of our steps we are obliged very much to identify what is involuntary with what is unconscious.

In a later chapter he explains further:

The true artist recognises, however dimly, the existence within us of a double world of thought, and his object is, by subtle forms, tones, words, allusions, associations, to establish a connection with the unconscious hemisphere of the mind, and to make us feel a mysterious energy there in the hidden soul. For this purpose he doubtless makes use of the known. He paints what we have seen, he describes what we have heard; but his use of knowledge is ever to suggest something beyond knowledge. If he be merely dealing with the known and making it better known then it becomes necessary to ask wherein does his work differ from science? Through knowledge, through consciousness, the artist appeals to the unconscious part of us. The poet's words, the artist's touches, are electric; and we feel those words, and the shock of those touches, going through us in a way we cannot define, but always giving us a thrill of pleasure, awakening distant associations, and filling us with the sense of a mental possession beyond that of which we are daily and hourly conscious. Art is poetical in proportion as it has this power of appealing to what I may call the absent mind, as distinct from the present mind, on which falls the great glare of consciousness, and to which alone science appeals.

It follows from all this that when we speak of the imagination we are speaking of something which is potentially extremely dangerous. Hidden in the midst of our conscious life, the imagination, taking its strength from things in us of which we are hardly aware, can destroy us by unsettling our normal sense of balance. I need not insist upon this: you have only to recall names like those of Kleist, Poe, Rimbaud, Wilde, to see how disintegrating the imagination can be when it accepts no sanctions but its own. Yet equally obviously there are names which can be set against these: names like that of St. John of the Cross, Pascal, Kierkegaard, Péguy, where the imagination, directed by a sense of purpose, almost frighteningly reinforces the cutting edge of a personality working for good. And of course there are the myriads in between these extremes—now working for good and now for evil—the Keatses and the Goethes and the Baudelaires and the Unamunos—are they not equally manifestations of what Dallas calls the Hidden Soul?

If so—and I think it is so—there is only one way of making that Hidden Soul a good and useful thing. It must be trained. And by that I mean that it must be led to understand, and so to control, its own reflexes. If that is done effectively we need not worry too much about the freedom of the imagination, because the instinct of creation will be guided far more effectively than it can ever be by any exterior censor.

It will not, I hope, shrink from experiments, but it will quickly perceive which experiments are already proving a waste of time. And may not some such process of reintegrating the creative personality be just what is needed in order to give the imagination back the power which it has steadily been losing over the last century or so? For we have seen how writers and painters and architects and musicians have been getting out of touch with ordinary people. By insisting on their total freedom they have formed a little rebellious world of their own—a world so far apart from everyday reality that it has almost lost its audience, and so its power. I do not, of course, recommend a lowering of standards in order to reach a larger public; I am not thinking of such misleading simplicities as socialist realism, or the official art of those countries which try to turn all art into a means of propaganda. But in countries like our own in which the human personality is still given its high, and in some senses its absolute, place, I do not see why the imagination should not assume—freely and naturally—the task of thrilling ordinary people with a glimpse of the possibilities which lie within their range. That, after all, has always been the historic role of the imagination: from Homer to the middle of the nineteenth century. It is only very recently that any artist has wished to press his freedom to the point of excluding an audience for his work.

I am nearly at the end of what I have to say, and I should like to leave you on a Ruskinian note, were it not that Ruskin has fallen so far from fashion that his very name may awaken your apprehensions. Still, he had an idea—if in the end a confused idea—of order and seemliness in the connexions between art and life which it might be valuable to revive. I can construct no such idea out of my own head, but I can remind you that to the Christian and Catholic part of society a sense of order ought to come far more easily than to a harassed nineteenth-century Evangelical. If that order can only be real enough we need have no fear of misapplying our imagination, and we need anticipate no reductions of a freedom which will take care never to degenerate into licence.

I think my yardstick of the appropriate will be useful here. Anything can be said, any subjects raised, any adventure of the mind entered upon so long as the means are appropriate to the end, and that the end is one of which we can in conscience approve. And supposing the end is not merely permissible but actively desirable. Supposing Ruskin's preoccupation with beauty as an active principle can be revived, and harnessed to the daily duties of life as Ruskin conceived it, and fortified by all the new techniques which have come to the aid of the imagination since Ruskin's day: supposing all this, can we not hope to see at last that revival in the arts which has been awaited for so many years? The imagination has never been so rich with possibilities as now—possibilities which have scarcely been exploited at all, like television or—to take a more far-fetched example—the new skills of musique concrète. Free to use all that is new and good, and sensible enough to reject the second-hand and the second-rate, the reformed imagination of the future need have no reason to waste its energies developing an inferiority-complex at the thought of the past.

THE ARTIST'S PURPOSE

One of the first questions put to Mr. Pryce-Jones was how he would define the artist's purpose to which he had referred. Did he consider it to be a conscious purpose? This question arose from discussions in preparatory sessions in the preceding months during which a division was evident between those who insisted on the conscious meaning of a work of art as an integral part of it and those who considered that this conscious meaning did not inhere essentially in the work of art as such. The division could also be expressed by saying that the first group of people made no radical division between art and craft, whilst the second looked on a work of art as something which achieved a status over and beyond the craftsman's purposeful achievement. The second case is argued in Dom Illtyd Trethowan's paper, although this is incidental to his central theme. Mr. Eric John presents an opposite view. Other references to this discussion occur throughout the book, notably in the paper of the poet, Mr. Saunders Lewis.

Mr. Pryce-Jones considered that the artist's purpose is indeed conscious and that no radical distinction is possible between art and craft. He pointed out, however, that there is an element of the automatic in all work. Behind the conscious purpose there is and should be subconscious activity.

EZRA POUND AND JAMES JOYCE

Discussion about Pound and Joyce arising from passages in the paper showed that at least one person did read Pound at length and found him easier than Milton. The puns and inconsequence of these writers were also compared to similar effects of Latin writers in seventh-century England, when a treatise on virginity could quite happily break out into acrostics or into puns more complicated than Joyce's. This 'Aldhelmian' Latin had to be rejected in favour of Bede's Latin, but its historical justification might lie just here, in affording a necessary contrast. The influence of James Joyce on David Jones was shown; and there seemed to be little doubt that in a somewhat similar way, Joyce, if in himself a kind of cul-de-sac, yet had an immeasurable and vital influence for good on others.

I

HISTORIANS LOOKING
AT THE ARTS

3. The Origins of Christian Art

LILIAN GUNTON

A group of three papers witnessed to the place which the arts have had in European society at various times in the past. Miss Gunton, who has made a special study of catacomb art, described some of the principal themes of the Christian community of the first four centuries.

I WOULD state, as axiomatic, that no great art springs spontaneously into existence. On the contrary it must be the result of development: an expansion both of substance and of form coming to maturity within a framework of tradition faithfully though not slavishly maintained. Therefore it is not herein claimed that art which may correctly be called Christian was at its inception other than commonplace in form although it was indeed great in its capacity for growth, expanding as all true growth must do from the content with which it is animate.

The earliest Christian art was sepulchral, adorning the subterranean crypts. The cemeteries, or catacombs as they came to be called, were long narrow galleries in which the graves, called *loculi*, were cut into the walls. Opening from the galleries were rectangular *cubicula* and it is chiefly in these that the paintings are found. The classical style is evident in the earlier period while in the later Byzantine influence predominates. From contemporary pagan art the Christian painters borrowed freely for their purely decorative motifs: vases of flowers, garlands, trees, birds, ornamental heads representing the four seasons and geometrical designs filled the background. But the real subjects of their art were utterly different from those of the pagans. They were scenes and persons drawn from the Holy Scripture such as had never been depicted before and for which they *had to invent new forms*. That is an important point to remember. It is also to be borne in mind that as theirs was a sepulchral art it had to be in direct relation with the deceased whose tombs were to be adorned, and the themes chosen illustrated those fundamental dogmas of the Faith which in the mind of the believer led to eternal life: belief in the necessity of the sacraments of baptism and of the Holy Eucharist; in the divinity of Christ as revealed in his Incarnation and in his miracles; belief in the resurrection of the body; belief in the intercession of the saints. These dogmatic themes were not left to the individual interpretation of the artist. They were regulated by ecclesiastical authority and this explains the repeated use of the same subjects and their uniformity of presentation, characteristics which have been derided by super-ficial critics of art ignorant of Christian ideography and its skilful admixture of symbolism and realism.

In the initial stage we find decorative motifs interspersed with one or two biblical characters. In the most ancient part of the catacomb of Domitilla the prophet Daniel, wearing a short tunic, stands with arms extended in prayer upon a small mount on each side of which is a well-drawn lion. There is no suggestion of location, no subsidiary figure. In an adjacent *cubiculum* is a ceiling decorated with simple geometric designs having in the centre the idealized figure of Christ, the Good Shepherd, carrying the lost sheep upon his shoulders, the most popular of all the catacomb figures. Daniel in the lions' den, the Three Young Hebrews in the furnace, Susanna accused by the Elders, and similar incidents from the Old Testament, were introduced as types of the liberation from the danger of death by the direct intervention of God, symbolizing to the Christian the liberation of the soul of the deceased by Christ from spiritual death and the power of Satan. Thus they illustrated the prayers for the dead: 'Liberate, oh Lord, the soul of thy servant . . . as Thou didst liberate Daniel. . . .'

To turn now to the frescoes that depict the sacraments. For baptism there are both symbolic and actual examples. The principal symbols are Moses striking the Rock to bring forth the life-giving water; a fisherman with line or net; and the paralytic carrying his bed. For this last, Tertullian gives the explanation: 'As the angel troubled the waters of the pool of Siloam for the healing of physical deformity, so when God is invoked the Spirit descends from heaven and sanctifies the water and thus baptism purges the soul of its malady, sin.'

Of actual baptism there are two representations, that of Christ and that of a catechumen. The distinguishing features are, in the former, the presence of the Dove of the Holy Spirit and the raiment of St. John, who wears either the working-man's tunic, the *exomis*, or simply the loin-cloth. In the baptism of a catechumen the baptizer wears the long tunic and the pallium. In both cases the sacrament is administered by immersion, which was the rule then, and still is in the Eastern Church. In the crypts of Lucina, near the catacomb of St. Callistus by the Via Appia there are two communicating *cubicula* known to archaeologists as X and Y. Upon the communicating doorway there is the oldest representation of the baptism of Christ. St. John, wearing the *exomis*, clasps the hand of our Lord to assist him as he comes out from the river while the Dove descends from above. In all later examples Christ stands motionless in the water.

As in the practice of the early Church Holy Communion followed baptism, so in the frescoes we find the two sacraments in proximity. Upon the wall facing the entrance to *cubiculum* Y is a painting of major importance. To the right side and to the left is a large fish together with an osier basket containing loaves marked with a cross, and in the interior of each basket there is a glass chalice with red wine. According to most authorities there is here represented the two species of Holy Communion placed in considered connection with the mystical Fish, the Icthus, that symbolized Christ.

In the adjacent catacomb is a gallery from which open six consective *cubicula*, called by the guides 'the chapels of the sacraments'. In the second, Moses strikes the Rock whence flows the water from which a fisherman is drawing out a fish upon a line.

In the language of the Fathers the newly baptized were referred to as 'the little fishes born of the great Fish, Christ'. Upon the next wall is the baptism of a catechumen; and above, on the vault, is an altar-table supporting two loaves and a fish, while placed around the altar are seven baskets of bread. These baskets have reference to the fragments gathered up at Christ's command after the feeding of the multitude in the desert. In the next chapel there is a baptism of Christ in the Jordan between the symbols of the fisherman and the paralytic. Upon the opposite wall seven persons sit before a table spread with fish and bread, while the baskets stand in the foreground.

As to the fish and bread upon the table, such food had not of itself special significance and may be found in pagan banquets. In Syria fish was a regular food for the dead and in Babylonia fish-sacrifice was used two thousand years before the birth of Christ, so that it was not intrinsically a Christian symbol but was taken into Christian symbolism at an early date, probably first in Alexandria, and has so persisted throughout the centuries. It is therefore necessary to distinguish between those banquets which have Eucharistic significance and the banquets which were the funerary meals eaten at the tomb of the deceased on the anniversary of his death, a custom that continued for a considerable time in the Christian community and of which some seven examples are known in the catacombs. Until recent times archaeologists were inclined to see in these family banquets, in which the number of the persons participating and their attitudes vary, a symbol of the future joys of paradise, but today it is accepted that they are more literal in character. To sum up: the essential elements of the Eucharistic meal are the number, seven, of those present (seven being understood as a collective and not a literal number) and the presence of the baskets of bread upon the ground. In the third century a complementary scene to that of the miraculous feeding of the multitude in the wilderness was introduced in the action of Christ turning the water into wine at the marriage of Cana. Bordering the Via Labicana is one of the less-frequented catacombs, but one exceptionally rich in well-preserved frescoes.

It is now known as the catacomb of Saints Peter and Marcellinus who were buried there. In the lunette of an *arcosolium* tomb the episode is depicted in narrative-symbolic form. While the guests recline at a *sigma* table a young servant approaches from the left carrying a large dish of meats cut to convenient mouthfuls as was the custom in Roman banquets. In the foreground is the tall figure of Christ touching with his rod of divine power the rims of six large water jars set at his feet. In the late third century the Eucharistic representations become simplified and often present the solitary figure of Christ touching with the rod either seven baskets of bread or six water-jars.

And now to consider those paintings that depict the Incarnation. Since the festival of Christmas first began to be kept liturgically about A.D. 340, we do not find the stable in Bethlehem represented in Christian art before that date, and in the catacomb paintings there is (despite frequent erroneous statements to the contrary) only one very late fresco, in the catacomb of St. Sebastian, that depicts the manger. But Epiphany, that manifestation to the gentiles that lifted from the pagan soul its particular fear of death with only the hope of shadowy and diminished consciousness to follow ('Ah, do not try to gild death for me, Ulysses'), Epiphany was one of the earliest of New Testament subjects to adorn the cemeteries. The action chosen was that of the presentation of the symbolic gifts. The three Magi (not *kings* for centuries) appear as beardless, identical figures advancing in single file with their offerings on their outstretched hands. Wearing travelling cloaks to indicate their journey and Phrygian bonnets their nationality, they run towards the Child held always in the arms or upon the knee of his mother. In the frescoes the nature of the gifts is indeterminate, but in the reliefs upon the sarcophagi they are distinct and the gold is proffered first, in the form of a crown.

The other early representation of the Incarnation skilfully combines the prophecy of Isaiah, 'Behold a virgin shall conceive and bring forth a son', in one concise episode with its fulfilment, of which a beautiful but faded example may be seen in the catacomb of Priscilla. It is interesting to compare this with a similar conception in the twelfth-century sculpture in the tympanum of the church of Donzy-le-Pré in France.

Of Christ's numerous miracles of healing a charming example is in a *cubiculum* in the catacomb of Saints Peter and Marcellinus. The delicately delineated figure of Christ turns with outstretched hand to the woman kneeling at his feet as she seeks but to touch the hem of his garment. There are no other figures, no suggestion of the pressure of the crowd, but the quiet benignity of the one and the humility and eagerness of the other are wholly convincing. In the same *cubiculum* our Lord appears again, seated upon the rim of the well, talking to the woman of Samaria who stands before him. In such episodes Christ's courtesy and gentleness towards women is well exemplified. It is worth noting that when working miracles of healing he touches the sufferer with his own hand. In such, seeming, trifles the student of Early Christian art can perceive the care expended in the creation of its iconography.

As to belief in the resurrection of the body, that was, naturally, a subject widely portrayed in the cemeteries. A popular symbol was found in the dramatic history of Jonas. Of this there are normally three episodes: Jonas cast from the ship to the expectant sea-monster; the return journey in which head and shoulders protrude from the creature's jaws; and Jonas at rest within an arbour shaded by a gourd. It may be assumed that the artists had no worries about this story as regards the capacity of a whale to swallow a man, since they merely borrowed a mythological monster familiar in classic art. Mention of the gourd recalls the argument between St. Jerome and St. Augustine concerning the precise species of the plant beneath which the tired prophet took his rest, St. Jerome seeking to clinch his contention that it was an *ivy* by referring, incorrectly, to the catacomb frescoes which he remembered seeing in Rome in his youth. But the symbol, *par excellence*, of belief in the resurrection of the body was found in Christ's stupendous miracle in raising Lazarus from the dead, of which there are still well over a hundred examples extant in the frescoes.

With political peace given to the Church by Constantine in A.D. 312 Christian art arose to express triumphantly the glorious victory of the Faith. This enthusiasm penetrated to the catacombs where many new subjects were introduced, especially in the Christological cycle. These include Christ teaching doctrine to the apostles; giving crowns to the martyrs; handing the scroll of the New Law to St. Peter, counterpart to the action in which the Hand of God the Father comes out from the clouds of heaven to give to Moses the Tables of the ten commandments. Also a conception well suited to cemeterial art, the individual judgment which in Catholic belief immediately follows death. An interesting fresco in the catacomb of Domitilla depicts the soul of the deceased, represented as an *orante*, at his or her personal judgment: within the arch of a lunette Christ is seated *in cathedra* between the twelve apostles, while in the lunette is the soul accompanied by two powerful advocates, St. Peter and St. Paul, distinguished by their traditional features.

By the mid-fourth century, belief in the advocacy of the martyrs had become a popular subject in sepulchral art. There is a fresco, again in the catacomb of Domitilla, that adorns the grave of a lady named Veneranda and shows her in the company of St. Petronilla who is introducing, it would seem, the deceased into paradise.[1] Upon the ground is a *scrignum* filled with scrolls and above it an open book. Probably the former referred to the teaching of the Old Testament and the latter to that of the New, since both were closely interwoven in a catechumen's syllabus. This is one of the first representations of a book as opposed to a scroll, and the artist did not neglect to include the thongs with which it would be fastened.

In quiet reproof of a devotion to the memory of the martyrs that might have grown to excess, for a custom had arisen by which older graves were being destroyed by those desiring to be buried in proximity to the tomb of a saint, Pope Damasus caused to be inscribed on his commemorative tablet in the chapel of the popes in the cemetery of St. Callistus: 'And here, I, Damasus, would fain

1 See Plate 1.

have laid my bones but I feared to disturb the holy ashes of the saints.'

After the invasion of Rome by Alaric in A.D. 410 burial in the catacombs, outlying as they were, virtually ceased, but those in which vindicated martyrs had been interred remained places of pilgrimage until the ninth century, as is proved both by the itineraries and by the style of the later paintings. One of the last was possibly that of St. Cecilia in the crypt in which she was buried.

Now before considering the companion subject of the carvings on the sarcophagi, reference must be made to the quite recent discovery of a catacomb hitherto unknown. This came to the notice of the Pontifical Commission of Christian Archaeology through a landslip in the Via Dino Compagni in Rome while building was taking place. There is no record of this catacomb in the ancient writers, but as Father A. Ferrua, S.J., who has been closely associated with the work of exploration explains, the writers of antiquity did not concern themselves with the artistic value of a cemetery in which no martyr had been buried. The area is small but the variety and novelty of the subjects depicted is astonishing, as is also their excellent state of preservation (one of the advantages of oblivion) and their advance in technical ability. A safe dating seems to be to the late fourth century, for there is affinity between many of the frescoes and the sculptures of the later sarcophagi. The majority of new subjects are from the Old Testament and include Lot fleeing from Sodom with his daughters; Noah when inebriated; incidents in the history of Samson; Pharaoh's daughter finding the infant Moses; and the Flood, with God the Father pouring water upon the earth from a window in heaven. Important as these paintings are to the historian of art, it is unfortunately impossible, from lack of space, to give descriptive details here, and the interested reader is referred to Father Ferrua's article in the April 1956 number of La Civiltá Cattolica.

We will now turn to the other branch of Early Christian art, the sculptures upon the sarcophagi. And here it should be stated that the examples described and much of the information are drawn from the great corpus of the late Mgr. Joseph Wilpert: *I Sarcophagi Cristiani Antichi*, although inspection and study have also been given to original monuments.

It has frequently been said that sculpture in its highest form, the statue, was forbidden to the Christian sculptor in early times. The Church may have felt some bias against statuary, but the real reason for the decline in the art was due to quite other causes, to the increasing predominance of East Christian culture as it spread via Byzantium and Ravenna into the West. And East Christian art, not altogether untouched by iconomachy, was chiefly decorative and colouristic, so that under its influence sculpture everywhere lost virility to wait attendance upon architecture. Apart therefore from a few fragmentary statues, scattered in various museums, very little early Christian sculpture in the round now exists, not forgetting the charming statuette of the Good Shepherd in the Lateran Museum in Rome, the unrestored part of which probably dates from the second century. But the reliefs upon the sarcophagi of the Roman and Gallo-Roman schools are numerous, and fortunately a large number are well preserved.

In content and in purpose these sculptures differ fundamentally from those on contemporary pagan sarcophagi, but there are evidences of early efforts to attach to familiar themes a Christian significance. A sarcophagus found in a catacomb on the Via Salaria and now in the Lateran Museum reveals this transitional stage wherein a philosopher lecturing to his students has been adapted to the instruction of a catechumen in Christian doctrine.[1] This is exceptionally interesting as an early example, in plastic form, of the Christian endeavour to cross that difficult bridge from the natural to the supernatural order—surely the heart of the matter for the Christian artist in every age. It is known that Justin Martyr continued, after his conversion, to teach Catholic dogma wearing his philosopher's pallium, open on the breast, as does the doctor depicted on this sculpture. Justin Martyr died in A.D. 168 and it may well have been contemporary. Another

[1] See Plate 3.

3

interesting detail is the veil worn by the catechumen: the
flammeum worn by Roman brides and by Christian women dedicated to virginity. This veil can be seen again in a fresco in the
catacomb of Priscilla, where a young woman is taking her vows in
the presence of the bishop seated *in cathedra*.[1]

Since the biblical characters in the sculptures are in many cases
similar to those in the frescoes, we will mention chiefly the
innovations. Amongst these are the creation of Adam and Eve by
the co-operation of the Blessed Trinity; their actual expulsion
from Eden and their reception of the emblems of labour; an
ingenious conception in which the Three Young Hebrews refuse
to adore a statue of Nabuchodonosor and fuse their identity with
that of the Three Wise Men who adore the true king, Christ; also
Ezechiel giving life to the dead bones foreshadowing Christ's
power to raise from the dead. In the Christological cycle are
included incidents in the Passion and two representations of the
resurrection of Christ, the one symbolic and the other narrative.

As already stated, the Nativity in Bethlehem entered into the
iconography about A.D. 340 and was at once a popular theme
with sculptors. That the stable was in a cave was well known in
Rome in the second century, since Justin Martyr, who came
from Palestine, taught expressly that 'Mary gave birth to Christ
in a cave near to the village'. Caves provided with mangers were
common in the Roman campagna and usually the entrance was
protected by a small roof supported upon posts. This seems to
have been the model for the sculptures, as similar roofs on posts
appear on the sarcophagi to indicate the stable, and it is noticeable that it is this roof that reappears throughout the centuries in
the pictorial art of the West, whereas in that of the East the cave
itself is depicted. As to the manger, this is sometimes a wicker
basket, a realistic detail from Italian peasant life, sometimes a
trough set upon trestles. Into the scene a shepherd is frequently
introduced, and the ox and the ass are invariably present, not, as
in later times, as picturesque subsidiaries but liturgically present
illustrating the prophecy of Habacuc: 'the Lord shall be recognized

1 See Plate 2.

between two animals'. Our Lady's position is always at the head
of the manger. The earliest, existing, appearance of St. Joseph
in a Nativity is probably on the ivory book-cover in Milan
which may date from the close of the fifth century. There he is
seen wearing the *exomis* and holding his carpenter's saw like any
working man of his time as he sits, slightly withdrawn, at the
foot of the manger, where he is to be found for centuries until
the whole conception changes and descends to a less spiritual
level.

One other detail that should not escape attention concerns the
head of the Child and his unnaturally adult features. This, again,
was of set purpose and not due to lack of skill. Since the head was
considered the seat of knowledge, it was deliberately enlarged to
denote this Child's knowledge of and acceptance of the stupendous doctrine of the Incarnation. Not until the semi-pagan
humanism of the Renaissance was the physically attractive infant
substituted for the spiritually developed one. Thus, in an age
when reading was the accomplishment of the few, did the Church
instil her teaching.

Of the numerous Nativities in the sculptures a very charming
one adorns a monumental sarcophagus now in the cathedral at
Ancona. The Epiphany has much more detail on the sarcophagi
than in the frescoes, although the basic formula is the same.
Apropos, a remarkable cover of a sarcophagus was discovered
during the recent excavations in the sepulchral chambers beneath
what is now the lower basilica of St. Peter in Rome. The
exceptional feature is the introduction of a cross standing upright
behind the group of Mother and Child. This linking of the
Passion with the Incarnation was expressed by Christian poets of
the fourth century, but is here incorporated for the first time (to
the writer's knowledge) into visual art. This almost certainly
dates the sculpture to the late fourth century, an attribution
borne out by the scene on the opposite side which depicts
an incident in the history of Joseph and his brethren, biblical
characters not represented on earlier sculptures nor in the
frescoes of the cemeteries until their appearance in the newly

discovered catacomb. This important and beautiful sculpture is now in the central aisle of the lower basilica.

Three episodes of the Passion together with a symbolic Resurrection adorn a fine sarcophagus in the Lateran Museum. The judgment before Pilate occupies two sections on the right side. The calm impressive Christ contrasts with the nervous perplexity of Pilate as he turns away his head while a slave pours water into a basin. In the sections to the left are two historic actions subsequent to the judgment passed: the crowning with thorns and the walk to Calvary. But the crown is of laurel held respectfully above our Lord's head by a soldier and the cross is carried by Simon. It is the triumph of Christ, not his suffering, that is emphasized: that triumph over sin and death which, after Constantine, became the dominant note in Christian art. In the centre is the symbolic Resurrection. The conception seems to have been based upon the military standard, the *labarum*, after Constantine had surmounted it with the sacred monogram. At the head of the cross was placed the Chi-Rho within a wreath of laurel; beneath the arms of the cross two soldiers are seated, representatives of the guard around the tomb. Two doves that perch upon the cross symbolize the apostles, 'The witnesses of Christ's resurrection' according to the words of St. Peter. Upon a splendid sarcophagus now serving as altar frontal in a church at Manosque in France the cross with its monogram and guards is flanked by six apostles on either side, each with his right hand raised in acclamation. In the background is the heavenly firmament, sun, moon and stars illustrating Psalm 148: 'Praise him, oh ye sun and moon: praise Him all ye stars and light.' Upon a fifth-century stone altar that originally stood in the church of St. Victor in Marseilles twelve doves bow their heads towards the Chi-Rho, recalling the twelve white doves that accompany Christ upon his cross in the lovely apsidal mosaic in the basilica of San Clemente in Rome.

Towards the close of the fourth century this symbolic Resurrection gave place to the historic episode of the visit of the holy women to the sepulchre on Easter morning. A sarcophagus now in

Milan has this incident skilfully conceived: above a perpendicular tomb hovers an angel addressing the women: 'Whom seek ye? He is not here.' While one turns her face towards him the other looks down to the threshold where a fold of the cerecloth is lying.

As to depicting Christ in the hour of his rising, it was long before so difficult a theme was attempted by any Christian artist; but from the first awkward attempts when Christ is assisted by an angel from an horizontal tomb he holds a bannered cross, the standard of his victory, that has its far-off origin in Constantine's *labarum*. This provokes the reflection that to find the origin of any relevant detail in Christian art one has to go back very far indeed.

Apart from Christ, the one personality singled out for special notice was St. Peter, who appears in some twenty-seven different scenes in the sculptures. A favourite theme chosen for the more monumental sarcophagi was that known as the *Dominus Legem Dat* wherein Christ standing upon Mount Zion hands the scroll of the New Law to St. Peter who receives it reverently on hands veiled by the *orarium*, a conception obviously taken from court etiquette.

For our last example we take the important sarcophagus known as the Dogmatic on account of the Catholic doctrine which it illustrates.[1] This was found in a cemetery not far from the grave of St. Paul, on the road to Ostia. The episodes are arranged in two zones: in the centre of the upper is a shield enclosing the busts of the husband and wife whose tomb it was. In the top zone, from left to right, first the Blessed Trinity are in the act of creating Adam and Eve: God the Father is seated in the *cathedra* draped with cloth; God the Holy Ghost stands behind the *cathedra*, and God the Son in front with his hand upon the head of Eve who is upright while Adam lies upon the ground. The Three Persons of the Trinity are bearded and identical in feature. Alas, the Fall soon happened and in the next group Christ, now young and beardless, is handing to Adam a sheaf of wheat and to Eve a lamb, for man must dig and woman must spin. Behind Eve is the tree encircled by the serpent holding the fatal apple in his mouth. But in the fullness of the divine mercy Christ came to bring the 'food

1 See Plate 4.

of immortality', and so the Fall is followed by the two Eucharistic
symbols, the turning of the water into wine and the multiplication
of the loaves and fishes. These last are handed to Christ by two of
the apostles, while the baskets for the fragments stand upon the
ground. The upper zone then closes with the raising of Lazarus
and with Martha or Mary adoring at Christ's feet. In the lower
zone, beneath the Creation, the Magi advance to present their
gifts, but with two important innovations. Behind our Lady's
cathedra, similar to that of God the Father but lacking the cloth
of honour, stands God the Holy Ghost with his hand on the back
of the *cathedra*, while to emphasize the doctrine of the Trinity
the first of the Magi points to *three* stars enclosed within circles.
This is followed by Christ giving sight to the blind, a miracle
understood as having both literal and moral significance, and then
comes an elaborate scene of Daniel in the lion's den with his
dinner brought to him by Habacuc. The series closes with episodes
in the life of St. Peter: his denial of Christ, with the tell-tale
cock at his feet; then his first arrest and the scene which usually
accompanies it, the symbolic baptism of the centurion Cornelius,
who is represented drinking from the baptismal water that
gushes from the Rock struck not by Moses but by St. Peter. This
Moses-Peter theme, frequent in the sculptures, also appears in
fourth-century frescoes and on the gilded glasses found in the
cemeteries whereon the figure striking the Rock has the name
Petrus inscribed beside it.

To any unbiased student of early Christian iconography not
only the presence of St. Peter in Rome but his accepted primacy
is surely beyond question.

The fatal year A.D. 410 affected not only the principal inhabitants of Rome but also the artists who seem to have joined in the
general exodus from the city. To trace the development or, more
correctly, the decline of sculpture it is necessary to repair, as
some of the masons may have done, to Ravenna where from the
fifth century to the seventh sarcophagi were carved in large
numbers, of which some sixty still exist in the various churches
and museums. They are distinctive in style, massive in form, and

with the decoration widely spaced over an unfilled background. Representational subjects soon gave place to Oriental symbolic-ornament, until that also petered out into complete ineptitude.

Before the rebirth of sculpture as a major art there is a gap of five centuries until its tentative new beginnings in the tympana of the new French cathedrals. But that carries us beyond the scope of this inquiry.

In this short survey of the origins of Christian art we have been concerned of necessity with its infancy in the catacomb frescoes and upon the carved sarcophagi, and remarkable is the extent to which this circumscribed activity succeeded in expressing the faith and the mind of the Church as of the individual Christian. But although both painting and sculpture had declined aesthetic-ally, when the Church gained her freedom she was not at a loss for a medium through which to illustrate her liturgy or her doctrine. After the peace of Constantine, churches arose wherever the Faith had spread, and for their adornment was developed an art specifi-cally Christian, in the new use of mosaic for whole wall-surfaces so that these brick buildings, so unpretentious externally, glowed with meaningful colour within. Perhaps in no other art medium have East and West so successfully united in spirit and in achievement.

When Constantine built for Pope Sylvester his episcopal church of the Lateran the nave walls were adorned with a series of mosaic panels forming a concordance of Old and New Testa-ment scenes. This opened on the one side with the expulsion of Adam and Eve from paradise and closed with Jonas escaping from the sea-monster. The opposite series opened with the Good Thief entering paradise and closed with the symbolic Resurrec-tion of Christ. When the visitor to the Latern basilica today looks up at the series of stucco panels upon the walls of the nave he sees, although he probably does not know it, the same concordance in *Baroque* dress, revealing the constancy in the basic themes and inspiration of Christian art.

Miss Gunton stated that themes were set by ecclesiastical authority. On being challenged she gave as her authority that of Wilpert's books,

Le Pitture delle Catacombe Romane *and* I Sarcophagi Cristiani Antichi. *It emerged, however, that Wilpert's statement was based solely on circumstantial evidence. There was no direct evidence that ecclesiastical authority set and controlled the themes and their treatment. Miss Gunton stated on the same authority that it was thought that copy books were passed round from artist to artist (pages 53–54 of* Le Pitture delle Catacombe Romane). *Whilst this seemed reasonable enough—especially since it is likely that pagan sculptors had on occasion to carve Christian themes and that new converts who had to carve these themes might well require direction—all the same it was again clear that there was no direct evidence for this. It was asked whether these 'books' were made of wax or parchment held together with leather thongs, or what. The conclusion was that an alternative hypothesis could be that the similarity of theme and treatment was due primarily to the artists themselves, who began from the first to build up an accepted convention in the way usual to all artists. For their material they would go naturally to the themes most frequently treated by Christian teachers and preachers, so that whilst it could be said that these authorities were responsible in this indirect way for the particular themes chosen, yet they did not in fact impose them in some formal way, or by means of a legalistic direction of the sort to which Catholics of later ages have become accustomed.*

The fact itself of the similarity of themes and the treatment in all early Christian art was also challenged, and it was suggested that it is really only a broad similarity, typical of all artistic conventions, and corresponding to the discipline for which the artist always in fact seeks. The variety of technique and theme was considered by some to be very wide as between city and city, but the evidence available was small, and the point in the end appeared to be a matter of opinion. But it seemed clear that the similarities did not necessarily involve imposition formally from above, and that they had not prevented a marked variety in each individual work.

With this conclusion, however, Miss Gunton did not agree, again maintaining that the fundamental similarity both of choice and treatment of biblical themes was strong evidence of a unity of purpose which she considered improbable, if not impossible, in free-lance painters and sculptors over a period of some three hundred years.

4. Faith and Works in Mediaeval Art

ERIC JOHN

*Mr. Eric John, a Lecturer in Mediaeval History in the
University of Manchester, carried the historical witness on
through the thousand years till the Renaissance.*

It is perhaps more difficult to detect the part of faith in mediaeval
art than in the art of any other period, just because in the external
sense the Middle Ages were an age of faith. Almost every *objet
d'art* is only secondarily a work of art, primarily it is an object of,
and an aid to, devotion; almost every work of art had an altogether
Christian and Catholic context. The relation of art and the Church
in the Middle Ages may be compared to the relation of Phèdre
and Venus: *C'est Vénus tout entière à sa proie attachée.*

The mediaeval Church, in the West at least, in its institutional
shape was without immediate and local competition. On the
surface everything was piety, devotion, orthodox and settled: in
art as well as faith canons were fixed, traditions were established,
and a vocabulary of numerous and universally understood symbols
was useful as well as obligatory, for mediaeval imaginations were
incurably pictorial and didactic. Every picture was a visual aid
and the most improbable objects were made to point the most
involved lessons. The incidents depicted and the lessons conveyed
were almost invariably drawn from sacred sources, they were
illustrations to divine science. Virtually everything bears on its
surface the imprint of faith. Nominally, mediaeval works of art
were wholly Christian: commissioned by Christians, executed by
Christians, looked at by Christians, and concerned solely with

communicating a Christian message. But when everything presents a Christian surface how can we single out any one thing as an example of a specifically Christian splendour, of a specifically Christian truth? We cannot refuse to single out, we cannot admire in the lump because truth and beauty must be sought in the particular—'God resides in details', as the best students of art as well as of faith have always insisted.

In fact the signs of a lively faith in many mediaeval works of art are not wanting, but if we wish to interpret them correctly we must avoid two common pitfalls.

The first is that of attempting the characteristically modern way of an interior approach, in which the student looks at the individual work of art, recalls what he knows of the doctrines he supposes the artist to have subscribed to, and infers all sorts of things about his state of mind and conscience. But almost all mediaeval works of art are anonymous, or have little more than a name attached to them if they are not. We can have no idea of the degree of assent which these artists gave to the conventional doctrines of their time, and apart from what the works of art themselves tell us when properly questioned we can know nothing of their creators' opinions or manner of life. The difficulty arises because we cannot tell from an isolated work of art what is conventional, borrowed from others, and what is new and intentional, or why it is there. We cannot then pick out the single work of art and readily penetrate beneath the surface and point to the way in which the artist's faith entered into and controlled his skill and its application. Not even the most ingenious Frenchman could write a little study called *Presence du maître du livre de Kells* as ingenious Frenchmen can and do pour out studies on these lines of Péguy, Bernanos, Jacob *et hoc genus omne*. Even less can we evade the difficulty by positing a chimera called 'the mediaeval artist', who believed everything, painted everything, was everything, that the amateur of mediaeval art thinks he can discern whenever he looks at a book of reproductions of MSS. illuminations, church carvings, and so on. We really know little about the genus 'mediaeval artist' or even whether the term can be used at all meaningfully. We do not know who they were, how professional they were, how specialized. Some of them must have been simple journeymen illustrating an ideology thrust upon them from above, but by no means all of them can have been. The illuminator of the Lindisfarne Gospels was a bishop; the twelfth-century abbot of St. Denis, Suger, took an expert and professional interest in the decoration of his abbey church, which he obviously thought a natural part of his monastic vocation. Dr. von Simson has recently suggested that the architecture of the greater Gothic cathedrals was much more closely connected with the intellectual developments of the times than any view of their architects as simple journeymen will permit. We cannot, then, put the individual artist through an interior examination nor evade the difficulty of his anonymity by appealing to a set of general characteristics supposed to be true of all mediaeval artists, supplying the defects of our knowledge of the individual by our supposed knowledge of the general run.

The second pitfall comes from the purely contingent fact that mediaeval imaginations were pictorial and didactic at the same time as they were formal and abstract. This offers the modern critic a dangerous opportunity of evading the impasse by thoroughly misunderstanding the part of faith in mediaeval art. Most art criticism now presupposes that the representational view of art is necessarily opposed to the abstract, and that all artists can be assigned to one of these two schools. Anyone can see that mediaeval art is at once abstract and representational, simultaneously formal and narrative. It is fatally easy to imagine a tension here and to identify one tendency with faith and the other with art. In this way we get the Victorian nonsense, which, identifying faith with the representational, dismissed Giotto as barbaric and exalted Raphael as *the* standard of religious art while nowadays we get the equally absurd view which sees only flaccid pagan artiness in Raphael and Michelangelo, and can find no faith outside Giotto and Fra Angelico.

The truth is that mediaeval art exhibited, from its source and throughout its entire course, a necessary artistic heterogeneity which is at once one of the sources of its power and a sufficient reason for refusing to locate the interplay of faith and art just here; this artistic heterogeneity was an inevitable consequence of the circumstances of the conversion of western Europe. The newly converted peoples already had a highly formal• art characterized by complicated, sophisticated patterns with a minimum of representational effect. The missionaries brought their own hybrid art with its classical tradition of naturalism tinged with oriental and hellenistic influences—the kind of art we loosely call Byzantine—which was now the standard Christian art of the mediterranean world. It is not surprising that the resulting tradition of art should combine a concern for representation with a passion for pattern and that mediaeval pictures frequently consist of patterns made to look like, seem, people, incidents or stories, with the shape of the human form violently or subtly distorted to bear out a deeply felt design. The *tympanum* of Vézélay is a famous example, but so too is Botticelli's *Nativity* where, if the distortion is subtle, the pattern is obvious, violent, and itself contributes to the narrative. We must then accept this heterogeneity as part of our *data* and look elsewhere for the *imprimatur* of faith than to an isolation of integral, altogether necessary elements.

What then is to be done? If we avoid facile distinctions, if we are denied the opportunity to psychologize, if every surface is uniformly orthodox, how can we detect the presence of faith? The answer is, I suppose, obvious enough. Every age is an age of sin as well as of faith, and there were tensions in the Middle Ages as obviously to do with the eternal combat of *civitas terrena* and *civitas dei* as those of our own day. Sometimes these tensions touch the mind and conscience of the artist as revealed in the work of art itself. At the same time mediaeval orthodoxy was not as static as people liked to think, and it is possible to see something of the interplay of art and faith in the adaptation of the grammar of symbolism to cope with developments in theological opinion and spiritual outlook. It is also possible to detect unevenness on what at first sight looks like the smooth face of mediaeval orthodoxy, and by looking at faith and art *in situ* and in motion, as it were, to see something of their mutual relevance. It is perfectly possible but it is a delicate and subjective business and it would be folly to pretend that one could come naked to the task. Two highly personal things are presupposed: an understanding of the content of faith, which is necessarily limited by talent and character; and a sensitivity to the work of art in question, which depends ultimately on that most personal of all things, sensibility. One must experience a properly sensuous awareness of the work of art at the same time as one's feelings are schooled within the discipline of whatever is relevant in Christian revelation. Things being what they are, one fails of course, one is too stupid and too insensitive—but since revelation is revelation and sensibility is to what is *there*, on the page or wherever, there should be some rigour in the enterprise, and in the end one should be in the right way, one's conclusions should have a little validity.

Let us begin with the shape of the church, I mean the physical shape of church buildings. A single church taken by itself will not tell us very much about the consequences of faith for architecture—although we know that the cruciform plan common in the West was imposed on architects for ideological reasons. The scope of the architect is defined by the function of the building: to parody le Corbusier, a church is a machine for liturgy; and whilst there are good machines and bad machines, it is technical skill, not interior convictions, which makes for the difference. But a study of technique will not help us much either. Undoubtedly a history of church architecture written purely from the point of view of developments in building technique would be profitable and interesting, but it would risk fundamental irrelevance. What is basic to church building is the faith of the Church expressed in its liturgical and communal life, and the architect's job is to set this expression of faith worthily and conveniently. If we look at church-building *in sequentia* then certain consequences for architecture which followed certain spiritual developments are obvious. A romanesque church and a church in the earlier pointed styles are precisely machines for liturgy. They provided a dignified *venue* for the people of the neighbourhood to perform their proper acts of public worship; differences of function and rank were marked but these were combined into a more or less harmonious whole. This type of architecture may be described as wholly functional and its function is liturgical. If we now turn to later mediaeval church buildings, to the hey-day of flamboyant, perpendicular, and the later decorated styles, this is no longer true. Church architecture is still functional but its functions are no longer simply or even primarily liturgical. The word *Church* was now mainly a collective noun for clergy, it was rarely used to mean either the Body of Christ in the Pauline sense or the communion of the faithful without distinction of rank, race, time or place. Not surprisingly, a great church would then have a choir and sanctuary heavily differentiated from the nave. The place of the clergy must be fenced off, and the choir screen as a massive barrier between layman and cleric became usual. (The *iconostasis* of Eastern tradition, in spite of superficial resemblances to the choir screen, belongs to an entirely different liturgical pattern and is irrelevant here.) In some of the later cathedrals this alone impaired the liturgical architecture of the church, since when the liturgy was celebrated the congregation could neither see nor hear what was going on unless another altar was erected in the nave. But not even the greatest architect can design a nave which is subordinate to a co-ordinated whole and which is yet expected to fulfil the whole functions of a church at the same time. Liturgically the church was no longer a unity, and architecturally an overall coherent design was no longer possible. Moreover, later mediaeval churches were no longer machines for liturgy; they were, rather, repositories for relics and machines for the celebration of private masses.

The cult of relics is ancient, natural, and (I believe we should agree) salutary—which is all the more reason why it should not be corrupted by excess. And no one can reasonably deny that mediaeval churchmen did take the cult to excess, when we find a saint like Hugh of Lincoln carried beyond the bounds of decorum and even principle in his lust for relics. His biographer tells us that Hugh was shown an alleged bone of St. Mary Magdalen at Fécamp and was so overcome with pious greed that, unable to break it off by hand, he bit off two fragments of bone and gave them to his attendants to preserve.[1] If St. Hugh behaved like this, what were the rest like? After the murder of St. Thomas, the monks of St. Augustine's, Canterbury, elected a monk of the cathedral priory as their abbot because, as a kind of dowry, he could bring with him St. Thomas's brains and a portion of his blood. Their intention was plainly to secure their share of the pious tourism which the shrines of St. Thomas attracted. If I speak harshly of the monks of St. Augustine's, nevertheless I speak justly: they sold phials containing a drop of St. Thomas's blood, greatly diluted, to wealthy and favoured pilgrims. But at least what they sold was authentic; it is to be feared that the passion for relics was sometimes met by forgery and deceit. After Glastonbury had been burnt down in the twelfth century the tombs of Arthur and Guinevere were conveniently revealed as a means of parting the faithful from their silver pennies.

The shape of the church was suitably distended as the heaps of relics mounted and there was need of altars to serve as sacred pantechnicons. At the same time the increasing individualism of mediaeval religion was transforming churches from centres of communal worship to places of privately endowed and privately celebrated masses. This, too, called for more altars, and later the mediaeval churches break out in a rash of side chapels to serve for both relics and private masses. The effect of all this on architecture was devastating. No one can deny that late mediaeval churches are beautiful, but if Durham Cathedral, the one great English machine for liturgy left substantially untouched—except for the chapel of the nine altars and the absurd shrine of St. Cuthbert—is compared with a late mediaeval ecclesiastical box (say York Minster), it is obvious that more than a difference in style separates them: there is a difference in principle. It is true that in later cathedrals the side chapels can be disposed within the ancient, virtually obligatory, cruciform shape, but the cruciform

---

[1] *Magna Vita Hugonis* (Rolls Series), p. 317.

lines are difficult to make out and the general shape of the church is no longer an objective correlative of the Christian religion. The high altar has ceased to be the centre, the focus of the church. When there are so many altars, when the status of the clergy is obtrusively asserted by a choir-screen, how can a comparatively small high-altar dominate the church as it can and does in Vézélay[1] or Torcello—or even in St. Étienne d'Auxerre? Architects now commonly chose some adventitious, convenient but meaningless, feature to dominate their churches and a great east window is a common solution to this architectural problem. The contest between York and Gloucester for the largest east window in England would be ludicrous if it were not also tragic. It is no coincidence that church architecture of the high Gothic variety is all breath-taking views and high emotion with all coherence gone: Winchester cathedral is an obvious example. What are York Minster[2] and King's College chapel but a couple of tastefully decorated cartons? They may be magnificent but they are not Christian architecture in the sense in which Vézélay—and Pontigny too—are both Christian and architecture. It is not to be wondered at that the Christian architects of the age of Humanism, Alberti and Palladio, should have reacted so strongly against this eccentric, irrational and emotional architecture, and that the great humanist churches, say San Giorgio and Il Redentore, for all the differences in detail, share a unity of principle with the rational and theological architecture of Vézélay, Durham, and Torcello. I should like to conclude my remarks on Christian architecture by quoting a passage from Alberti's treatise on architecture which magnificently exemplifies the kind of principle I have in mind:

> The next chief point to be considered in the Temple, is fixing the altar, where Divine Office is to be performed, which should be the most honourable place, and this seems to be exactly in the middle of the tribune. . . . Whether or not it be proper to have more altars for sacrifice in a temple, than one, I shall leave to the judgment of others.

1 See Plate 5.   2 See Plate 6.

Among our forefathers, in the primitive times of our religion, the devout Christians used to meet together at the Holy Supper . . . in order to soften and humanize their manners by frequent conversation and communion with each other . . . in those ages they had but one altar, where they used to meet to celebrate only one sacrifice in a day. Next succeeded those times, which I wish to God some worthy man might arise to reform, and be this said without offence to our Popes, who, though to keep up their own dignity, they hardly suffer themselves to be seen by the people once in a year, yet have so crowded every place with altars, and perhaps too with . . . But I shall venture to say no more. This I may venture to affirm, that as there is nothing in nature can be imagined more holy or noble than our Sacrifice, so I believe no man of sense can be for having it debased by being made too common. . . .[1]

I have attempted in sweeping outlines and sweeping statements to sketch a parallel between certain changes in tradition of spirituality and a tradition of architecture. I have tried to show that a change in opinion as to what a church was for could create a revolution—in my opinion a collapse—in the conception of architecture. The change in spiritual tradition was, in terms of that tradition, peripheral; for a mass is a mass in whatever circumstances and with whatever intentions it is offered, but the change in architecture was fundamental. Faith is, after all, a tougher business than art: the Holy Spirit is a more powerful protector than a mere muse.

I should now like to turn to a second example of a rather different kind, and examine the articulation of a distinct belief within a tradition of thought and feeling.

The tradition of thought and feeling which we loosely term the Divine Right of Kings was originally far from meaning 'the right divine of kings to govern wrong'. It began when churchmen seeking peace and quiet, law and order, for themselves and their flock, desiring a world fit for not only heroes to live in, gave the full weight of their moral support to the one stable political

[1] *Ten Books on Architecture*, ed. J. Rykwert (whom I have to thank for drawing my attention to this passage), VII, c. 113, p. 153.

institution of the Dark Ages, the semi-pagan tribal kingship which the germanic invasions had firmly established all over western Europe. These kings were hailed as the *Caesar* of the Gospels; it was to them that St. Paul's teaching of the divine sources of secular authority was applied. It was originally in this sense, and in this sense only, that the king ruled by divine right; his divinity was conferred by his office and was conditional upon its proper discharge. Thus the doctrine of the divine right of kings was no more than a piece of applied theology in a world in which there was too little authority and too much insubordination. The doctrine needed little development but a great deal of hammering home. In part, the early mediaeval theologian quoted texts, made inferences, and exhorted as his modern counterpart does in similar cases. But that was only a part of what he did. The doctrine was also expressed in a concatenation of symbols and a decorous elaboration of ceremonies. The pagan king had been little more than a successful warrior: 'Often Scyld Scefing took the mead benches away from troops of foes, from many peoples. He terrified the nobles . . . increased under the heavens and throve in honour, until all his neighbours across the sea had to obey him and pay him tribute. That was a good king.' Or so the poet of *Beowulf* thought.

When a pagan king was dying, if he was able he nominated his successor and handed him his weapons. But the Church was not prepared to think of a king as primarily a warrior. He was primarily a fountain of perhaps rather rough justice, but still justice; a shepherd of his people—when he behaved himself— and having first made him promise to be just, merciful, and to protect the holy churches of God, churchmen made him *Christus domini*, the Lord's anointed. For this purpose a quasi-sacramental coronation rite was devised. After the example of Samuel and Saul, the chief bishop of the kingdom anointed the new king with oil. Following the traditions of pagan kingship the newly anointed ruler was invested with symbolic objects representing his various powers and duties. The sword—of justice however—was retained, but the military character of the rest was slowly transformed. Instead of armour there were robes of state which were basically priestly, even episcopal, vestments. The helmet became the crown and its barbarous associations were replaced by analogies with the bishop's mitre. In other words, an intricate complex of symbolic ideas gathered round the coronation ceremony and they were no longer the old military ideas pure and simple; instead they were shot through with the Christian idea of justice. Some of the symbols used were so recondite that their meaning was forgotten soon after they were introduced, but mostly their meaning is obvious to the meanest intelligence. The rod of correction which the king carried, the white robe of purity, the golden robe of majesty, the gold and jewels everywhere, the holy oil and the *promissio regis* all added up to a trenchant exposition of the Christian doctrine of the just ruler—a man set apart to rule, called by God to rule, commissioned by God's ministers to rule, but to rule justly and for the sake of his people who are also God's people. A mediaeval king was obviously different from other men by the magnitude of his office, and on the greater occasions this was obvious at a glance from the clothes he wore and the symbols which covered him from head to foot.

For our purpose it is sufficient to notice how imperceptibly we pass from theology to art, from belief expressed in propositions to beliefs expressed in works of art. Early mediaeval *regalia* were works of art of the highest order, e.g. the crown of Otto I,[1] or the fantastic cameo by the master of the crown of Stockholm.[2] Where mediaeval *regalia* survive, their beauty is obvious, but it was a strictly functional beauty controlled very precisely by its context. These objects were made after the taste of a few very great artists, but after a taste limited by a number of rational and theological considerations. Faith, political philosophy, social utility, taste and art are here inseparable; what is more, they are indistinguishable.

But again in this field of mediaeval representation and speculation there is by the end of the Middle Ages a debasement of

1 See Plate 7.   2 See Plate 9.

thought accompanied by an important change in works of art. Many now think Richard II of England was the first monarch to think of himself as ruling explicitly by divine right, in the Stuart or Bourbon sense, and to attempt to rule in practice as absolutely as in theory he claimed he ought. He was in other words the first ruler to substitute a kingly pride of status for a kingly pride of function. The change was not unmarked in works of art. It is perhaps excessive to complain of the crown made for Richard's queen that, unlike the older crowns, its obvious symbolic intention has been subdued to mere prettiness, to a concern for *chic*—after all it is very *chic*—and we have to put up with the Imperial State Crown,[1] at once the most vulgar as it is the most expensive portable object in existence. Yet we cannot help but be disturbed by another object associated with Richard and his ideas of kingship, the Wilton diptych, all the more disturbed as it is quite pretty.[2] It is not likely that Richard ever saw the picture; it may have been intended to provoke a political cult of Richard 'the martyr' analogous to the *Eikon Basilike* and the cult of Charles king and martyr. But however aesthetically pleasing the diptych, the blasphemous impertinence of the artist is revolting. Not only is the smug, prissy, Richard introduced into the heavenly host by St. John the Baptist, St. Edmund and St. Edward with a ceremony which would be excessive for even a good man, but the painter in his partisan zeal has not scrupled to make the angels wear Richard's badge as they surround our Lady and draw the Holy Child's attention to the king kneeling in an unpleasingly perky fashion in front of him. A suitably patriotic touch is added by the angel who waves the banner of St. George over the Virgin and Child. It is customary to gloss this kind of impertinence as 'courtly', evading hard questions by a graceful word, but the fact remains that the Wilton diptych violates every canon of propriety based on the Gospels and the established norm of Christian tradition. Is it authentically Christian in any way to show a king being introduced into the heavenly host wearing all the rich robes of his calling? It is noticeable that John the Baptist is represented as the poor

1 See Plate 8.   2 See Plate 10.

relation in a group containing himself and two magnificently dressed royal saints, although our Lord said: 'Amongst them that are born of women there is none greater than John' whilst of the saintly kings one is now celebrated with a semi-double and the other is commemorated in the diocese of Northampton. One cannot help but recall the hard words in the Gospel about the rich man and the eye of the needle, and it is plain that the spiritual attitude behind the Wilton diptych is that of a thoroughly secular arrogance and pride. Is this impertinence in representation unconnected with the necessity which made a pliant pope translate archbishops of Canterbury to and from *partibus infidelium* at the request of victorious political factions in Richard's reign— or in the next generation tolerate with hardly a squeak of protest the hanging of an archbishop of York for no greater crimes than honesty of intention and political misfortune? Can we, moreover, separate our dissatisfaction with the implications of the composition from our final judgment on the quality of the diptych? I venture to think not; for all that must be conceded to the artist for his skill, our reaction to the painting will equally take in our reaction to the sermon it preaches: in this case, as for so many mediaeval works of art, there is no pure aesthetic response: the moral, the message, the story are an essential part of the total response to the work in question.

I should like to conclude with a third example and 'the Arian frustrate' with a brief discussion of a change in spirituality directly caused by works of art.

Around the year 1100 a striking change in opinion as to the point of the Crucifixion occurred. The question turned on the nature of the relation between redemption and human salvation. The older view of this relation between redemption and salvation has recently been summarized by Mr. Southern: 'Man was a helpless spectator in a cosmic struggle which determined his chance of salvation. The war was one between God and the Devil, and God won because he proved himself the master-strategist. That God should become Man was a great mystery, a majestic awe-inspiring act, justly acclaimed in such a triumphant expression of victory as the *Te Deum*. But there was little or no place for tender compassion for the suffering of Jesus.'[1]

In the course of the eleventh century a new piety centred on the sufferings of Jesus appeared all over the West. In due course a new theology also appeared whose success in displacing the old was final and amazingly rapid. The new theology is associated with three great names, Anselm, Bernard and Abelard, but it was St. Anselm's teaching on the atonement which was doctrinally the most influential. At first sight the treatise in which he set out this doctrine, *Cur Deus Homo?*, with its severely logical cast, seems to have nothing to do with either sensibility or pious devotion, but what was behind the treatise is revealed in a brief aside embedded in the logic: 'The unbelievers deride our simplicity, saying that we injure and insult God in asserting that he entered a mother's womb, was born of woman, nourished with her milk and other human food, and—not to mention many other things which seem inconsistent with God's nature—suffered weariness, hunger, thirst, blows, crucifixion and death among the robbers.'[2]

It has been shown by Mr. Southern that the origin of *Cur Deus Homo?* lay in a dispute between Anselm's friend Gilbert Crispin and a certain Jew who had recently come to England. It is the Jew's arguments that Anselm had in mind when he began to write. We know further that the Jewish objector had specifically complained of the representation of God 'as a wretched man, nailed to the Cross, hideous even to behold'. This manner of representing the Crucifixion, which is that to which we are most accustomed, was then fairly new. One of the earliest versions was made in England just before the Norman Conquest—it is an illumination for the *Gospels* of the Countess Judith—and everything suggests that the new piety had strong and early roots in England. Certainly there is no doubt that Anselm was familiar with and approved the new piety and wrote *Cur Deus Homo?* to defend it. But the dissemination of this piety was chiefly due to a new religious Order founded by

[1] Richard W. Southern: *The Making of the Middle Ages* (Hutchinson, 1953), p. 235. A good deal of what follows is taken from this remarkable book.
[2] *Cur Deus Homo?* i, 7.

an Englishman, the Order of Cîteaux, and it was the most famous Cistercian publicist, St. Bernard, who offered the most powerful rejection of the old theology. Bernard's views were, on this point at least, by no means as conservative as some have held. They had more in common with those held by Abelard—although they are far from identical—than St. Bernard would probably have cared to admit, and they had a great deal in common with Anselm's. A study of early Cistercian manuscript illumination is instructive; it is, for instance, in an early twelfth-century lectionary done at Cîteaux that the first Western representation of our Lady feeding the Holy Child is found. But it will be sufficiently obvious that the new piety and the new theology of the early Middle Ages were inseparable; that the piety came first; that what we call works of art were an integral part of this new piety. In all this again, art, faith, representation and teaching cannot be separated. Most of the innovating artists were themselves monks, and their clear anticipation of the movement of theological protest initiated by St. Anselm shows that a change in style could also be a spiritual revolution. 'Religious Art' is here simply one form of eloquent meditation.

I must now try to bring these rather scattered threads together. I have tried to illustrate rather than to argue and my theme has perhaps more range than order. But it will be apparent that a study of mediaeval art is far from requiring simple prostration before the undiluted splendour of faith; the Middle Ages had their tensions and mediaeval art has its sinful as well as its faithful side. It is, moreover, strikingly obvious that for mediaevals, theology was not simply a matter of the presentation of texts and the making of distinctions, it was also a matter of striking illustration, of the embodiment of convictions as well as ideas in patterns of symbols and ceremonial behaviour. The best of mediaeval theology is not confined to *Summae*, it is an appeal to the intelligent sensibility as well as to deeply felt speculation; it is a unity of opinion and feeling which makes it easy to understand why mediaevals could plant their opinions and disseminate their doctrines with a thoroughness no longer found, in spite of the

media of mass-communication which modern religious teachers
may employ. Likewise the great works of mediaeval art were for
those who made them applied theology as well delight for the eye.
No contemporary would have thought of them as 'works of art'
or would have cared in the least about 'significant form', but the
best of them would have cared a great deal about the expression
of firmly held and reasonably understood beliefs. I cannot help
but wonder whether this is really specially mediaeval or whether
it is perennially true of 'art' and 'faith'. I wonder if the present
state of religious art is not simply an aesthetic desert but a
profound symptom of the void in the heart of our faith as
professedly Christian people.

Certainly this lack of any clear distinction between 'art' and
'faith' was an immense source of strength to the artist. If I may
venture a personal and amateur opinion this is why magnificent
art could be turned out in such quantity in the Middle Ages. The
mediaeval artist, I think, began with an advantage over his
modern fellow—he didn't have to begin on a battlefield between
the disputed claims of tradition and originality. He had simply—
but what a simply!—to be original on and around a set theme
within a certain range of manner of treatment. Even minor
artists could produce splendid stuff under such conditions, whilst
a major artist could achieve something hardly possible any longer
—a major innovation in a great tradition. Indeed, coming from
any study of mediaeval art one wants to say that the great task of
the modern artist is identical with that of the modern theologian,
to discover the tradition.

I have tried to limit myself to an historical approach. Certainly
my history may be justly accused of being all philosophy teaching
by example, and at every point shortage of learning and time has
made me summary and dogmatic. In conclusion, having expressed
contrition, let me follow Luther's misunderstood advice and sin
strongly. If I had to express in a few words what seemed to me *the*
lesson to be drawn from the practice of art in the Middle Ages, I
should say that every picture ought to tell a story, that it ought
to be a story worth telling, that it ought to be obviously as well

as prettily told. To this I would add a rider taken from one of the
few modern artists possessed of many of the mediaeval virtues
and some of the mediaeval defects: 'Never trust the artist, trust
the tale.'

*Mr. John's paper was illustrated by some slides, and five of these
illustrations have been included in this book. It was objected that some
of the theological developments which Mr. John used to explain some of
the features of late mediaeval Gothic architecture had already taken place
in the 'romanesque period'. Mr. John conceded this but thought it hardly
affected the argument, which did not require strictly coterminous developments in theology and architecture, merely that at some point in the history of church-building, architecture was modified to meet prevailing theological opinions.*

*Mr. John's strictures on York Minster and the Wilton Diptych were
challenged in so far as they proposed a general principle which would
seem to deny that we can gain pleasure from art with whose function or
purpose we find fault. This view seems not to allow for pleasure in
art as something worthwhile whether or not it is educated and informed
about the historical background or purpose of particular works of
art. Can there be aesthetic enjoyment of a cathedral which is liturgically
incorrect?   In discussion he proposed an analysis of the response to works
of art, which was first a response to the thing itself, and secondly a
response to the thing in function which one seeks to understand. The first,
he said, was not valid in itself; the feelings have to be educated. This
approach was criticized as similar to the ethical fallacy that good
men make good art and bad men make bad art. It was agreed that
appreciation of a work of art could be deepened and modulated and
modified by information and knowledge of an objective or historical
sort about it.*

5. The Modern Age

JOSEPH RYKWERT

Mr. Joseph Rykwert, art critic and editor of Alberti, pre-sented the third paper in the historical section.

IT is almost useless to generalize about half a millennium of human activity: even if, as with the history of the arts since the waning of the Middle Ages, it has been considered from several points of view and thoroughly documented. The line of attack I wish to adopt—that is, to consider art as a *function* of society—may not be as familiar as a stylistic description or even one in terms of biography. I will therefore throw out this consideration to serve as a useful line of reference: that from the fourteenth century until our own times almost, men have been dominated increasingly by two complementary tendencies: to perfect the means of production in agriculture and industry, and to centralize economic power. This may seem restrictive; and in fact the tremendous by-product of these economic currents is much more important at the outset—the sharp revaluation of physical experi-ence through the growing ability both to measure and to control the natural environment. The process had begun early in the fourteenth century, as the tangible world of measurement and sensory experience worked itself loose from the pseudo-theo-logical categories, themselves depending on pre-Christian, mythical patterns. It was this move which occasioned the first unsettling in the ways of mediaeval artists.

What are now called The Arts—painting, sculpture, architec-ture, imaginative writing, music—have as their function to mediate between the raw confusion of sensory experience and the stark unfamiliarities of rationalization. Our emotional life is governed very much by inherited patterns of feeling and response. Any apparent shift in the pattern of cause and effect, any new sharpening of consciousness, will require mediation before it can be fully assimilated to our thinking as well as our feeling. In doing this the arts perform one of their most valuable social functions. That is why constant change has always been a characteristic of all artists' activity, and will remain so. The quick and violent artistic changes of recent times have been ascribed by some people to commercialization, the insistence on the fashionable, the need of jaded palates for a recently invented relish. It is part of my intention to show how much these apparent vagaries of artistic fashion are the product of the return of the artist to his traditional rôle, after the débâcle of the Industrial Revolution.

If it is the function of the artist to mediate, it is just as well to remember that this mediation is accomplished through the creation of physical objects. They are of a wide variety, from songs to railway stations, and together they make up the great complex of man-made environment. As the social conditions change, so the context within which the artist works will also change, sometimes radically. The increased prosperity of Europe which made itself felt so strongly through the thirteenth and fourteenth centuries saw the decay of corporate forms of organization. It was a slow but pervasive decay: quicker in the towns than in the country however. Collective trade and bargaining, collective industry, collective agriculture, collective games were slowly discarded. The pattern applies also to the religious life: monastic orders became increasingly elaborate and collegiate; liturgical worship became increasingly the act of private worship performed by several people in the same place almost by accident.

The artist, then, who had been the employee of a city, or corporation, or trade guild, or monastery became increasingly dependent on the good favour and taste of the individual patron: the rich merchant or banker, the prelate, the great nobleman or royal prince. And as those who exercised political power tended to withdraw from the direct exercise of arms, so this last kind of patronage, that of the prince as the *arbiter elegantiarum* of a court, became increasingly important, until it overshadowed all others in the seventeenth century.

I do not wish to imply, however, that there was a definite point at which some radical break with past ways had been made. When speaking of the social context of art at the end of the Middle Ages I do not want to insist too much on the shift to the direct influence of the patron who paid and who had the say as to what must be changed in a given piece of music or picture or building. That would be to obscure too much the indirect and perhaps, at that historical moment, the more important factor: the change in the sanction afforded by the community to the work of art. It was then that the delicate chantry chapels grew like parasites on the great body of the cathedral, and magnates with-drew their tables from the common hall to the private dining room. Slowly the paintings and sculptures which had filled the great public halls with their forceful rhetoric, and which had pointed the right and wrong of public acts, were reduced to the scale though not yet to the function of toys. The im-portant illuminated manuscripts of the early fifteenth century are not the great choir-books and lectionaries of earlier times, but the dainty Books of Hours from which an equivocally literate prince drew his meditations, even if he could not read the Office.

In so far as it is possible to speak of a unitary 'mediaeval art' it is essential to remember that a vast distance separates, say, the *Chanson de Roland* from *le Jouvencel*, Vézélay Abbey from the choir of King's College Chapel. In painting, the development is perhaps described more easily: genre and anecdote, portraits, landscape, the incidentals in fact slowly become emancipated from the didactic purpose of the work of art until they swamp it. In a sense, then, the great masters of the fifteenth century, from Masaccio to Piero della Francesca, returned to the older and simpler ways. Compare a scene painted by the chatty and precious Gentile da Fabriano with one done by Masaccio: a landscape more rudimentary than Giotto's, an architectural *mise en scène* which is simpler, more elementary. And yet there is a new spirit in the work of the fifteenth-century artists: a new rigour dominates the painter's vision.

This new and sharp vision of the external world is due to a method: that of setting out a space according to the optical laws of recession. It must be considered in relation to the progress in the manufacture of scientific instruments, and the consequent change in the whole view not only of the separate disciplines of geometry and astronomy but also of measurement.

The fourteenth-century mathematicians had taken geometry from its strict enclosure within the realm of speculation. With the great improvement of such instruments as the astrolabe and the normal surveying gear, and the introduction of the compass, all tangible material phenomena appeared measurable, and problems of surveying begun to occupy the minds of mathematicians. Perspective was the means which artists devised to mediate the emotional acceptance of the accurately measurable external world. It entailed, in turn, a revision of the previously accepted laws of harmony. The working out of the proportions of a building or painting followed an empirical geometric method of squaring or triangulation, which could be achieved with the help of the most rudimentary drawing instruments. However sophisticated the notion underlying such a procedure (that harmony will be achieved through recourse to mathematics), the method by which this was attempted was extremely simple— the most useful source of it is the little book *On Pinnacles* by the fifteenth-century German mason, Mattheas Roriczer.[1] But the elementary methods he describes were not adequate to cope with the elaborate distortions which occur in perspective. For this, the more complex procedure not only of ruling geometrically the plane of the picture, but also of determining in the horizontal plane the whole space in which the picture becomes a window was required. How extremely elaborate that procedure soon became has recently been instanced in an examination of Piero della

[1] Mattheas Roriczer: *Beuchlein von der Fialen Gerechtigkeit*, Nuerenberg, 1486; cf. also P. Frankl, 'The Secret of the Mediaeval Masons' in *Art Bulletin*.

Francesca's so-called *Flagellation*[1] in Urbino, where the key to the composition of the painting is a highly emotive allusion to the squaring of the circle, one of the set problems of contemporary geometers.[2]

Without dealing in causal or even temporal priorities, it will be obvious that a new notion of space will also require a different treatment of the human body from that usual in mediaeval painting. The human figure had appeared in most mediaeval painting as a flat shape, almost an arabesque, and was determined geometrically by rather naïve, two-dimensional, patterns, such as are shown by the thirteenth-century French mason, Villard d'Honnecourt in his notebook, the only document of its time and type to have survived.

In the painting of the fifteenth century, in those exactly measured and geometrically ingenious spaces the human figure had to be shown with precision, and in the round: and so the painters turned anatomist. Vasari tells us[3] that the Pollaiuolo brothers practised dissection on human bodies so as to draw up an exact *schema* of muscles, while Leonardo's enormous knowledge of anatomy, some half a century in advance of his contemporary medical authorities, is commonly acknowledged. How expressive, emotionally, this anatomical accuracy had become to the men of the Renaissance is attested by Vasari's story about Luca Signorelli who, when his son was killed in a street accident, sat all night drawing his naked body so as to be able to see in the work of his hands what nature had given him and evil fortune taken away.[4] The expressiveness lay not only in the anatomical precision, but also in the consequent and articulate re-creation of proportionally co-ordinated bodies. To this end, beyond the dissections mentioned before, painters of the fifteenth and sixteenth centuries recorded measurements of various human 'types' with a view to

[1] See Plate 11.

[2] R. Wittkower and R. Carter: 'Piero della Francesca's *Flagellation*', *Warburg and Courtauld Institute Journal*, 1953.

[3] Giorgio Vasari: 'Life of the Pollaiuolo brothers' in his *Lives of the most famous Architects, Painters and Sculptors*.

[4] Vasari in his 'Life of Signorelli.'

arriving not at some 'mean' measurement of a generalized human body suggested by the canon of Vitruvius, the Roman architect, but rather so as to be able to use bodies in movement in their paintings with the greatest degree of accuracy and therefore also of expressive power. The most thoroughly documented case of such an approach, always excepting Leonardo, was that of Dürer. In his *Unterweysung der Messung*, a highly popular book, Dürer set out the commensurate parts of human bodies of various types: babies and old men, fat and thin, tall and squat, and so on. The very popularity of the book leads one to suppose, even if the matter has never been properly analysed, that it was intended and used as a source-book by painters.

By the time of the Reformation there was, in fact, all the material available to construct any invented imaginative or devotional scene, even containing monsters, with the greatest anatomical rigour and precision; (the monster's whole anatomy would be delineated—it was no longer simply the extravagant chimera of the mediaeval manuscript) while space itself was expressively regulated. This great technical accomplishment was exploited by painters not only to provide fresh interpretations of the stock mediaeval themes; the devotional and scriptural narrative paintings, the allegories of good and bad government and the good and bad judge (such as the judgment of Cyrus), and elementary classics. It tempted the artist and the patron into systematic and highly atmospheric exploration of mythologies and fantasies which had hitherto not strayed from the borders of illuminated manuscripts and the bosses and gargoyles of cathedrals.

The century between about 1450 and 1550, moreover, was the greatest age of European art: Piero and Matthias Grünewald, Leonardo and Breughel, Michelangelo, Raphael, Bosch and Dürer were surrounded by a positive milky-way of minor stars and starlets. It was the age, too, of the greatest poetic and thematic invention in painting, while literature itself, as in England between Chaucer and Shakespeare, and in Italy between Petrarch and Tasso, was comparatively quiescent. The great age of poetic invention in painting was also the great age of sophistication of architecture. The schematic methods of the old master-masons were abandoned in favour of much more subtle methods of achieving proportion, by recourse to calculation, even if of the crudest kind, rather than empirical drawing procedure. It was this method which was brought to its greatest perfection by Palladio, in a system of polyphonic notations of dimension, as intricate and as varied as might be expected from a contemporary of Gaforio or Palestrina. If the change the century had brought about may be summed up in a cant phrase, we may say that whereas a mediaeval painting was a *presence*, painting after the fifteenth century presented a *temoignage*. The mediaeval painting was a substitute, a stand-in, for a saint or king; the element of recognition was provided by the iconographic incidentals (keys for St. Peter, etc.) or by some heraldic device. Only extremely rarely, and not until the end of the thirteenth century, was any actual resemblance even considered. In a famous manuscript of the *minnesingers*, in fact, some of the poets are shown in armour with their visors down, but are easily identifiable by their coats of arms prominently displayed. This dead-pan quality ruled the narrative cycles and scenes of universal judgment. The spectator read them, on the flat and solid wall, as he might read a written text: the world in the painting was a wholly other-world from the real one, there was no invitation extended to the spectator to walk into or to become part of the world in the painting: the gesture of our Lady in the Masaccio *Trinity*[1] painted about 1425, where, with a raised hand and eyes turned to the spectator, she invites us to contemplate her tortured Son, was inconceivable in terms of the art of Cimabue, Orcagna, or even Giotto. Soon after the picture was painted, Leone Battista Alberti wrote in his treatise on painting: 'And I like there to be someone [some figure] in the painting to announce what is happening in it. He may motion with his hand to come and see, or with an angry face and threatening eyes make as if he wanted the events to remain secret. Again he may point to some danger, or some wonder in the picture, and invite us to laugh or to weep with

[1] See Plate 12.

him. And whatever the painted figures are engaged in doing or watching should contribute to the action or point the tale.'

This practice appealed to the minds of most sixteenth- and seventeenth-century artists as much as to those of their fifteenth-century predecessors. Independently, moreover, Flemish artists had turned to a similar procedure. If you look at the signature on the portrait of the Arnolfini couple in the National Gallery, painted in 1434 (that is, two years before Alberti wrote his treatise), you will notice the unusual form, *Joannes van Eyck fuit hic*—'has been here'. Whatever the interpretation of this enigmatic inscription may be—and most of the bulky literature surrounding the painting hinges on its interpretation—there is no doubt that the artist was asking the spectator to be a witness of it, much as he painted himself witnessing it, reflected as he is in the convex mirror between the two figures, and standing among the detailed and intimate debris of an inhabited room.

The sense of witness, the sense that the artist was no longer providing his audience with a narrative like one of the early chroniclers, but that he was giving the spectator the sense of actual visual presence, was reflected in literature by two new and related developments: the emancipation of the vulgar tongue, as distinct from Latin, the literary or even academic language; and the increasing reliance, in all literary forms—though it began almost exclusively in prose—on direct speech.[1] The sense of immediate presence, which of course the *jongleurs* and itinerant singers must always have cultivated, passes into written literature in a rudimentary form in the early Italian *prosatori*, in Sacchetti, in Boccaccio, and is present too in some of the poets of the thirteenth century—in Jacopone da Todi, for instance. In the north it occurred later, and again followed the emancipation of the vulgar tongue. But, even then, Northern literature was, until well into the seventeenth century, totally consumed by the passion for allegory. No detail was too insignificant for a double or even a more multiple meaning. Look again at the details of the Arnolfini portrait: the single candle in the brass chandelier, the four

[1] Cf. J. Huizinga: *The Waning of the Middle Ages*, pp. 290 et seq.

5

oranges, the discarded clogs, the terrier in the foreground, and on the back wall of the room the rosary hung next to a mirror whose frame is studded with ten medallions of the Passion. Even if we had no knowledge of the attitude of mind of the painter and the client, surely it would seem obvious that it is all too intensely seen to be a narrative of visual incident of no relevance to the theme of the painting. This taste for the allegory of miniutiae was accompanied by the decay of the 'great' themes of mediaeval art. There is a lassitude about fifteenth- and sixteenth-century descants on the conventions of chivalry, courteous love, and the commonplaces of devotion which pervades all the arts:

> Hélas! on dit que je ne fais mes rien
> Que jadis fas mainte chose nouvelle;
> La raison est que je n'ay pas merrien
> Dont je fisse chose bonne ne belle.

laments Eustache Deschamps, a fifteenth-century Burgundian poet. The great mystics were still able to galvanize the popular imagination with new images urgently stated—Meister Eckhardt need only be mentioned here. In the south, moreover, a new patristic revival, promoted by the new device of printing and the contact with Greek Byzantine scholars after the Council of Florence, found splendid architectural expression in the new churches of Brunelleschi, Alberti and their followers.[1] It was too late, however, to infuse these new energies into the body-politic of Christendom. The demand for reform had become too insistent, and the resistance to it on the part of authority too obstinate.

When Luther burnt the Bull of excommunication on 17 December 1520, and the break-up of Christendom began in earnest, a catastrophic change occurred in the situation of the arts. The most obvious immediate consequence of the Reformation was the clearing of all or most sculptures and pictures from existing church buildings, and a general interdict on religious imagery in public places. Curiously, it was not painting and sculpture which

---

[1] Cf. for instance the Programme for the SSma Annunziata, by S. Lang, in the *Warburg and Courtauld Institute Journal*, 1955.

suffered first from this repression, but architecture. Until its northern revival under the more or less benevolent despotisms of the early eighteenth century, with all its echoes of French inspiration and undertones of a sophisticated, semi-arcadian sentiment, northern Europe suffered a stunted, heavy, over-seasoned architecture for some three hundred years. Architecture—or so it seemed—could not be deprived of its proper ornaments of painting and sculpture without wilting; however, painting and sculpture continued to thrive in the north of Europe, reaching a new climax in the two generations of Rubens and Rembrandt. I have already noticed the emphasis on incidentals, on detail transformed into allegory. With the separation of the arts, with the division of environment, in the north, there is associated, however, the new assurance about the external world. Not only had the world become a sphere, the universe had become in a sense decentralized—the earth was now a satellite of the sun, and the newly visualized motion of the spheres was to many philosophers, humanists and also scientists a demonstration of the platonic theory of the harmony of the spheres:

> Fair ordered lights, whose motion without noise
> Resembles those true joys
> Whose spring is on that hill where you do grow
> And we here taste sometimes below.

> With what exact obedience do you move
> Now beneath and now above!
> And in your vast progressions overlook
> The darkest night, the closest nook!

writes a seventeenth-century poet, and prays

> Settle and fix our hearts that we may move
> In order, peace and love;
> And taught obedience by thy whole creation
> Become, an humble, holy nation.[1]

There was an assurance in the vision of the apparently immutable movement of the universe, and assurance in the newly discovered

[1] Henry Vaughan: 'The Constellations'.

ability to navigate, which men owed to the compass and to the
scientific cartography which the discovery entailed.

> Whilst my physicians by their love are grown
> Cosmographers, and I their map, who lie
> Flat on this bed, that by them may be shown,
> That this is my South-west discovery
> *Per fretum febris*, by these straits to die,
>
> I joy, that in these straits, I see my west . . .[1]

wrote another seventeenth-century poet in the assurance of faith and
the language of cartographers. The poets now respond immediately, as do the painters, to the profusion of impressions around
them; they no longer see nature through the opaque screen of
conventions, some of them very ancient—the picture of four
elements at the basis of physics and chemistry, and the corresponding one of four humours at the basis of medicine and
psychology—which had for so long acted as the conventional
mediators between the inquisitive, reflective observer, and the
undermining and overwhelming impact of immediate experience.
But the profusion of nature had in turn become much more
controllable, much less menacing, and natural phenomena in all
their variety and incoherence struck the imagination of many
artists as interesting, and sufficient in themselves. And yet the
great emotional impact of this new and direct approach to nature
was not fully absorbed until the beginning of the nineteenth
century. In visual art, however, the effect was radical and very
destructive. I may perhaps be forgiven if, in spite of the very
interesting relation between the artists and scientists in Italy,[2] I
ignore it, and turn entirely to the Low Countries, in particular to
Rembrandt.

Here is the great tragic figure of post-Reformation art. There
can be no doubt of the religious intensity of Rembrandt's works.
The precision of the constructed programmatic composition was

[1] John Donne: 'A Hymn to God my God in my Sicknesse'.
[2] Cf. however Erwin Panofsky: *Galileo as a Critic of the Art*, The Hague, 1954, and
the last two chapters of Anthony Blunt: *Theory of Art in Italy, 1400–1650*, Oxford,
1940.

not for him, nor again could he produce the conventional portraits, genre exercises, or those appetizing still-lifes which in his time and later were so much in demand for prosperous dining-rooms. Look at his portrait of his wife Saskia as Flora.[1] The mythological element is almost ironical, so thinly is the symbolism spread: and yet how prolific and inexhaustible this plain, plump, pregnant girl, clutching her bunch of greenery is! But for this passion, for this intensity and immediacy of vision there was no religious context available. The portrait of Saskia, as well as those of the other members of Rembrandt's circle of friends and family in various biblical and mythological transformations show us the breaking-point between the programme, the theme as the content of the painting, and the manner of treating what is shown in the picture: landscape, still-life, portrait, as well as the very handling of the painting as the 'content' of a picture. For Rembrandt, and for most painters in the generations which were to succeed him, the content of the painting was not some new approach to the programme—on a parallel with the way in which the allegory of incident succeeded the narrative and symbol in the fifteenth century, but a break in the tradition. The content, the point of interest for the spectator, was now provided by the way in which the painter chose to treat isolated technical problems: light falling through translucent substances (water, wine, glass, etc.), the transmission of weight, the rendering of volume and so on, but without any particular regard to the relation between the technical achievement and the expressive power. If every picture still told a story, it was the telling and not the story that was of interest. The problem of technique became the artist's toy in a game in which sensibility was his only real rule and arbiter.

Two hundred years later this attitude towards painting achieved itself in Impressionism. Achieved and surpassed itself—since the Impressionist problem, as it was formulated by Renoir in his later nudes and by Claude Monet in his series of great lily-pond panels, was not to isolate a given technical point and resolve it, but to

[1] See Plate 13.

achieve the all-over texture of a *total* impression through the quick, direct handling of paint.

Wonderful though these paintings are, they were done without any possible concern for human and social context. No doubt if such a concern had been suggested to an Impressionist painter, he would be simply puzzled, as many contemporary painters are. The museum and the private art-collection were the accepted and unquestioned destination for their paintings. But pictures for a drawing-room or even a museum are physical objects among physical objects. And the juxtaposition of these objects, each one of which had originally been the record of a total impression can only confuse the observer, who passes from one to another without ever being able to achieve a poised relationship with his environment.

That relaxed relationship, the freedom to ignore the works of art individually but to accept them as the inevitable part of one's surrounding was something that Giotto, for instance, in the Scrovegni chapel, or Mantegna in the Eremitani chapel not fifty yards away, could take for granted. To provide the spectator with a visual context for his everyday actions, as well as with criteria for criticizing his experience in visual terms, was to them obviously a part of their job. It would not have occurred to them, perhaps, that their pictures might have a validity outside that of their functional context. But by the end of the nineteenth century, when environment—in western Europe, at any rate— had become more confusing than ever before or even since, the plastic arts not only failed to provide a coherent visual context for human activity, but even the means for criticizing visual experience were now lacking, since painting, the art which is most obviously the custodian of such standards, was concerned with an increasingly narrower range of experience. The Impressionists are not to blame for this situation. If the range of experience of which they could treat was narrow, it was certainly genuine at a time when vast quantities of academic painting contributed nothing to the environment, and attempted to remove painting from any direct contact with experience. Reading Henry

Murger's *Scènes de la Vie de Bohème*, where one of the themes is the sad fate of a large painting, an academic composition, at the end one is no wiser as to the quality of the painting, or indeed as to the quality of the work produced by any other artist mentioned in the book. The existence of artists, as it is described by Murger, is a 'dedicated' experience: the artists' standards, rule of life, norms of behaviour are not, cannot, should not be those of the commonalty. Nor is there a special part in Bohemia reserved for the great genius who stakes his claim to it by showing his supreme ability in his work—a place such as Vasari reserved for Michelangelo. Since artists are the people who deal in feelings, and have a monopoly of them, they are all apart and inspired, whatever the quality of the objects which result from the inspiration. Manet in the *Moulin de la Galette*, and Degas in his ballet paintings, saw themselves as outsiders, as uninvolved observers, though privileged ones, since they stood in the wings. But the curse which beset the Impressionists' literary contemporaries from Baudelaire to Verlaine did not overtake painters until the next generation: Van Gogh, Gauguin, and Toulouse-Lautrec were each cursed in an exemplary and public manner.

The 'set-apartness' of the artist was emphasized by his costume. It was not just that it seemed difficult to take a middle position between the aesthete's dandification and Bohemian *louche*. There was a definite uniform, which most of the time seemed to involve a floppy bow tie and a black velvet beret. The curious dichotomy which bedevilled the artist's existence, that he had the high prestige of a prophet, while he was treated as a totally unserious person wholly disengaged from the real business of living, had its apotheosis in the curious relationship between Wagner and the poor mad moon-king, Ludwig II of Bavaria.

Ludwig II, with his new orders of chivalry and puginesque jewellery and huge romantic castles perched on absurdly inaccessible rocks, brings me back to my central theme. The one point at which the modern world touched him, was through his interest in ingenious mechanical devices—synchronizing clocks, voice transmission, and so on. But it was an interest in the

ingenious solution of an abstract problem, the creation of a toy—
Ludwig's interest in mechanical invention was much like that of
any intelligent fourteenth- or fifteenth-century prince, though the
technical resources at his command were infinitely greater. These
had been developed in the interests of production, a vulgar
activity unworthy, so it was considered during much of the
nineteenth century, of the attention of the sensitive, the artistic,
and of ladies. Theirs was the realm of feeling. But the realm of
action and thought, the domain of real men was that of increasing
production, of progress.

That such a division exists is the great tragedy of contemporary
art; it is not a tragedy which can be blamed on the Renaissance or
even on the Reformation, or on any other single group or movement or period. The process had begun slowly, in the middle of the
eighteenth century, even before the application of steam power.
According to one authority[1] the production-line process had been
perfected by 1780 by an American miller, Oliver Edwards, who
applied the ancient principle of the Archimedean screw to
rationalize the process of milling and despatching flour to the
exclusion of human operators. That mass-production was introduced independently of steam-operated machinery is an important
notion; since we must realize that the Industrial Revolution was
not simply the advent of steam-power, but was a social and
economic change, in which steam was more of a powerful
catalyst than a prime cause: whatever we choose to call it, however, Adam Smith and Malthus were as much the fathers of this
revolution as James Watt. To have hung a whole culture on the
expansion of productive processes, and to have pushed everything
else into the background: to have centralized economic power to
such a degree that an empire could be organized on the assumption
that the mother country will live, to a large extent, on imported
foodstuffs; to have sanctioned competition to the death by elevating it into a biological principle, did indeed lead to a vast growth
of industrial activity. From all this activity the artist knew himself to be excluded. The profusion of the man-made was as

[1] Siegfried Giedion: *Mechanization Takes Command* (Oxford University Press, 1949).

menacing and as bewildering, in the nineteenth century, as that of the natural had been during the Middle Ages and before. And the artists seemed unable to perform their traditional rôle of mediators. Strangely enough, their return to that rôle was heralded not so much by their discovery of the beauties of machinery, but by the discovery of the art of the primitive peoples. The theory of the space-time continuum was formulated in Germany, while Picasso, Braque, and Apollinaire were discovering African and Polynesian art in the junk-shops and anthropological collections of Paris. Here was an art full of an emotional power which seemed to appeal to the whole of man; an art which was functional, which had effectively mediated between the man who had made it, and for whom it had been made, and a terrifying, prolific Nature. In primitive art the highly sophisticated artists at the beginning of our century found the elements of a new visual language of a simplification of form which allowed them to interpret the vision of nature which the discoveries of physicists and astronomers have given us. It is hardly surprising that, as matter was dissolved into electrical functions, so the object in cubist painting became the analysis of dimension and of movement. The period of forty or so years which separates us from the cubists has been a time of much experiment, some of it absurd, some diverting, and some absolutely splendid. This paper is too confined for the sort of 'who did what first' kind of history which it is fashionable to write nowadays. What matters to us most about it all is that these experiments have slowly, painfully, and at times through apparent accident, led to the creation of a popular visual language. This visual language may not be popularly accepted in its most concentrated form—in the paintings of Mondrian or Kandinsky, say. But it is the visual idiom of street advertising, the newspapers, the factories, and the sports stadium. And it is the only visual language in which we may speak to our contemporaries of those things which too many of them regard as specialized experience and which must again be placed within the context of everyday life. To those who hesitate to adopt so latitudinarian an attitude to the gross and jangling—as they think it—modernity of some of our contemporaries, I should like to quote in conclusion these lines of one of the great experimenters of modern literature:

> Nous voulons explorer la bonté contrée énorme ou tout se tait
> Il y a aussi le temps qu'on peut chasser ou faire revenir
> Pitié pour nous qui combattons toujours au frontières
> De l'illimite et de l'avenir
> Pitié pour nos erreurs pitié pour nos péchés.[1]

The artist has always been condemned to the part of a frontiersman of consciousness, and to acknowledge that such is his place is to restate his traditional function. It is his duty to create a language in which the things which have not yet been said but need saying may be said, and to purify the speech of his contemporaries by abandoning the dead weight of vacant conventions. Such a process has been going on at a particularly rapid rate perhaps over the last fifty years. To reject the visual language which has been produced as a result of this process, is not to make a decision about tradition and experiment, or about the desirability of novelty, or any such grand issue. It is simply to cut oneself off from one's contemporaries, rendering oneself mute, when one is obliged to speak out.

[1] From 'La Jolie Rousse', by Guillaume Apollinaire, in *Zône*, 1914.

II

THE WITNESS OF THE ARTISTS

6. *The Poet*

SAUNDERS LEWIS

Mr. Saunders Lewis, a Welsh poet honoured in his own land, lectured on mediaeval Welsh literature in the University of Cardiff until 1957.

INVITING me to take part in this symposium Mr. Todd wrote: 'I am inviting you to contribute as a poet. Your contribution could include some indication of how in your view art mediates truth, both to the artist himself and to those who listen to his work. How would you describe the experience of artistic creation?'

May I take that as my agenda? The fact that none of you knows anything at all of my work is an obvious advantage; it gives me a sort of anonymity. I can say 'he' as though it were 'me'.

I suppose it is normal to begin writing verses in adolescence, perhaps in the last two years of school life. It is a consequence of being taught poetry. A poet is a schoolboy who likes poetry even after being taught it. Lines and verses stick in his mind, are exciting, and he tries to do something similar. Then he discovers that the most absorbing of all verse is that of his slightly elder contemporaries. Poets are largely formed by their something seniors, whether in their image or in revolt against it.

May I pass-by the question, how does a poem start? There are so many answers by so many poets in as many languages. I venture a generalization: however the poem starts, what sets the poet working at it is the realization that what is vaguely in his mind has the promise, the shapeability, of a poem. A poet is a man who has formed the habit of making poems. By practice he acquires proficiency in recognizing and collecting the sort of material that is capable of being shaped into a poem. He lives on the watch for it. In mediaeval Wales and Ireland the material of poetry was part of the curriculum of the poets' schools. Today it depends on the caprice of fashion and the caprice of the individual.

But whatever it be, the matter of poetry is not an unwritten poem in the poet's mind. It is not a completed experience for which the poet has to find adequate symbol. A poem is not the expression of anything already existing, nor of anything that has already occurred unexpressed.

When you are making a poem you are aware of two activities, both essential and continuous. The first is complex. Your poem has started, perhaps a line, perhaps more, perhaps—in spite of Mallarmé—an embryo idea. So you begin churning up, inventing, discovering, phrases, half-lines, lines, sentences that grope into the right rhythmic shape, or else that won't, and your poem builds up. You depend, of course, on what the doctors call your foreconscious for memories and associations of all kinds and periods of your life, and you find you are fed with images and suggestions of matter appropriate for that or this particular point of your poem. You don't know what may not turn up. It is not that you've got an idea but cannot find the right word for it. It simply is that you haven't yet the idea, you are suspended, waiting, willing, experimenting, evoking, perhaps by chanting a phrase repeatedly to yourself, fishing for the thing, despairing; and then when your headache is so bad that you give up and think to go to bed, suddenly it comes—or no, it doesn't come, but there it is, proton-like and Proteus-like, having crossed no intermediate space, impossibly virginal, nothing like anything you expected, but so absurdly inevitable that with glaring untruthfulness you dub it *le mot juste*.

So the poem is not the completion of anything foreseen or preconceived. It is not the carrying out of a previous intention. Certainly it is necessary to have some initial intention, but you launch your intention, you entrust it to the co-operation of all that seems chance or at least is unknown and incalculable in the foreconscious and the unconscious. So that the poem does not recollect or recreate an experience. The poem is the experience:

it creates the experience for the poet just as much as for his first audience. The Dante of the *Inferno* was not a man who *had been* through Hell, but a man who went into Hell a-making.

Yet I must not suggest that it is all a game of tennis between the conscious mind and the foreconscious. There is a third player; let us call him *technique*. Poetry is normally made in verse, all kinds of verse, from such strict forms as sonnet or *englyn* to *vers libre*. Verse, all and every verse, implies rules, relations, semantic and phonetic relations, formal construction, both rhythmic and metric. These are never ornaments of verse in the sense of being superfluities, but essential and major concerns. No craftsman of verse can give his constant attention to these factors without observing that they profoundly and incalculably contribute to the texture, to the themes, to the development, to the ultimate shape of the product which is the poem. Paul Valéry once wrote that Racine would change the character of one of his *dramatis personae* if a rhyme demanded it. That is not a *boutade*: it holds truth, though it might be more carefully said. It is not that a rhyme for Racine modifies a character already decided, already entire, but rather that the rhyme discovers the character, contributes to the character, adds it own unforeseen quality to the character. When Monime tells Mithridate:

> . . . cet aveu honteux, où vous m'avez forcée,
> Demeurera toujours présent à ma pensée.
> Toujours je vous croirais incertain de ma foi;
> Et le tombeau, Seigneur, est moins triste *pour moi*
> Que le lit d'un époux qui m'a fait cet outrage,

both Racine and Monime are surprisedly discovering that she has become this kind of person, that there are in her these unplumbed depths, and hence to the end of the play he has to treat her accordingly.

Characters don't have the same sort of life in the dramatist's mind before he starts writing and after starting. Characters take flesh from the words fastened to them, from the rhymes they find, out of the unfolding situation. They grow into and through the technique.

Some modern critics have written blame of Aristotle because in his discussion of tragedy he said that the thing of first importance was the plot. They are shocked that he did not give priority to characterization. That is a sadly academic criticism. Aristotle was examining how plays were made. He was analysing tragedy from the point of view of the practical maker, and I think he was right and most percipient to put plot first. Plot also is technique, and for the working playwriter it is the exploration of the plot that contributes most to the shaping of the tragic hero. I remember reading the advice of an English literary critic to young aspiring playwriters. Put half a dozen living characters together on the stage, he advised, get them talking, and then see what happens to them. For my part I cannot imagine even a Pirandello play being written that way. You don't put living characters into a play. You start your plot with mere ciphers or ghosts. You fasten words to them while you fasten them into a plot. Then, if your words have life, they may emerge from the plot living characters. I think that is as true of *Uncle Vanya* as of *Oedipus Rex*.

Technique, in this view, is the poet's major ally; the technical controls of verse, far from being restrictions or impediments, are an ever-present fount of happiness. Rhymes create character and alliteration may tangle a hawk in a sprung rhythm. The poet is a craftsman who has learnt to trust technique. This, I suspect, is a point at which I ought to bow to the ballet dancer.

The second constant activity in the making of a poem is that of critic. 'Would he had blotted a thousand' said Ben Jonson rightly of his better. You cannot control what the foreconscious offers. Half-lines leap up, phrases, new combinations of words; images and memories take word-shapes, sometimes nimbly, sometimes sluggishly. But there you are, the appraising critical you, alert, watching, rejecting, selecting, moving the pieces about, building the chosen into a satisfactory unit, testing them on your ear, speaking them in different tones, scrutinizing them on the paper. Have you got the necessary patience? Can you reject steadfastly enough or do you surrender to what you know is second-rate? Can you lie in wait long enough, like a fisherman over a dark pool? Is the critic in you—the essential poet in you— resolute enough, inflexible, fine and subtle enough? Everything depends on that. Making poems, like making a picture, is applied criticism. A single line may destroy a lyric or a painting. Even to recognize when your poem is finished is a vital critical decision. For I have said that I do not understand a poem as the reproduction of anything previously complete in the mind. Therefore to find the poem finished is to be critically satisfied with the whole shape of it, since there is no criterion outside the poem itself. That is why fixed forms such as sonnet or ballade are so tempting, and why success in them is now all but impossible. Technique can also betray. One needs immense critical sureness to succeed with the fixed forms.

Mr. Todd's second question was: how does art mediate truth? I am no philosopher and I must try to avoid the snares of the metaphysicians and the analysts. The account I have offered of poetic composition posits that the poet does not 'tell the truth'. He is not a witness in any legal sense. He is not relating or recollecting or symbolizing a previous experience. The fact that memory provides very much of the unshaped material of a poem does not, I trust, invalidate this account. One may remember the Abbé Brémond's theory of the relation of poetry to prayer. It seemed to me a most depressing theory in its implication for poets. I am anxious to avoid giving my two nouns, poetry and truth, capital letters, and I am more interested in poems and in plays than in poetry. And yet, truth in poetry—the phrase has its honest meaning, just as it is sound sense to talk of sincerity in a poem. Any poem, even the slightest lyric, is a complex thing. Let me go to neutral territory and consider for a moment 'The Banks o' Doon' by Robert Burns:

> Ye flowery banks o' bonnie Doon
> How can ye blume sae fair!

It is a hackneyed theme. In six simple verses the poet uses images that had been used a thousand times before him. Nothing is new;

6

the rhymes are most obvious, the rhythms those of commonplace song. Yet it is one of the lovely and immaculate things. Truth and sincerity are words you need to describe its quality. An adjective too literary, a smear of sentimentality, might have toppled the thing into a falsehood. Burns goes serenely by his dangers and achieves a song that is as pure as a crocus.

So I would offer for your consideration that the truth of a poem is the recognition of the poet's critical control. It is the criterion of the poem's spiritual unity. The truth, the integrity—and I thank Goodness for this—are not all in the poet or in his mode of life or even in his immediate mood, but they are in the poem, in the thing made, which, once completed, stands independent of the poet. Integrity is not a virtue of the poet transferred to the poem as though the style were indeed the man, but is a quality achieved objectively in the poem through the poet's craftsmanship and critical control. Even so, I do not offer that as a dogmatic statement about all poetry. I offer it as a means of protecting my own integrity. Poets are not as good as their poetry and are not served by being identified with their poems. There is a wisdom in *Hamlet* that there never was in William Shakespeare. The truth of the poem depends on no reference outside itself. Its validity is its one-ness, and its truth is its being. It has the truth of a thing, a *res*.

I do not deny, of course, that there is a large body of poetic work in many languages that is autobiographical, that poets have had experiences which they have recorded in poems. What I am trying to maintain is that the making of the poem changes, transforms the experience, frames it in a new context so that its truth now is the truth of the poem. It cannot be veracious, it cannot be witness, just because art demands an absolute unity, and every poet knows that in composing he surrenders his experience to the poem. I venture to maintain that this is true even of the Song of the Ascent of Mount Carmel.

A good poem is an impersonal thing; whereas bad verse is personal. I wonder will the dancer tell us that at the supreme moment of a well-achieved dance she is like Wordsworth's Lucy:

> She neither hears nor sees;
> Roll'd round in earth's diurnal course,
> With rocks, and stones, and trees.

I believe it must be a common experience for a poet, having some time written something good, to read it again after an interval and to say to himself, 'How did I ever happen to write that? I cannot even imagine myself today thinking or saying anything at all like that.' When you come out of the dance you are just ordinary and normal. It is when you surrender your being to the technique that you achieve things beyond your knowledge of yourself.

I stop here. I know that there are implications unexplored in more than one of my paragraphs, but I have tried not to trespass on the philosopher's ground. Nor have I discussed 'poetic vision' as a means of approaching Truth. Frankly, I do not know what poetic vision means. It is the adjective that I don't understand.

7. The Dancer

MARY DRAGE

Mary Drage danced in the rank below ballerina with the Royal Ballet Company at Covent Garden until she married in 1958. It was only with difficulty that she was able to spend a few hours at the symposium, in between performances and rehearsals.

WHEN a dancer is asked to say something about what it feels like to be a dancer, or what makes her want to dance, she has an immediate sense of impotence. What *can* be expressed by dancing just cannot be expressed in words; and, anyway, so much of what she does is completely intuitive. A rash journalist, seeking to probe behind this apparent spontaneity, got what he deserved when he asked a famous ballerina what she thought about while she danced. She replied, 'My next meal', and the interview ended!

The only thing I *really* know about my feeling when I dance is that it is then that I seem to become most truly myself. At no other time do I have such a certainty and conviction of my own reality, my particular and separate identity, the very nature of myself as a person, a dancer—and something more than a dancer too; but that 'something more' is the part of one that can only be expressed in dancing.

This statement may seem a bit far-fetched at first—it seems to make the other dancers, even the audience, seem quite redundant. But it is a fact that the sense of being oneself when dancing can be attained quite apart from the other dancers or the audience; it can even be attained when practising alone provided that there is the music to inspire one. Even one dancer alone can produce this impression, or feeling, but when a whole group are combined in a ballet, dancing with their utmost powers and before a receptive and responsive audience, the experience is magnified a thousand-fold.

This surrendering of oneself whole-heartedly to expression in the dance cannot be achieved truly, nor even perhaps partially, in the corps de ballet. There it is one's business to dance to the best of one's ability but always exactly in unison with the others. One has to be continually watching the lines of dancers and the patterns on the stage, and any kind of individuality in timing or expression is out of place and even reprehensible. Any effect produced or emotion expressed must be the joint effort of the group, and the more single-minded and united the artistes, the finer will be the result.

In dancing a solo role, however, the important thing is to bring one's entire individuality and concentration into dancing this particular character or that particular sequence. In both cases the essence of the dance is so much more than just a matter of choreography and technique, of learning a series of steps and executing them perfectly, that without this extra feeling for the rôle itself, one dances badly. A purely mechanical performance is a bad performance, however brilliant technically, and for the dancers themselves it is a degrading experience. A sense of frustration will pervade the whole performance if it has become nothing but a succession of senseless acrobatics. The trouble is that so many different things can affect a performance and reduce it to the near-mechanical level. In this negative sense the presence of the other dancers can make an enormous difference. Performing well, they raise the entire performance through their support; but if they perform half-heartedly, they can actually put off the other artistes. Nothing is more destructive to atmosphere than to come face to face with another artiste whose mind is quite obviously elsewhere, or who is just going through the motions of a rôle.

This applies, of course, to all the people concerned in the performance: the conductor, the orchestra, the stage staff, and the audience—all can help or hinder the production by their attitude. You are very conscious, too, when a work is going badly, that it could and should have lifted you out of yourself, should have drawn on that inner part of yourself without which you cannot feel that you have done your best. You feel, and everyone else with you feels, let down and cheated. The magic has failed to take hold. Onlythe greatest artistes can pull a performance together. By their personal magnetism and the loyalty they inspire, they can cause a poor first act to be followed by a brilliant and inspiring second act, and wring from a dull and unresponsive audience a warmth and enthusiasm that they never knew they could feel.

I hope it will be clear from this that the more one loses oneself in the dance, the better it is from the audience's point of view. The less one is conscious of the steps themselves, so long as they are faithfully executed, the better one's performance. When one is consciously trying to give the audience something, and the more one is consciously pretending to act a part (acting in the bad sense of the word) the worse one's performance will be. It is in this that the Russian Ballet is supreme. The dancers *are* their parts, quite simply; they live with their rôles, constantly thinking of the people that they portray, and even cry real tears over their tribulations. It is true, conversely, that outside the ballet, and when not talking about ballet, they seem very odd people indeed to us Westerners, shy, reserved, and absolutely uninterested in the ordinary business of living. Their tradition is still one of absolute religious dedication to their art, and it is for them almost sacramental. Their artistic standards are so high that they would not dream of putting someone on to the stage at short notice. Dancing is above commerce and, anyway, money is no object to them, so if the dancer of one of the principal rôles is ill, the whole performance is cancelled. It would be regarded as a kind of blasphemy to make someone else learn the steps and go on to the stage without the usual exhaustive preparation; indeed, it would almost be regarded as an impossibility, ballet not being merely the mastery of a certain technique of dancing, but the understanding and interpretation of a character. It is an artistic experience, and as such cannot be turned out as printing presses turn out copies of a picture. Each performance has to be an original artistic creation like the actual painting of a picture; and each performance is, in fact, exactly like that for the dancer. Here again the Russians score with their much less frequent performances, each of which is approached with all the enthusiasm (as they themselves admit) of gifted amateurs. Even when just talking to them we felt like commercial and disillusioned old 'pros.' by comparison with their unbounded love of their work.

Every performance, then, is 'live'. There cannot be any mirror-like repetition of a ballet in the way that you can make a good print of a picture, one which, however inferior to the original, nevertheless brings it happily to mind. No, dancing is always 'first hand', newly created by each artiste at each performance. Day in, day out, one is involved in this endless creation, and so it is that dancing, of all the arts, is so often half tragic and extremely frustrating. At every performance one leaves a part of oneself on the stage. Sometimes this is something which felt so wonderful that one longs to have it back again, so that one might be able to *give* it once again, and sometimes it is the exact reverse. A performance that has been utterly mechanical or technically second-rate one longs to be able to erase, as an artist is able to destroy a picture which has failed, to obliterate its memory by burning it up, or as a poet can tear up his words. But the wretched dancer cannot undo what has been done. Something is left behind on the stage which is incredibly personal, a part which is gone for good, but which, so long as one can feel that it was received into the hearts of the watchers, it is happiness to lose. To be told that one has *moved* the audience is the finest and most longed-for compliment that a dancer can receive. No mere concrete record of achievement or prowess can give a dancer the same satisfaction.

It may be asked how all this can be true of the purely abstract ballets. It seems quite understandable that in a story ballet the dancer must merge in the character portrayed in the same way as an actor does, for the more importance that is given to the story itself the more convincing will be the performance. But can this be applied to pure dancing? Here again, one must aver that the Russians excel in the story ballets. Ulanova really becomes Juliet and the little peasant girl Giselle. It has taken her years of loving thought to reach this standard of perfection. In Russia, two years are usually given to the study of any new part. For the first year one dances alone, memorizing the steps, perfecting the technique, and thinking about the rôle. Then for six months one works with a partner or ballet-master, to criticize and polish, and finally, when the artiste feels ready, the rôle is danced before the director of the Ballet Company, who then decides whether the result is good enough to warrant being seen by the public. The ensuing performance has a reality and power to excite and move its audience unparalleled in the Western theatre.

But to return to our question: how does all this apply to abstract ballet—the ballet of pattern? It applies to almost the same degree; and the finer the ballet, the more wonderful the music, the easier it is to reach the same plane of self-forgetfulness. The simple classic steps and pure white tunics worn by the dancers in César Franck's *Symphonic Variations* is to my mind the perfect example of the abstract ballet. In this, the dancer must lose his *own* identity and be in some way identified with the music. He becomes a mediator of the music to the audience, an inter-preter who is yet part of the representation of the piece. He must be completely receptive to the music, not so much a human being as a reflection of mood and sound—the more musically sensitive he is the better. Perhaps one could say that in a story ballet the artiste is like a stained-glass window which modulates the light, but in the pattern or abstract ballet he must be like a completely clear pane of glass.

One is aware that the audience is, or should be, very closely involved with oneself. This is so much the case that I feel myself that ballets which are solely tales of man's malice and portray nothing but evil and horror with no relieving light, are a bad thing. To name one, *The Miraculous Mandarin* has always seemed to me to be quite unnecessary. There is nothing in it which the audience did not know before, and as an essay in modern brutality it is simply a record of evil deeds with no possible artistic justification. It can only depress and degrade its watchers; this fact separates it completely from the ballets in which other emotions are mixed with the evil themes and in which the tale itself is more human, as in *Miracle in the Gorbals* or *The Rake's Progress*. A really sordid ballet seems to be even worse than a really sordid play, because there is a deeper and more physical identification of the audience with the subject through the actions of the performers. Equally I think that there is something particularly ennobling in a ballet with an heroic theme. Take the love-even-unto-death of the hero and heroine of *Swan Lake* or the unselfish and undying devotion of the Khan Girei for a Christian maiden in Pushkin's *Fountains of Bakshisarei*. They really leave one feeling a better person. A good performance of something like *Les Sylphides* can give one almost a sense of being purified. In ballet all the senses are assailed at once, and so it is hardly surprising that it should be able to produce such a strong effect on one's feelings.

Sometimes it becomes virtually impossible for the choreography to rise to the heights of the music, when this attains a grandeur and feeling which no single dancer nor even the finest ensemble could ever adequately interpret. There is a theme in Richard Strauss's *Don Juan*, at the entrance of the heroine, La Morte Amoureuse, which is such a heavenly passage that it is almost impossible to imagine a justifiable translation into dancing. One fears that nothing the human body can do could adequately express all that the music conveys.

Dancing demands a continual search and striving after the perfect performance. This is not just an idea fostered in us by high-minded philosophers and critics of the dance. Most ballet dancers would not think of putting into words what I am trying to say, for we very rarely stop to analyse our motives in dancing, but if they did I am pretty certain that they would feel the same about what I have been trying to explain. They are certainly always striving after the ideal performance. Occasionally, for various reasons, people fall into working without any real interest, but they cannot remain in this state for long and still continue to dance. Either their love of their art reawakens or they drift off into other things. This need of single-mindedness and the absolute necessity of a vocational attitude towards dancing raises grave problems. For the Russian dancers these problems hardly exist—they are heirs to a great tradition, stretching back to long before the Revolution and quite indifferent to politics; a tradition which treats dancing vocationally and respects it almost as much as the icon painter revered his art. The means for a completely dedicated life are there. In the past at any rate, it has not been unusual for a great dancer to marry, have a child, and come back to dancing—or even to suffer a grave illness, recover, convalesce, and return in her own time. She is considered so much a part of the company, and her artistry is so valuable, that she is allowed to take such things in her stride. Tensions there must be of a personal kind, as there always are in human life, but there is no basic problem of how to manage to be both a dancer and a human being. Society is agreed in regarding the artistes as deserving of the best conditions of work and recreation, and, of course, a pension at forty! The latter gives a great sense of security and unhurriedness to the artistes, who feel that they can develop at their own tempo. Many of the finest dancers, mimes especially, go on working long after this age, adding greatly to the performances with their superb artistry and knowledge of the theatre. These conditions are the reward of the artiste's absolute loyalty to the chosen vocation.

In the West today it is a different matter. For most people ballet is just a technique, a very exacting and difficult technique which one must start to learn very early; it may even be called an art, but it is an art which is no more than a part of the many provisions for entertainment in any capital city. So it is that a dancer's life here is a special strain. There is always the temptation to hold oneself back slightly tonight because tomorrow or the

day after one will be playing some even more exacting part. In
private life there is always the question of whether one can fulfil
elementary family obligations because one's energies are already
taxed almost to their limit. One begins to have the feeling that in
order to be a great dancer one should not marry and that one
must devote all one's energies exclusively to dancing. And this
leads one to suppose that a great dancer could not be a true
Christian. For how could he devote all his strength selfishly to the
development of his art when the demands of charity or justice
knock at his door requesting him to visit a sick relation or join
in some other corporal work of mercy?

I am speaking here on a problem which must face every
artiste. In delving deeper and deeper into his own nature, in
developing his own personality, he risks becoming completely
self-centred and egotistical. In searching for reality in his art may
he not be losing the supernatural reality of the life of grace and
missing many chances of getting to know and love God more? I
do not know the answer to these problems, but it is certainly
true that here in England today a dancer who is striving to be a
Christian is acutely conscious of the pull between the two
demands. His aching limbs, his fear that his strength may not be
equal to the day's demands tell him to stay on in bed while his
conscience tells him to get up early and go to Mass.

Do really great artistes, then, have to be self-centred? Does
what they do on the stage justify a special way of life because it is
done for others? Perhaps it does; and when I say that dancing
makes me feel more truly myself than at any other moment of my
life, is this not the 'I' whom God intended me to be and am I not
doing his work by using the gifts he has given me? I know that I
take no steps on the stage but with his assistance; the harder the
rôle, the more fervently I pray beforehand for his strength and
grace to bring me through. Never am I more aware of his loving
care than when I stand trembling with fright in the wings before
a difficult solo. Afterwards, too, I realize with gratitude and
humility that if there was anything good in the performance, it
was his doing and not my poor efforts.

Is it true, then, to say that I am being simply egocentric? I often think so, and there is very little either in secular society or in religious teaching to assure me that this artistic experience has any normal religious validity. And yet without this recognition, dancing must simply be described as something people do in that world of 'art' which has nothing much in common with the lives of ordinary folk. That, I feel sure, just cannot be true, when so many ordinary people draw inspiration and happiness even from the imperfect work that we present to them.

As in the case of the discussion after the novelist's paper it was impossible not to feel a certain dissatisfaction with the conventional reassurances provided for the artists by their fellow Christians; these hardly measured up to the difficulty. 'The dancer's life is justified if it is all lived for God.' The objection that most dancers are not Christians was answered by saying that their dedication to the dance is a kind of religious dedication without their knowing it. But this hardly helps the Christian faced with a division of loyalties. The tension which a Christian artist working in such a milieu must suffer is great; but at least it is only a heightening of a tension that must be faced by every Christian artist. It reaches its most extreme form in the dancer. Miss Drage summed the matter up here when she said: 'My body is my instrument.'

8. The Singer

DAVID GALLIVER

David Galliver, a concert singer of lieder and oratorio, who is often heard on the B.B.C., contributed this paper on the interpretative art of singing.

'THE singer is of no account in the scheme of things. It is the composer who lives; the singer is one of the Ephemeridae. Invaluable to anecdote, immaterial to history, he belongs to reminiscence, not to record.' So Harry Plunket Greene prefaced his book *Interpretation in Song*. The advent of large-scale gramophone recordings has to some extent modified this judgment; we can now pass down to posterity the performances of great singers, and their achievements can thus be subjects for reminiscence and record. But the judgment is still valid, distinguishing as it does between the artists of the first and second degrees—between the composer and the performer. It is to the composer that the first place must be always given—he it is who has created the work of art. The performer in his instrument bringing his creation to birth in the world.

But both composer and performer are essential. If the song remains enclosed in a few sheets of manuscript paper, it is lost to all but its composer and perhaps the musicologist, who turns over its pages and hears in his mind how it would sound if someone were to sing it. The singer is scarcely less dispensable to the song than the song to the singer: only when it is sung has the song reached its full expression.

The music and words of a song are the artistic expression of the composer's vision of some aspect of life or experience; through his work of art truth is conveyed, truth which may be of

greater or less significance according to the value of the composition. The greater the work, the more universal its application
and its truth. Thus Schubert's song cycle *Die Winterreise* is more
than the sad story of a rejected lover; it is a study in human
misery. This truth the singer has to convey; a mere rendering of
the notation is not sufficient, its inner meaning must be comprehended and projected. Here the singer stands as an artist in his
own right, and makes his independent contribution to the
expression of truth; his is the responsibility of conveying the
truth and beauty of the musical creation; his task is to present
beauty in song, and to present beauty in any kind is to draw the
attention of men ultimately towards the Supreme Beauty.

Most people like to sing at some time or other when they're
together; hymn singing and community singing are the natural
expression of this fundamental human urge. But the singer likes
to sing alone. This is not exhibitionism: he does not sing
primarily for the riotous applause which he hopes may follow his
sustained fortissimo top note, nor indeed for the appreciation of
a more discerning audience. He sings because he has to, because
he finds in his singing that artistic expression which his personality
demands: he is like the Italian peasant who sings to express his
joie de vivre as he sets about his work. But whereas the peasant's
singing is the expression of an unconscious urge, the professional
singer brings it into consciousness with his craftsmanship. Art is
the disciplined and consciously developed expression of fundamental talents—these for the singer are the possession of the
desire to sing and a voice of pleasant quality, coupled with an
innate love and understanding of music, and the capacity to
appreciate and express the beauty of the words he has to use. But
if the singer does not trouble to develop these talents, as any other
craftsman does his skill, he may find one day that they are gone,
and he is left with nothing, not even his urge to sing. How many
musical prodigies have been lost in this way, how few have
reappeared as great artists!

Before the singer is able to begin to give a true interpretation
of the composer's creation he must work at his craftsmanship. He

must learn to develop and control his voice, to acquire the technical mastery which will enable him to express not only the notes, the words, and the tempo of a song, but also each shade of mood and colour implicit in it. It is a task which is never finished: no singer, however great, will say: 'I am the complete master of my voice, I have reached perfection.' As he advances, the goal of perfection becomes clearer, but so does the realization of the difficulties involved in reaching it. They are mistaken who say to the singer: 'What an easy life you must have! All you need to do is to open your mouth and the sound pours out!'

Side by side with the study of voice goes the study of music itself, so that innate musicality may be guided and developed and the field of activity for the singer may be enlarged. And hand in hand with study of music, the cultivation of the appreciation of words: for, whereas instrumental music is pure sound, vocal music is the marriage of words and music, the singer being the only artist to wed the two. And words are essential to the meaning of the song—the singer cultivates a true feeling for the significance of words, not just the technical acquirement of good diction. How disappointing for him if the only compliment he is paid is: 'I could hear your every word'—it is like telling an actor how well he looks in his costume.

These are the tools of the singer's trade, and the more skilfully he is able to use them, the more beautifully the artistry within him is free to express itself: he has then really begun to sing. The better fashioned his craftsmanship, the more easily can it takes its rightful and secondary place. The song has been studied, its difficulties mastered, its inner meaning comprehended. All these are in the singer's subconscious when music claims first place to give wings to the burden of the song.

> In the dim light of the golden lamp the singer stands and sings,
> And the songs rise up like coloured bubbles on birds with shining
>   wings,
> And the movement of merry or plaintive keys sounds in the silent air,
> Till the listener feels the room no more but only music there.[1]

[1] Edward Shanks.

But, indeed, this picture of the singer's art is an ideal one. Unlike the painter and the writer he cannot choose time and place for his creative work. He may be performing in a great cathedral or in the smallest hall: the enthusiasm of those around him may create an atmosphere which will inspire him to the greatest heights, or he may have to sing in circumstances where inspiration sadly fails—then it is that he must bring his craft to bear more consciously, and strive to make up for the lack of spontaneous light within him by the perfection and conscious artistry of his rendering: and in so doing he may recapture the mood which has eluded him. But it is only rarely that the singer experiences the fullness of that inner exaltation which is the final proof to him that his hours of preparation have been worth while: however, those few occasions suffice.

Nor is this the whole story. The singer's ability to project his art does not depend alone on the artistic factors we have considered, but on the whole presentation of his personality. True, one's personality is individual, and cannot be basically altered, but such feelings within oneself as lack of confidence or purpose in life (as distinct from purpose in art) can have a stultifying effect upon artistic development. This is particularly unfortunate for the singer, since affection of the voice—and not only the singing voice!—is one of the first signs of such conditions. Thus the artist has the responsibility of ensuring—as far as he is able—that his house is in order personally as well as artistically, or, rather, personally so that it may be so artistically. The connexion between the two is clear and definite. How fortunate he is who has been allowed to find his artistic fulfilment as a Christian. In this way all needs of personality may be satisfied, and art win its way to true freedom of expression. It is all too easy for a singer to acquire a false set of values; the Church gives him the true one. To take a small illustration: it has stayed in my memory how I went along to, I think, my second instruction, more concerned with the prospect of getting a cold which might prevent my appearance at a forthcoming university concert, than with the comprehension of the Truth of the Catholic Church. And my

Jesuit instructor, realizing this, said to me with a kindly smile:
'My dear boy, if you saw things as they are in reality, you would
understand that your getting a cold wouldn't really matter for
you.' It is thanks to that priest, who pointed out reality to me in
that way, that I have not been unduly worried about what we all
know to be the singer's *bête noire*; not, of course, that I knowingly
sit in a railway carriage with one so afflicted, or have quite that
feeling of affection for members of my family when they are
stricken with coughs and colds!

William Byrd, that great English and Catholic musician, once
wrote of singing: 'The better the voice is, the meeter it is to
honour and serve God therewith: and the voice of man is chiefly
to be employed to that end.' From what I have said one might
perhaps think that praise of God and the art of the singer are
connected primarily in a wide sense. When I sing a Schubert song
or take part in a Mozart opera I am indeed praising God—my
singing is the expression of his divine will, just as the music is
part of his divine plan; but so is every human activity:

> Who sweeps a room as for Thy laws
> Makes that and the action fine.

But the singer has an advantage: for not only indirectly but
directly also he can use his talents to the greater glory of God.
His songs are not only secular but sacred too: for many of us, much
of our work consists in the singing of sacred music—of oratorio
and Church cantatas. And since this is an aspect of the singer's
art which I think to be of special interest in the present context,
I will consider it in a little more detail.

Here in the singing of oratorio is an inspiring task for the
Christian singer. Here he can feel fully that he is singing *Ad
majorem Dei gloriam*. When the great Johann Sebastian Bach had
finished writing his Mass in B Minor, he wrote at the bottom of
the last page of the manuscript the three letters D S G—*Dei solo
gloria*; and the singer must have similar feelings when he takes
his part in a performance of Verdi's Requiem or one of the Bach
Passions. The greater the work, the greater his responsibility to

7

play his artistic part worthily. 'Better than any sermon' writes the music critic in his account of the concert in the next morning's paper. Misguided though it may be, such a judgment gives an indication of the significance of such performances, and not from the artistic viewpoint alone.

For a Catholic singer, it must always be a particular joy to take part in Elgar's *Dream of Gerontius* with its majestic concept of Christian life. I shall always remember the first performance of this work in which I sang: under a fine conductor its realities became apparent, the prayers of the friends around the bed of the dying man, the evil of the demons' chorus, the serenity of the Angel's farewell. When taking part in it, one seeks to communicate not only the purely artistic but also the wider religious feeling of the masterpiece.

But participation in the performance of such works not only gives inspiration but also challenges the singer. As an artist he must, of course, possess flexibility of imagination to comprehend and project in his art the philosophy and atmosphere of works which are not primarily his own; he must be prepared to interpret with equal conviction and sincerity Brahms' lieder and Greek Ionic hymns. Thus a true artist will be able to give a satisfying interpretation in Handel's *Messiah*, whether he is a believing Christian or not. It is primarily if he is a Christian that he surely cannot remain detached from and unmoved by the implications of his work, for it will awaken his Christian conscience. But to draw the conclusion that, because of this, the more holy the Christian artist is in his personal life the more convincing will be his work, is to tread dangerously on dangerous ground. It is true, of course, that every human activity is enhanced through the grace of God; as Thomas à Kempis wrote: 'When the grace of God cometh to a man, then he is powerful for all things; and when it departeth, then he is poor and weak.' But it is not similarly true that my singing of oratorio (and all other music) must vary in quality according to my state of soul. If one were to believe this, who would dare to sing at all? The truth surely is that here again is a special gift of Providence to the singer himself, so that he may be reminded in an obvious way not to forget his real purpose in life, or allow his art to become an end in itself. It is a reminder to him, not primarily as an artist, but as a man. Providence does indeed seem very kind to singers: but, you know, there is an old German saying *Dumm wie ein Tenor* ('as stupid as a tenor'), and perhaps we singers have an especial need of hearing the obvious stated!

So we have seen something of the art of the singer; but what of his audience? They are necessary to him, they share in his activity, for them he paints his picture, and the consciousness of their appreciation enables him to approach his goal ever more nearly. They may have come to hear him for pure diversion's sake, to enjoy something new: they may be there to enjoy the sound of his voice, for, as Byrd wrote: 'There is not any music of instruments whatsoever, comparable to that which is made of the voices of men, where the voices are good, and the same well sorted and ordered.' Or they may be guided to him by sheer love of hearing music. But whatever the motives which have brought him his audience, the singer has but one aim, as we have seen, to convey in his art his message of truth; through it his audience will be transported into another world.

> Bright is the ring of words
> When the right man rings them.
> Fair the sound of songs
> When the singer sings them.[1]

But is this just escapism? At first sight it might appear to be so. The listeners find solace in being transported to another world, for a while they will forget their immediate cares and worries. In 'A Song for St. Cecilia's Day, 1687' Dryden expressed the power of music most beautifully:

> What passion cannot Music raise and quell?
> When Jubal struck the chorded shell,
> His listening brethren stood around
> And, wondering, on their faces fell

[1] R. L. Stevenson.

To worship that celestial sound:
Less than a God they thought there could not dwell
Within the hollow of that shell,
That spoke so sweetly and so well.
What passion cannot Music raise and quell?

If this is escapism, it is escapism not from reality but into reality; temporary cares are put aside in the contemplation of the everlasting. For music has its own truth to tell; and there is nothing negative in it, for it brings a new awareness, a new sense of being alive.

To his music plants and flowers
Ever sprung; as sun and showers
There had made a lasting spring.[1]

To see the rapt faces of an audience after a fine performance of a great work is proof enough of this.

But performances do not need to be faultless for music to reach the hearts of those who hear it. Each sincere rendering brings with it something of the spirit of music: I have spent memorable evenings in small concert halls or churches, with small choirs, where the merits have been enthusiasm and love of music rather than technical accomplishment. And who shall say that the spirit does not dwell as much there as in great halls with first-class choirs and orchestras? It is the singer's privilege to be able to take his part as an artist in so many performances of different character, each one new, each one giving him—as it were in return for his own contribution—something fresh to add to his store of experience. It is a way of life both personally and artistically supremely worth while. *Omnis spiritus laudet Dominum.*

The discussion revolved round the relationship of religion to art; and it was clear that religious belief affects an artist's work fundamentally. Mr. Galliver insisted on the autonomy of the art of singing, its validity

1 Shakespeare: *Henry VIII*, III, i, 6–8.

as a discipline in itself; and in this sense musical interpretation has nothing to do with belief. A Buddhist could sing a Christian piece as well as a Christian. But singing is not pure music and a singer may not be able to help himself if he has strong beliefs about the nature of life; he may find it difficult to sing religious music if his own beliefs militate against everything religious. Equally religious belief must affect one's whole attitude to one's art and to dedication to it.

It was suggested to Mr. Galliver that in spite of its excellences The Dream of Gerontius is in some ways not as Catholic, musically, as Bach. Whilst the subject is Catholic, the music lacks the depth and integrity which in Bach make one think of it as finer music 'theologically'. Mr. Galliver agreed.

There was some discussion about those artists whose gifts depend directly on their bodily fitness, such as singers and ballet dancers. As these artists are physically more vulnerable than any others, what happens to them when they lose the physical capacity to follow their art? Is teaching a possible way out for them, and can they direct their creative energy in teaching? Mr. Galliver pointed out that many singers could go on singing professionally till quite late in life, so that the problem did not always arise. However, when it did, it seemed that while some could be happy teaching, many could not. Mary Drage witnessed that this was true, only more tragically so, in the case of a dancer, for her retirement from the stage was often an unmitigated tragedy. Sometimes the creative energy could go happily into teaching, but often not. It was perhaps, at this point, that the inadequacy of the common approach to art today was most plainly laid bare. Treated as an end in itself, as a religion instead of a function of religion, art may leave its devotees eventually prostrate.

9. The Painter

EDWARD WRIGHT

Mr. Wright spoke as a painter who sees his painting as part of a whole life and not simply as an isolated 'art'. He teaches at the Royal College of Art.

THE easel picture according to Panofsky is a 'man-made object demanding to be experienced aesthetically'. In other words it is an object which requires intuition and an attitude of mental re-creation on the part of the spectator. The man who makes this object is known as a painter, although he may not use paint always nor even use it at all. His picture may consist of ready-made coloured substances glued together; it may include a whole magpie's nest of relics from other crafts and industries whenever technique is used as a creative process. If it is a painting one expects it to look like paint or like sand, feathers or sacking if they are the real physical ingredients. At times when an un-obtrusive film of paint represented the window into which the spectator looked, the technique could be self-effacing and smooth (Van Eyck, Piero della Francesca, David). It did not mean that the paint had been used with the intention of misleading the spectator into the belief that this was not paint. But such an attitude is no longer valid for our time. Panofsky also says: 'Where the sphere of practical objects ends, and that of "art" begins, depends, then, on the "intention" of the creators. This "intention" cannot be absolutely determined. In the first place, "intentions" are . . . incapable of being defined with scientific precision. In the second place, the "intentions" of those who produce objects are conditioned by the standards of their period and environment.'[1]

The Painter

So, the physical ingredients of a painting only turn it into an image because the painter intended it to be that thing. And who is the painter? He is, to begin with, a maker of images and his identity is always modified by exterior and interior forces, by the time and the society to which he belongs, by his faith and doubts, by his material limitations, and finally by the accumulating evidence of the works which he produces. A creative process includes both 'task' and 'play', and the 'play' element is also revealed in the *persona* which the painter acquires. Picasso, for example, is technically so brilliant and so articulate in inventing and handling visual symbols that he becomes the archparodist and transformer of his predecessors' themes; giving us surprising variations and comments on the works of Cranach, El Greco, Poussin, Delacroix, Courbet, and many others. This kind of play can also be recognized in the jazz music of Jelly Roll Morton, Oscar Petersen, and Dave Brubeck among others. Given the time and the necessary scholarship it would be interesting to trace the history of the *persona* of the painter. Many writers about pre-history agree that the image-maker of the late palaeolithic or ice-age was the priest or magician of his social group. Kühn, describing a painting in the cavern of the Trois Frères says:

> Above them all is the picture of the magician himself, the portrait of the man who may, indeed, have executed some of the engravings. With his large, dark eyes he gazes at the visitor. It is impressive, it is even alarming to look steadily into those eyes which for millennia have stared down from a height into vacant space. This shaman wears upon his head the mask of a stag with its antlers. Bear's paws cover his hands and a horse's tail hangs from his waist. One leg is raised as in a dance.[2]

1 Erwin Panofsky: *Meaning in the Visual Arts.*
2 Herbert Kühn: *Rock Pictures of Europe*. See Plate 14.

Prehistoric men believed in a mystic identity between human being and animal; this belief was celebrated in a ritual play performed by the magician, disguised in animal form. This also shows that from earliest times painting had been used to depict simultaneous aspects of one being and the idea that a single person can have more than one nature. The painter participated in the ritual when he made his images of it. Kühn even suggests that both priest and painter may have been the same person. A relationship between ritual and play in primitive society has also been suggested in *Homo Ludens* by Johan Huizinga: 'In play as we conceive it the distinction between belief and make-believe breaks down.' He adds:

> The concept of play merges quite naturally with that of holiness. Any prelude of Bach, any line of tragedy proves it. By considering the whole sphere of so-called primitive culture as a play-sphere we pave the way to a more direct and more general understanding of its peculiarities than any meticulous psychological or sociological analysis would allow. Primitive or, let us say, archaic ritual is thus sacred play, indispensable for the well-being of the community, full of cosmic insight and social development but always play in the sense Plato gave to it—an action accomplishing itself outside and above the necessities and seriousness of everyday life. In this sphere of sacred play the child and the poet are at home with the savage.[1]

THE PAINTER'S TASK

Poetry is saturated with the play instinct and at the same time the poet has a task. Now according to Mallarmé the task of the poet is 'to purify the language of the tribe'. We are the tribe; through fumbling confusion of thought or evasion of reality, from day to day we devalue and deaden our words. The poet recreates them and in a spirit of play gives them back to us, alive again. Something similar can occur with our images when they are used as visual symbols to embody our ideas. Most of us are now verbal and visual symbol consumers. The painter is still an image maker but as a visual symbol creator he has now been outpaced by graphic artists, anonymous package designers, film directors, and

1 See Plate 15.

advertising men. In a way the easel painter is still the image
maker of the tribe, but what he makes is now usually reduced
and altered on the moving belt of mass-symbol production.
Hundreds of thousands of people can enjoy good coloured postcard reproductions of modern paintings; millions more can
occasionally enjoy less faithful reproductions in the mass-
circulation weeklies. The graphic artist, the designer, and the
ad-man are influenced by the easel painter on a stylistic level, and
the easel painter is often influenced by their day-to-day choice of
symbols. This is normal since their task, native to the environment, is to supply visual symbols to the symbol-consuming
millions, to whom they also belong. They work as designers and
they must foresee their end-product accurately and within a given
time on film, on glossy art paper, or in neon lights. The easel
painter cannot foretell the appearance of his image until it is completed. There was a time in the nineteenth century when
ambitious painters went in for set-pieces or 'machines' intended
to dumbfound the spectator by a display of technical organization
and efficiency. To achieve this type of work it was necessary to be
businesslike, programmatic, and to keep the end-product well in
view. In our eyes this cast-iron method is no longer worth
pursuing. As the American painter, Corrado Marca-Relli has
said, 'Everything is in motion, until the final touch; everything is
subject to modification by its neighbour until the very end.'[1] For
the easel painter the play element outweighs the task element in
importance. During the ice-age both painter's task and painter's
play were sacred. The task included a given theme, site, and
materials. The interpretation of the theme, the use of materials,
and above all the use of the site, were vitalized by the instinct of
play. Nowadays the painter is not given a theme nor is he asked to
create visual symbols for his society. In spite of this the will to
make images survives.

The Painter's Play

In a curiously oblique way people are still ready to look at new

[1] 'Marca-Relli Paints a Picture': *Art News*, Nov. 1955.

images and even absorb them because they are still needed. The
painter is now his own taskmaster and his *persona* has acquired
surprising elements of the surgeon, the explorer and the cook,
among others. The Italian painter Burri probably considers his
materials from a rather surgeonlike point of view. This is illustrated by an extract from the article 'Burri Makes a Picture' in the
American magazine *Art News*.[1] 'The plastic blobs on the protuber-
ances had become tacky and it was time to proceed to their
"slabbramento", a term often used in the sense of "opening a
wound". With a palette knife incisions were made in the blobs
along the curving ridge of the swellings, and the edges of the
plastic were retracted and secured with straight pins (later
removed).' Such disguises are usually a part of the painter's
creative play misinterpreted by self-conscious observers as an
attempt to evade their critical pigeon-holing. The painter's play
develops with his time and environment but many 'art-lovers'
cling to devalued attitudes. One uses certain faculties to absorb a
painting, faculties which can only be made poorer if they are not
used every day on the things which surround us. Domestic
appliances, advertisements, and people's everyday gestures need
not be placed in a caste system below that which includes
sculptures, easel pictures, and mime. We can't withhold feelings
for rare occasions and at the same time keep them alive. But many
people think it necessary to have a special attitude in front of a
fine-art object. A special attitude which is usually induced by a
device such as an elaborate picture-frame. This attitude is now
vestigial, a remnant out of a vast wardrobe of gestures belonging
to the days when people wore wigs. In fact, as Huizinga points
out, the practice of framing pictures in a certain way was con-
temporaneous with the vogue for wigs in the seventeenth
century.[2] The frame is used to isolate the picture and pay
homage to it as the wig frames the face and makes it appear
nobler. It is very easy to detect the shrine-creating impulse at
work in people's houses, and the 'pin-up' is just another proof of
our need for images. The appearance of elaborate frames and glass

[1] *Art News*, Dec. 1954.   [2] *Homo Ludens*.

cases implies that the impulse has lost touch with reality and a 'special attitude' is being fabricated. A curious example is the stuffed fish in a glass case. What could be more natural than to go fishing, catch something, and have a record of one's catch? It is equally natural to eat what one has caught, and photography might appear the obvious means of recording one's catch. But this is not enough from the angler's point of view, as a photograph is not the same as a trophy. So some people prefer to embalm the fish in a glass case rather than eat it. They are even ready to spend several hours cleaning it, to let six weeks elapse while it dries, to spend another week mounting it, and finally to devote a great deal of time, labour, and expense to trying to make the embalmed fish look alive in its cumbersome glass case. A primitive impulse is concealed in a clumsy nineteenth-century illusionistic technique very much in sympathy with repository art. The extraordinary thing about the stuffed fish in a glass case is that the embalming and model-making techniques destroy all one's awareness of the fish's real nature and of the moment when it was snatched out of its element and died. The remnants are there but utterly disguised by the illusionistic faking. Japanese fishermen have their own way of making trophies. Known as *Gyo-Taku* it consists of rubbing the catch with India ink and taking an impression before the ink dries. You can have your fish and eat it. The fish goes to the kitchen and a brief, tactile and lively image remains to be contemplated. Usually it is very difficult to see the complete transition from an idea through creative technique to the end-product of the process, the image, although it is becoming less difficult and less unusual than before. The image in the process of becoming is illustrated in another example from Japan, on the lid of a writing box by Shunshō. It represents a woman squirting black tooth-stain from her mouth on to a screen and writing the characters Koi-wo-shinobu or 'perseverence in love'.[1] One sees how the ideogram on the screen has assumed a particular form as a result of this painterly game with the tooth-stain straight from the woman's mouth. Idea and form, thought and feeling are joined in

1 See Plate 16.

a calligraphy which uses no hand or instrument. This is creative technique at play and the image is found within the unusual limitations. A painter learns to be economical like a farmer, like a cook, and his equipment influences his development, impels him to work by arousing senses of smell and touch. The tubes and tins of colours, the bottles and containers of turpentine, oil, and varnish, the dry crusts of paint, the brushes, knives, and rags are a physical part of his environment, completed by the presence of the work in progress. This accumulated work is also a witness to be accepted or denounced. It is capable of crowding him out, forcing him to react, or nauseating him and making his life unbearable unless he renews himself. Whenever a person or a group of people absorb an image or a sign, they tend to modify, increase, or devalue its content, and some painters have been unable to overcome the crisis created by their devalued accumulated work or to reconcile themselves to their own limitations. They have killed themselves. Perhaps play had stopped; it may have done so, or more probably the game had now become as some games are, one of life and death.

Mr Wright showed slides of a number of pictures, a few of which are reproduced in this book. His paper produced a long and interesting discussion. He was asked how it is that modern paintings never seem to be finished works of art, if set beside Old Masters. Two points arose from the answers and discussions about this question.

(1) Today the painter suffers from an inhibiting sort of freedom. Commonly he is not commissioned; he is asked to paint in no particular style or discipline; there is no longer a clear integrated tradition or form within which he will naturally produce his work. He is not therefore a craftsman, in the sense that the eighteenth-century portrait painters were. But his work is still the ancient craft of symbol-making. Even when he is 'experimenting' in the most unusual way he may succeed in producing valid symbols for his society. An obvious example, referred to a number of times during the symposium, is Mondrian, whose spatial geometry has had a strong influence on architecture, typography and industrial design.

(2) *No work of art is ever a 'finished' work of art in the sense that an aeroplane is 'finished' when all its parts are put together as they should be. The end of a work of art comes when the artist decides to stop; this was indicated by Mr. Wright himself and by Mr. Lewis, the poet. The painting is the record of the artist's gestures, and part of his art is precisely knowing when to stop. When there is a highly specialized tradition it is possible to make of these gestures something which has the appearance of being 'finished', an achievement to which nothing more could be done. Such is the result of the highly disciplined traditional gestures of the Japanese calligraphist.*

10. *The Novelist*

ANTONIA WHITE

Miss Antonia White, author of Frost in May *and other novels, of which the most recent is* Beyond the Glass, *spoke of the problems which face the Christian novelist.*

THE inclusion of a novelist in this symposium is a generous admission that the novel, in spite of the impurity of its hybrid form, has some claim to be considered a work of art. The very nature of his material involves the Christian novelist in problems very different from those of Christians who work in a purer medium. Before dealing with his specific troubles, I would like to begin with the common problem he shares with other Christian artists. Not only is it the one which preoccupies me personally more than any other, but it is the very one we are meeting here to discuss. And if there is one thing on which I desperately need some light, it is this very question of the status of art in human life, which for us can only be synonymous with Christian life.

Almost since I was a child, I have been puzzled by the source and function of this strange activity called art. Where, if anywhere, does it fit into the Christian life? Is it to be included among those symbolic talents which we are forbidden to bury in napkins? Or does it come under the heading of that scandalizing right eye that must be plucked out if we are to enter into salvation? The Gospel gives some guidance to those engaged in other occupations, to the shepherd and the fisherman, the tax-gatherer and the soldier, but never so much as mentions the artist. The Old Testament, it is true, contains the most minute instructions to those engaged in the plastic arts as to what they are to produce for the adornment of the temple, and thereby at least implies

divine approval of art as a human occupation. But the New Testament seems to ignore the artist so completely that it does not
even suggest whether his activity is legitimate or illegitimate.

Yet every artist is aware of his odd, and possibly suspect, gift
not merely as a powerful impulse but as an allegiance to which
he feels bound. And that allegiance not only imposes strict laws
on him but demands an engagement of his whole self comparable
only to that of religion itself. These laws appear to have nothing
to do with moral behaviour yet their transgression induces
something remarkably like moral guilt in the artist who trans-
gresses them. So strong is this sense that art is autonomous that
St. Thomas Aquinas can speak of a crime being perpetrated
against art by the artist when he intends to make a good work and
produces a bad one.

To what realm, then, does art belong? It almost seems to be a
no-man's-land, belonging neither to God nor the devil, with its
own hierarchy of values and its own independent laws. Yet, for
the Christian, this is a possibility he cannot admit.

May I leave abstract generalizations and state the problem in a
very crude, concrete way as it might appear in actual human
experience? I hope you will forgive if, to do this, I quote a
passage from one of my own novels. It describes the bewilderment
of a very young girl, who, as a Catholic, believes that everything
must have some moral or religious significance yet finds herself
confronted with something that seems to have neither.

> What had begun to disturb her was the sense of a realm into which
> she penetrated now and then quite involuntarily and whose existence
> did not seem to be officially recognized. And this realm, though it
> seemed to her to be connected sometimes with truth, sometimes with
> beauty, seemed to have no connection with morals. A poem might
> be the key to it, or some lovely sight or sound, but quite often she
> would suddenly find herself in it for no apparent reason, waiting to
> buy cakes in a stuffy shop or on those evenings in Paget's Fold
> listening to the aunts' gossip. During these experiences she was not
> aware of 'right' or 'wrong': the words simply did not apply. How
> could they, since during these brief moments she was not aware of

herself at all except as a kind of sensitive film? If they came from God, why were they not accompanied by a rush of fervour and a desire to be better? And if from the devil, why did they not provoke her to wicked thoughts and rebelliousness? But they seemed to have no results; if they left any wish at all, it was a desire somehow to express them. They seemed to be nothing but a sudden intensification of life and she could not control them in any way. Sometimes she had dared to hope that this was what Christ meant when He said: 'I came that you might have life and have it more abundantly'. But since she had always been assured that this meant the supernatural life of grace, something abstract and mysterious which one believed by faith but did not feel, she put the idea away as blasphemous.

That passage states the problem as it dimly presented itself to a girl of fifteen. Yet, in my own late fifties, I find myself no nearer a solution of it than she was.

For a time, I believed I had found, if not a solution, at least an accommodation. Solution it could not be because it completely altered the terms of the problem by denying the priority of religion. During a long period, in which I completely renounced Catholic belief, I saw both art and religion as purely human activities, modes in which the human spirit expressed its profoundest intuitions of what Santayana calls the realm of essence. Which mode was chosen depended entirely on the natural bent of the individual. Art was perhaps the purest of all human activities since it aroused no desires, inculcated no dogmas, and incited not to action but to contemplation. In my new hierarchy of values, the saint was a kind of artist who used his own nature as his raw material. What made him one degree less pure was that he looked for some reward beyond the achievement itself.

But since, for the past seventeen years, I have mercifully been back in the Church—I hope, and believe, with a much deeper conviction of faith and what it implies—the old problem is there as disturbingly as ever. For faith is not the cosy comforter the non-believer so often pretends to envy the believer. As Père de Lubac so profoundly says in his preface to *The Drama of Atheist Humanism*: 'Faith disturbs us and continually upsets the beautiful balance of our mental conceptions and our social structures. Bursting into a world that perpetually tends to close in upon itself, God brings it the possibility of a harmony which is certainly superior but is to be attained only at the cost of a series of cleavages and struggles co-extensive with time itself.'

I would like now to come to the specific problems of the Christian novelist as opposed to those of other Christian artists. The first and most acute of these is not only his subject but the inevitable dichotomy between the way he perceives that subject as an artist and his reaction to it as a Christian. The second concerns his presentation of that subject which, in the modern world, is bound to be conditioned to some extent by extraneous things which do not trouble the painter, the sculptor, and the musician.

Taking his first problem, the subject itself, this lands him straight on the mined territory of moral values. The raw material of his craft is nothing less than human behaviour. As a Christian, he cannot regard human behaviour with the purely aesthetic interest of a painter confronted with a landscape. Yet, as a novelist, this is precisely what he wants to do. Indeed, things that shock him religiously, both in himself and others, often stimulate him far more than those that edify him. He delights in imperfection, in things as they are, not as they ought to be. He is more interested in nature with all its flaws, inconsistencies, and weaknesses than in nature perfected through grace.

I will give a rather sinister example of this dichotomy between one's attitude as a Christian and one's attitude as a novelist to the same piece of human behaviour.

A great friend of mine died in peculiarly distressing circumstances and I had to break the news to her mother. The mother's immediate reaction showed not a tinge of even apparent grief at her daughter's death. All that she said was: 'And only last week I lent her five pounds. I don't suppose I shall ever see *that* again.' As a human being, I was naturally shocked. As a novelist, I was delighted at this sudden unguarded revelation of something I had never suspected in the mother's character and which illuminated all kinds of things in her relationship to her daughter that had puzzled me before.

Moreover, was not my own behaviour far more unChristian and inhuman than that of the mother? My grief over my friend's tragic death did not prevent me from rejoicing, as a novelist, over what I had perceived as a result of it. And that brings me straight back to my old original problem, the very nature of that peculiar, compelling, what one can call amoral mode of perception which distinguishes the artist's consciousness from that of other people. When that mode of perception operates not on any outward appearance to which the terms good and evil do not apply but on human conduct itself, is it surprising if the Christian novelist sometimes wonders if he can only achieve salvation by plucking out his right eye?

He cannot even compromise by putting a shade over that right eye when not actually engaged in writing a novel. For being a novelist is not a part-time acitivity confined to a certain number of hours spent at a desk. In a sense, one is writing most of one's waking hours and quite a number of one's sleeping ones, for dreams are highly interesting to that implacable right eye. Wherever the writer goes, whatever he does, that shameless observer watches his own behaviour and that of others with avid yet impersonal curiosity. It is accumulating a thousand invisible notes which are grist to the novelist's mill. The novelist is not, as so many people imagine, consciously searching for material out of which to make a novel. Nor has he any intention of literally reproducing anything he has seen or heard, for that would reduce him to a mere reporter. What makes him any kind of artist, as opposed to a manufacturer of fiction as a saleable commodity, is precisely this peculiar awareness and ability to select and combine perceptions into an organic whole.

And this brings me to the Christian novelist's second problem, that of presentation. For, owing to the nature of his material, he cannot simply present it as a shape or a pattern. Whether he likes it or not, since the novelist is dealing with human behaviour, human conflicts, human motives, he is bound to give some interpretation to these things. A painter does not have to interpret his subject but only his vision of that subject. The unfortunate novelist has to do both. And since he himself is involved in the very predicament he is attempting to describe, the predicament of human life, he cannot even momentarily stand apart from it and see it as pure form; or, as Santayana would say, intuit it as pure essence. The poet can be caught up in a timeless moment in which he sees life *sub specie aeternitatis* and crystallizes that transcendental experience in a poem. The novelist is earthbound in that realm of existence which Santayana defines as 'such being as is in flux, conditioned by external relations and jostled by irrelevant events'. The very nature of his work is not to crystallize, but to attempt to transcribe that very flux, while still immersed in it. True, the novel may have its transcendental moments, but the novelist cannot possibly sustain the high temperature that burns away the dross of his own private obsessions and preoccupations. He simply cannot avoid giving himself away. I doubt if anyone could deduce from any painting of Cézanne's the fact that Cézanne was a believing Catholic. The Catholic novelist cannot avoid betraying it. It is not a question of 'dragging' religion into his work, or even of deliberately pushing it out. It is simply *there*, part of his preoccupation, part of his vision; and part, only too likely, of his deepest private conflicts. And it is this last fact that exposes him to something he fears far more than being contemptuously dubbed 'one of the Catholic squad' or using the novel as a vehicle of religious propaganda. 'What a pity,' a friend said to me, 'you have to spoil your novels by dragging in all that Catholic stuff. But I suppose your priests insist on it.'

In fact, the case is almost exactly the opposite. What the Christian novelist is far more likely to dread is that instead of being an apostle, he may be a Judas. Being himself such a struggling and very imperfect Christian, he may betray what is most sacred to him by his personal distortions of it. Consciously or unconsciously, his own inner conflicts will be projected into his work. In his religious life fear may predominate over love, acceptance in principle go side by side with rebelliousness in practice. He may be willing to die for his faith yet barely attempt to live in charity with his fellow Christians. He can enter only too intimately into the consciousness of the sinner and he is probably unable to imagine, even dimly, the interior life of the saint. In view of these difficulties an eminent Catholic critic, Martin Turnell, goes so far as to advise modern Catholic novelists to keep religion out of their work and write only in a lighter vein, since 'when they grow serious, they come to grief'. Yet surely this is a counsel of despair. For those who have no aptitude for the 'lighter vein' (can you imagine a 'light' Mauriac or a 'light' Julien Green?) this would mean giving up novel writing altogether. For the rest, it would mean side-stepping the problem by taking no risks. And, if the parable of the talents does apply to the novelist, it was the man who took no risks whom the Master so ruthlessly condemned.

All that I have said so far might apply to any Christian novelist in any age. My last two problems concern some of his troubles in our own. First, it is impossible for any Christian writer, and most of all for a Catholic, not to be self-conscious in an age which is not so much sceptical or agnostic as violently anti-supernatural. A young woman said to me the other day 'Religion *embarrasses* me just as some people are embarrassed by bad language.' Now this self-consciousness, this feeling of being cut off from the main stream, is a very severe handicap to a novelist, since the novel is, above all, an attempt to communicate common experience to other human beings. I think it accounts for much of the violence and even clumsiness of the intrusion of the supernatural in modern novels by Catholics. The writer cannot go into long explanations of what would once have been taken for granted. He has to use shock tactics: to foreshorten, over-emphasize and distort in a way that upsets the balance of his work and creates a discordance between himself and his reader. For the novel is the one art whose content is accessible to everyone, though only a comparatively few may have the slightest appreciation of its form. Essentially, the novel is only an elaborated form of the told story, and people do not tell stories to themselves. A novel implies a reader, even if only one. The reader—or listener—will accept the wildest fantasies if they are presented as fantasies. He jibs when what seems to him fantastic is presented as truth, or when something which seems to him abnormal is assumed to be normal experience. This lack of common background between the Catholic novelist and his non-Catholic, very likely non-Christian, reader is particularly acute for anyone writing in English. In Europe, even the atheist knows the common terms of Catholic reference and understands, even if he does not accept, their implications. In England, where the Catholic tradition has so long been broken, it is not so much a question of rejection, as of uncomfortable bewilderment on the part of the reader. He feels the novelist is cheating him as much as if he suddenly introduced passages in a foreign language into his work. And this necessarily embarrasses the novelist and tends to make him (especially as the chances are that he is a convert) either over-aggressive or over-apologetic whenever he deals with religion.

Secondly, he is faced not only with such a change in mental climate that religious belief now appears to many as an anachronism, but also with a revolution in psychology that has profoundly affected the moral one. The question of motive for any human act assumes a new and formidable aspect since we now know that the conscious motive may be only a deceptive mask for some very different unconscious desire. The great psychological novelists of the past, such as Dostoievsky and George Eliot have intuitively perceived this, but the modern novelist knows it more explicitly. Though lacking their genius, he cannot revert entirely to the old simple presentation of a character in terms of its conscious desires. This is a problem common to all modern novelists, but a particularly thorny one to the Christian who is committed to a belief in free will. Yet, without accepting Freud's determinism (which, incidentally, sees both art and religion as sublimations of primitive impulses), he cannot doubt the truth of many of Freud's discoveries concerning the unconscious forces at work in human nature. If he has been analysed, he has become painfully aware of these dark forces in himself. And that knowledge must inevitably affect his interpretation of the characters he attempts to create. More than this, since one might almost call some form of psychological maladjustment the occupational disease of the novelist (it may even be the very source of his faculty) may he not infect his reader with his own sickness? To some extent he is bound to project his own unconscious conflicts and fixations into his work. The theme he chooses (or rather which he feels chooses *him*), the characters he uses to illustrate it, will inevitably reflect his innermost preoccupations. Whether he studies his characters direct from life or fondly fancies he 'invents' them, they will all be characters in his own private drama. Consciously or unconsciously, he involves the reader in that drama, forces him, in imagination, to *act* in it without the least idea what effect on him this will have.

It is this question of influence, though usually stated in much simpler and more forthright terms, that brings the Christian novelist to his final problem—the attitude of his co-religionists towards his work. There are still very many Catholics who judge a novel entirely on the question of whether or not it could conceivably 'give scandal' and entirely ignore any other standards of criticism. A very eminent Catholic archbishop told me how, when dining with two—also eminent—members of the Irish clergy, he had talked enthusiastically about *The Power and the Glory* as one of the finest Catholic novels of the century, and met with a marked lack of response. This was not altogether surprising, as they turned out to be two of the Censors who had banned the book in Ireland.

Pushed to its logical extreme, this dread of giving scandal would prevent a conscientious Christian from writing anything but edifying tracts in fictional form. Indeed, after those terrible retreat sermons of my childhood on 'bad' books, I used to wonder how Catholics ever dared write novels at all. For a 'bad' book was *any* book which might even unintentionally cause any reader one moment of moral uneasiness or theological doubt. And the penalty for writing one was to remain in purgatory till the last

copy of the offending book was out of circulation. Perhaps I may
add, in parenthesis, that my own solitary attempt to write a novel
which should be deliberately apostolic ended in disaster. It was
confiscated at a point before my sinners had been sensationally
converted into saints. Too frightened to explain my ultimate
intentions, I was branded as a bad influence and asked to leave my
convent school.

This absurd incident was actually neither as absurd nor as
irrelevant as it sounds. It gave me such an appalling sense of guilt
about writing that for nearly twenty years I never attempted to
write another novel. Only two or three times in all those years
did I even attempt, and then with tortured misgivings, to write
anything of 'my own'. I worked entirely to the order of others,
producing magazine articles and advertising copy which involved
no personal risk. Even to this day, this sense of guilt persists when
I attempt to write a novel. I feel that, in spite of myself, something sinister and suspect will creep into my work and bring down
the wrath of heaven and earth. It appears to me as a terrifying and
dangerous task I would be only too thankful to be let off. Yet, if
I do *not* write, I feel even more guilty. I am convinced that no
amount of other work, even for the direct benefit of my neighbour, will absolve me from having shirked it. I can most truly
say with Dr. Johnson that I write out of the terror of a guilty
conscience.

It is obvious therefore, however much I try to argue and reason
about it, that I instinctively feel that this faculty of mine, however small, is something given me by God—a responsibility which
I cannot evade. Dare I say that I even feel it is actually connected
with my salvation, that in some way I shall be judged on what use I
make of it. I do not simply mean that, as I am sure every Christian
artist does, I pray about my work and at least *try* to do it honestly
for God. I mean that God may somehow put my writing itself in
the balance and perhaps excuse some of the egotism, vanity,
irritability, sloth about good works and even common duties to
which the writer is so prone.

Yet, even if, as I so deeply hope, this symposium will establish

art as a true function of Christian life, I do not expect to go away
with all my problems solved.

While not agreeing with Martin Turnell that belief destroys
talent, the conflicts it creates certainly tend, in the novel, to
destroy perfection of form. Yet the novel has always mirrored
conflict, not a vision of order and peace. Perhaps, by its very
nature, it can never achieve the 'wholeness, harmony and
radiance' which, St. Thomas says, signalize the true work of art.
Indeed, the deeper the novelist tries to go, the more truth as he
perceives it he tries to include in his work, the more likely he is
to mar the harmony and consistency of its formal pattern. In
wrestling with his particular daimon, he is bound to be maimed in
the fight. Yet, if the daimon be Jacob's angel, though lame he may
still be blessed.

*Miss White's principal theme, the dichotomy between art and religion
was central to all the discussion. Art requires the 'innocent eye'; but
religion brings in a moral conscience to prejudice this innocent eye. Miss
White said that she had written* Frost in May *at a time when she had
ceased to be a believing Christian; she said she would certainly have
written less frankly and omitted the event of the safety-pin in the child's
ear had she been writing the novel as a practising Catholic. Those
present were somewhat horrified at this fear of giving scandal and assured
the novelist that her guilt feeling was not justified.*

*After all the reassurances, equivalent to those of a kindly confessor, the
novelist, like the dancer, was hardly satisfied. Her problem was that of
Mauriac and Bernanos, and behind it lay the whole problem of the
domestication of the supernatural, the special characteristic of Catholicism.
The conclusion of this discussion, as indeed of the whole symposium, was
that art is indeed a true function of religion. But the artist must sing the
song of his own age and—to turn the sculptor's words—how can one
sing an uncertain song with the certainty of faith? The answer may
perhaps be found in the final paper where it is implied that the artist's
vision, like the mystic's, inspires hope rather than certainty. The man of
prayer, like the artist, progresses by a road of asceticism and negation.
Discussions at the symposium turned more than once to Keats's reference
to the poet's 'negative capability'.*

11. The Sculptor

PETER WATTS

Mr. Peter Watts is a stone carver in Bath. He learnt his craft before the war; after demobilization he chose to establish himself independently as a carver, working for a market which he describes as 'sectarian and regional'; he carves a great deal for churches, also for the needs of public bodies and an occasional private person in West of England districts where stone is still used. His witness is that of a man who earns his living as a sculptor.

WE live in a world of ghosts where noise counts for more than silence, the name counts for more than the thing, the shadow is more regarded than the substance. Everything God makes has a stamp on it, the stamp of Being. God never repeats himself, and every stamp is different. Custard is a dish made from eggs, custard powder is quite another thing. Oolithic limestone is fossilized sea-bed, but artificial stone however much it may look the same is again entirely different in substance. We like to fancy they are the same, we like to ignore God's stamps. I believe that we are in danger of losing altogether our sense of the reality of earthly things. We jumble rocks and stones and trees together and call their appearance a landscape, a thing of shadows. We forget the separate identities these objects receive from their Creator, the Being they share with him. Before we can make anything ourselves, we must learn to see the things outside us as they really are; that is, as things that God has made. Otherwise we shall be in danger of denying God.

I am a carver and my theme is stone. God made stone to teach us something about his own strength; his Church, he said, was to be made as impregnable as a Rock. We all know that stone decays, and may be blasted into smithereens. Whole hillsides may be carted away and ground into paste for spreading on the roads or smearing on the face. Nevertheless, stone itself is a creature of God, given us as a promise that he will be with us always, and also as a proof that he has been with us from the beginning of Time, for why else should he have so neatly packed it with little samples of his achievements from the protoplasm to the Peking man.

No one should touch hammer and chisel who has not first of all studied the action of the elements on stone. The rain and the frost and the wash of the tides lay bare great crags and boulders which they then mould into shapes. These shapes disclose the structure of the stone, its bedding and its lines of fracture, essential knowledge to the carver. If he should then choose to carve stone into the shape of leaves or hands or hair, it will be almost as if they had appeared naturally by some freak of weathering. Substantially the forms will be stone forms. By looking at them you will learn little enough perhaps about the things they represent. But you will learn something about the stone of which they are made, and what is more important still, something about the man who made them, himself a creature of God. I don't mean geological facts or traits of character, I mean the much more important kind of learning—I mean manliness and stoniness. It is the reality of Michelangelo and his marble, not the realism of David's ear that counts.

When I was a boy and returned year by year to school from holidays spent by the sea, I always carried with me in my pocket a small pebble picked at random from the shore. It spoke to me of the sea whenever I felt it or looked at it. All the power of the moving waters at their priest-like task seemed to be contained in that smooth hard shape. The sea had made it. It was a piece of stone, but also it bore the mark of the sea. Its shape had energy, the energy of a wave; its surface had lustre, the lustre that aeons of pure ablution had bestowed. It also represented for me the sea-beach fifty miles away to the south where I had found it, but

this was only by association. This was sentimental, and I knew it.
Any scrap of flotsam would have done as well to represent the
place, and awaken wistful recollections. But the pebble had a
higher sadness. The pebble was a sea-dirge, and all the sounding
shores of the world reverberated in my ears. Its value as a souvenir
was soon forgotten.

The stone statue of the carver, then, has power to move us not
by association with the subject, though we may find this pleasing
and helpful, but by the way it reflects the carver's own being
through his sympathetic handling of the stone. The expression of
the face, the attitude and proportions of the figure, may or may
not correspond with our ideas of what is appropriate, but that is
not the point. It is the shapes themselves that will proclaim the
thing a masterpiece, a reality. And having once grasped the
fact that for some mysterious reason this carving has as much right
to be as a daffodil or a mountain, then its particular connexion with
a subject no longer matters. We no longer worry that it should
fail to represent clearly, when we discover to our joy that in a much
larger sense it *is* that which it attempts to show. The ordinary
plaster products of the repositories are not lacking in pious
associations, the shop-windows where these are displayed positively exude the aura of piety like a chimney vapour. But because
they have no true substance as things they have no part for the
sculptor in the state of prayer. On the other hand, a Madonna by
some virile Baroque master may be anything but pious. It will be
more likely to remind us of my lady's boudoir or the grand opera
stage than of *prie-dieus* and gardens of the soul. But it was made by
a man who had this much familiarity with the ways of God that he
understood Making, and therefore it has the heavenly trade-mark
upon it. It is a prayer to contemplate.

I wish to repeat and to make clear what I believe the sculptor's
message to be. We have grown heavy-handed and heavy-hearted
with our love of science. We have lost the love of common things,
the world is nothing but a dreary jumble of minerals. Cheese is
only chalk with something added. The shadows crowd upon us
and make everything look the same. We are so lost and confused

that we cannot tell what is and what is not. Indeed we no longer understand the verb 'to be'. In this dark night it is the sculptor's job to be a maker of sign-posts. I take this piece of stone, he says, and I make something and it is, and there you have a sign that God is and that I am and that the world is. From the day the cave-man first set up his image in the farthest recess of his labyrinthine home, the sculptor's aim has been to imply no less than this. The primitive idol did not picture God, but in a sense it was God. You touched it before you went out hunting because it *was* and there was no escaping it. And as long as it stood there everything was right and there was always meat for breakfast.

Sculpture, then, is heavy and uncompromising stuff, a hard and ponderous obstruction in the rabbit-run of progress, a load indeed upon the minds of those who like a clear scamper. We see it in municipal art galleries, in the halls of technical institutes and modern secondary schools, in the foyer of the press lord, in any place where there is an excess of funds private or public. We no longer touch it as we pass but we feel its challenge. It requires understanding, it demands of us that we live up to it. It has the insistent call of an influence like the spring to which the heart is lifted and responds. It calls us back to the soil, the furrow, the seed cast into the dark earth with hope, the harvest gathered in with joy. It is the ancient voice of the stone thing in the cave, the thing that is. We remember how that thing presided over the agonies of birth and death and over the joys of maturity and fulfilment, for countless centuries before the coming of Christ. And then we think of mass education and daily papers and television critics, all the flitter and the flutter, the squeak and the gibber of modern existence, and more than ever it seems that unless we can learn to cherish the values of hard voluminous form, reality will soon be lost to our sight for ever.

I have heard it said by those who delight in prophecies of gloom and doom that when civilizations decay the arts of sculpture and poetry are the first to perish. There is this much truth in it, that when you once abandon the search for form, whether in verse or stone, then the whole matrix of civilization loosens and begins to crumble. Where the love of form is strong, there you will be likely to find strong institutions, laws of justice, and a united people. If the poets and sculptors sicken and grow tired, it means that the sense of form has gone and the nation's life is near its end. I do not believe that it ever vanishes entirely, there are plenty of good things from the Hellenistic and Dark Ages and plenty in our own time as well. But it is no longer a source of strength, it has lost its binding power. The flowers of statuary and song grow rather among ruins that are well-founded than upon walls new-raised in shifting sand.

It is a time for sculpture. The days of public monuments are over temporarily, but this is a thing that cannot be helped and does not greatly matter. From the arches of the late Emperors to the building of Vézélay there was a gap of six hundred years when no great monuments appeared in Europe, but there is enough Byzantine carving in Italy to prove that sculpture was far from dead. It was the work of the monks that kept it going, men devoted to training, training the heart, the mind, the hand, the eye, training the whole man to a perfect instrument of God's grace. Working tirelessly for a lifetime upon one small task, watching the sense of form develop, generation after generation in a process so gradual that if an aged man could say, looking on the work of his youth, 'I can manage this leaf a little better now, a little better than the man who then taught me', he was satisfied. Thus, and thus only was the period of renaissance in the eleventh and twelfth centuries made possible.

All this makes nonsense of the current theory that art grows, that it is organic to the soul and flourishes according to specific climate and environment—flourishes like grass, in the rash declaration of one eminent critic (with a disappointing crop of wild oats to his credit). If there are certain times when it appears to grow spontaneously, that is only because centuries of patient and assiduous exercise of the will have given it the roots. Again, if there are times when individual artists fly off the perch in obedience to what seems a blind impulse, that must not be interpreted as a defiance of tradition, but as a certainty of their

being able to transcend the traditional laws. The present is most
certainly not the time for encouraging the young to fly off the
perch. Far from being able to transcend the laws few of them
have more than a smattering of practice in them. Yet in many of
our more progressive schools all the really laborious processes,
such as carving, are being excluded, and quicker methods of
working such as modelling freely in slow-drying cement are
taking their place. The reason is of course to give impulse and
caprice a freer rein, and the result is as morbidly chaotic as one
might expect.

It is a time for stiffening the sinews if we wish the sense of form
to survive. To this end the technique of carving affords a most
excellent discipline. You have before you an arbitrary mass of
stone. You have to visualize within its boundaries a figure of
compact and rhythmical shapes. By means of drawings, or sketch
models cut from plaster or soft stone, you must make yourself
absolutely familar with the general outline and massing of this
figure before you may make so much as one cut in the stone itself.
When you do begin you must work all round, remembering that,
unlike a sonnet or a piece of music, a statue is composed not in
time but in space, and therefore has no beginning and no end, but
is there whole and entire from the moment the carving begins. It
may be that one view is more important than another in the sense
that it will receive most attention, but such is the complexity of
three-dimensional form that you will find with every fresh stage
of the work the number of varying aspects has multiplied itself a
hundredfold, and that you cannot afford to neglect one of them.
Eric Gill used to say that the work should look good right from
the start. This is an attractive theory, but it depends much on
the method of roughing out. I regret to say that my own method
must be far from ideal, for I find my earliest results anything but
encouraging. To me there is no agony like that of trying to fix the
general position and proportion of the shapes, no joy like that of
giving them final form and crispness.

The work should have finish, but only just so much finish as is
required to bring out the quality of the stone and give to it an air

of completeness and authority. No amount of polish can make a
dull work shine, but up to a point the value of a good work may
be enhanced by it. These are the veriest platitudes of instruction
such as any student of the arts will receive in his first term. Yet
how often is the corruption of taste that abounds everywhere
attributable to nothing but their neglect! It is true to say, I think,
that carving enforces a stricter adherence to these homely precepts than most other methods and media. You may 'get away
with it' in oils or in clay, but never in stone or wood; just as you
may get away with bad grammar in English or even in French, but
never in Latin or Greek. Above all, the discipline of having to
work from the general to the particular without destroying the
wholeness of the shape and without slurring the forms, is one that
cannot fail to have a good effect upon the intellect and outlook of
the young student of carving. Set your pupil to work quickly and
roughly in some shoddy material, he may produce ten results in
the same time as it would take him to produce one in a good
piece of stone. The results may be promising but they will give
him no sense of achievement. I believe that one simply cannot
underrate the psychological value nowadays of this so-called
sense of achievement. Millions suffer hardship daily without hope
of victory or reward beyond the wage-packet. Mere hardship
merely hardens. But to have wrestled with a task, to be brought
face to face with an overwhelming mass of trials and perplexities
and irrevocable decisions, to be beaten to one's knees on the very
verge of despair, to rise and return to the assault, and then
suddenly to find the one thing done—this is to make of hardship
a fine tempering process. Spent and exhausted but with the work
before you coming swiftly now to its conclusion, you find the
experience was supremely worth while, and you are satisfied—
for the moment.

The mortal sickness of the world is non-fulfilment, which is the
soul's destruction. This it is that peoples all the land with ghosts,
this it is that turns reality into a dance of shadows, a soft alluring
fantasy in the antechamber of Death. Make something that shall
stand in the doorway and have power to be, and you destroy the

spell, you switch on the floodlight and the shadows vanish. One substantial achievement to the sculptor's credit and he sees the world as God saw it on the seventh day. Yet how many of all the thousands in our art schools are ever given the chance to achieve anything final? I went one day to the local academy to ask for the assistance of some experienced pupil in a simple matter of roughing-out. They shook their heads and said that no one had the skill to assist me. My ears are still ringing with the astounding reply that followed. They said: 'It is not our business to train craftsmen, but teachers of art.'

The old monk with his page of manuscript or his foliated capital was wiser, and his works remain. If anyone suggests that he might have been happier had he had greater opportunities for self-expression, and that in this case his work would have seemed to us more human, more alive—well the answer is that what made him so happy was the fact that he had no self and therefore no desire to express it, and that this very freedom made it possible for him to achieve an expression of serenity such as no one for over five hundred years has even approached. *In silentio noctis*, in the stillness of the Dark Ages, the nightingales were singing.

Today it is all a clamour of rooks; to be a voice is something, to croak above the rest is the all-in-all. What one chiefly notices is the lack of anything to sing about except—What a big noise we are all making! I have the pathetic memory of students coming to me with tools in their hands saying: 'What shall I carve, what shall I do?' I was always tempted to reply: 'Go home and help your mother with the washing-up!' Instead I felt greatly sympathetic, but could never bring myself to tell them quite bluntly that they had mistaken their vocation. They would never have believed me, anyway, they would have impressed upon me their certainty that they were called to art. In which case I should have had to explain to them that art was not a vocation in that sense at all, that if you became an artist it was not because you felt the call, but because you had something to say. Then they would have burst into tears and said that they only wanted to be teachers of art anyway.

For my own part I have to admit that I never felt the call of art, least of all did I feel drawn to sculpture. At the age of twenty-one I was quite ready to become a poet or a playwright or an actor or a journalist or a painter or an architect or a designer of stained-glass windows, because I thought that in any one of these trades I could work for a whole lifetime without drying up. It was only a chance acquaintance with a hammer and chisel that decided me, and the fact that stone was handy in these parts. What should I carve? Kings and prophets and saints of course, and the curious little comedies of everyday life that were enacted beside them in the branching capitals. Wells was a short bicycle ride, and there were pictures of Chartres and Vézélay in the library of the school where I worked. The fact that five hundred years separated me from this wonderful tradition did not alarm me in the least, nor did the danger of being sneered at as a mediaevalist deter me. It was the only work of the district that was any good; it was every bit as lively as Chaucer and the thought of it made you sing as you walked up over the Mendips or down through the cider orchards below Dulcote hill. The old master-masons were centuries dead, but when I took up the trade and learned it with the screech of modern machinery in my ears, I always had their example in mind. Believing in the same essential truths, working the same stone and with very similar tools, I was never once conscious of the immense gulf of time. I just wanted to carry on in the same spirit.

London, in spite of its ugliness and grim bustle, is a European not an English capital. I went there and worked in studios, in stone-yards and in the schools. The master-masons of Somerset seemed very small and very far away. Very near me instead were the most enormous and unapproachable wonders, things that threatened to crush me like a worm whenever I stood by them. When Keats first saw the Elgin marbles it was mortality that weighed him down. But they were his kindred and his was the agony of a master-spirit delivered too late into the world. They were his brothers and his equals and they were lost to him like everything else he loved, poor fellow. When I saw the great Theseus fragment from the Parthenon pediment it was my total

9

lack of any possible claim to kinship with it that distressed me. If this was sculpture where was I? It was god-like in its posture and in its shapes, even the knee was god-like and carved by a god too, or by some creature who would never have recognized me as a man, but would have spurned me as an insect. Yet a mild-faced official came and talked about it in a reedy voice exactly as we have heard doctors talk to their students about the patient on the table. One might have asked him, if only one had thought of it, what had the Parthenon and Wells Cathedral in common with each other. In my mind's ear I seem to hear an embarrassed snigger as the only reply. Had the world gone differently, had it been an earlier Parthenon and a later Wells—who knows? But as it was, of course there was only one possible answer—each was a moment in time and place.

And I was another—another moment in time, that is—but my place was Wells. London was a great vacuum where time and place were suspended and only talk went on; on and on past midnight, trivial, fragmentary, and over-serious, with nothing of the jovial intimacy of real discussion.

> In the room the women come and go
> Talking of Michelangelo. . . .

Yes, and of Mino of Fiesole, too, and the Pisans, Giovanni and Niccolo, of Jacopo the Oak Man, of Ghiberti and Donatello the twin marvels. Yes, there was no denying it, Rome had conquered the world a second time, not with soldiers, but with sculptors and painters. Who then dared talk of Wells, of Dinder and Croscombe and Compton Martin, and—the ruined glory of them all— Glastonbury? From the day that Torrigiani landed, Torrigiani the bruiser who broke Michelangelo's nose with a blow of his fist, whom the traitor Henry called over to build tombs in his father's chapel at Westminster, from that day onwards the master-masons were finished, cut off in their prime just as the English Renaissance was flowering again after the troubles of the fifteenth century, as it had flowered a hundred years earlier after the Black Death, but this time with promise of unprecedented glory. Forced to work, as at Hampton Court, under the supervision of

Italians. Forced, as in this part of the country, to accept the plans of upstart amateurs like Thynne and Sharrington. Forced to become dry and studious and second-rate, the lost provincials once again of a world empire.

There had been a time, of course, when England was really herself, and that was when the official language was still French. *The Canterbury Tales* and Wells Cathedral were both essays in the art of being English. Unsuccessful as art perhaps, but positive and searching as expressions of what it felt like to be in England now that April was here. Obviously, it seemed to me, that was what an English sculptor of the twentieth century should be aspiring to do. It was not an original idea; certainly there had been others, far better men than myself, who had tried, who had failed gloriously, and who were now labelled as cranks. Looking back, indeed, it seemed as though the past was strewn with failures in this very field, from about the year 1850 onwards. William Morris, for example, so prolific, so versatile, so expert in all he did, and yet at the same time so slight and superficial and unconvincing. Enthusiasm run riot, no strong basis of reality, a sentimental outlook that made him think of all men as brothers in art, it was so easy to find the reasons for his failure. Much less obvious to account for was his true greatness, his victory over the second-rate. It was this, that whereas he had a blurred vision of his fellow-beings as one great family, he had a brilliantly clear and level vision of all the rest of Creation. He did not believe in God, but I really think that he did see the world as God saw it on the seventh day. He saw everything separately, and he saw right into each thing, he understood its very being. Rocks and stones and trees and grass and fabric and flowers. But there were depths in himself which he feared and covered up.

Provided I could overcome the fear of self, and provided that I did not expect miracles of enlightenment in those about me, that, I thought, was the sort of sculptor I should wish to be. At least a glorious failure. The only alternative was to go abroad, like Alfred Stevens, and spend years studying the finest examples in the world, to make myself a kind of composite master of masters, and then to come home and produce something utterly beautiful and utterly dead, like the Wellington Monument. I had no ambition at all in that direction. What I wanted above all was to realize the fruits of my boyhood in Somerset and my Benedictine upbringing which taught me to love the beauty of my Father's House. And this meant working in the spirit of that ancient tradition which the monks had so carefully fostered and tended, and which had rooted like the wild rose in all the little villages about the Mendips.

From the worldly point of view this meant also limiting myself to regional and sectarian interests. I could never represent the age or the nation as a whole, fulfil the *Zeitgeist* as I believe they call it. Why? Because the spirit of the age was one of scientific inquiry, and of doubtful speculation not upon the nature of transcendental things but upon the possibility of their existence. How was it possible to be certain, as I was, in a spirit of uncertainty, the prevailing spirit? I was trying to see nature as God-made, others were trying to see it as if it had been made by themselves in a dream which might or might not turn out to be true. There was much to admire in the splendid flights of fancy of some of our leading contemporaries, though an equal admiration was also due to the audacity of supersonic test-pilots. But it was not for me to emulate them, I had another job to do. If I can tell chalk from cheese, I thought, I shall remain here with the Somerset mud on my boots and prove that immortal difference to the laggards and the yokels.

We are all fond of laggards and yokels, as much as we all detest the Common Man, that overbearing autocrat who is for ever trying to grind us down into a polished uniformity. There was a time when the Common Man was a foolish and endearing sort of character, 'A commonplace type with a stick and a pipe and a half-bred black-and-tan'. But he has now abandoned these simple attributes and has acquired a new and sinister dignity in cap and gown. He has no religion, of course, but he has a compact and compendious philosophy and the Great Mystery holds no terrors for him. A severe fundamentalist at heart, he likes to reduce everything to a basic simplicity of form, especially in the matter of art, because he finds it does facilitate judgment so enormously. But being entirely innocent of prejudice, which is reactionary, he has no very rigid preferences in painting and sculpture. The Common Man knows all about Art, but he does not know what he likes. He merely appreciates what he knows.

And the sculpture he knows and therefore appreciates the best is that which the *Daily Blurb* calls 'abstract' and the weekly *Onlooker* calls 'non-figurative', although my own name for it is Basic Sculpture. How well it suits the Common Man this nice adjustment of political idealism to the world of art! Sculpture with its Greek heroes and its Gothic saints, its disturbing symbolism, its awkward fuss of gesture and expression, always seemed to him the most untidy and unhealthy of the arts. How satisfying to have it all cleaned up and set in order, purged of all those uncomfortable associations, reduced to a smooth hygienic drama of shapes! How soothing to the jaded nervous system, how full of meaning to the subconscious mind! You see, the Common Man likes pure formalism in a work of sculpture because the whole thing depends on a formula, which to him is always the complete answer to everything. He likes the formula to take the place of the subject because he is far readier to appreciate the roundness of the statement $x^2 - y^2 = (x+y)(x-y)$, than he is to understand the jagged meaning of 'I am the Resurrection and the Life'. This is an example of his short-sightedness, for you have only to repeat the formula twice and it becomes a cliché, whereas the text will never become a platitude. So on the whole I think it fairly certain that Basic Sculpture, whatever its official favour at the moment and however it may please the Common Man, is doomed to pass away from sheer dryness, and that within as short a space of time as it takes the simple inventive faculty of the human brain to exhaust itself.

If we see a work that we particularly like, we do not immediately inquire about the subject, it is of secondary importance to us. There is perhaps a certain urgency and force about the figure which is so striking that there can be no doubt as to the

artist's meaning. Later when we come to associate that meaning
with a title, we may find the connexion interesting or not as the
case may be, but it will anyway have little or no effect upon our
judgment of the work *per se*. It would be reasonable to suppose,
then, that subject-matter is of secondary importance to the
artist also, and that he generally makes up his composition first
and then works-in the necessary associations. I have no doubt
that figure-subjects done for exhibition at the Academy have
frequently been dished up in this way, with subject interest
added for spice at the end. It is a matter of personal taste or habit
and I have no wish to decry the methods of highly skilled and
gifted composers in sculpture. It would certainly not suit me,
and my sort of work, because if I am asked by a priest to make a
statue of St. John the Baptist, say, I have two things at once to
start thinking about in conjunction with each other: namely, the
subject of the statue, and the requirements of its place in the
church. The first is a pile of dry tinder to set my bonfire alight,
the second is a lengthy prong to stir it and keep it under control.
I have never been able to understand how anyone could get
started without the inspiration of a subject to make a brisk flame.
And yet I have seen men labouring heavily at compositions with no
care at all for subject, but from sheer habit of exercise, like the
men one used to see in the early morning running round Battersea
Park. There is, as Mr. Christopher Fry has cruelly observed, a
dreariness in dedicated spirits, they burn so slowly.

Sculpture is one of the most boring subjects in the world to write
about, especially for someone like myself who has the excitement
of actually doing it every day. I have tried to keep this paper
interesting, and I am very conscious of the fact that in doing so I
have risked a great many half-truths. But in any case the whole
truth can never be known, the last word can never be said. There
is a great deal I should like to be able to say, but I cannot find the
words. There is the dark side, without which of course all
sculpture would fall flat. I cannot touch upon that side, indeed I
have only recently become aware of its existence. It has to do with
oneself, and it adds very considerably to one's difficulties. The

funny thing is that there seems to be no way round it, but no sooner have you realized that a dark and unexplored place exists than you must go through it. I go through, and I find it is just like becoming a helpless novice again. There is an awful struggle in the stone of something trying to come, and after hours of fruitless effort I begin to think that the end is near and the stone must be abandoned. Then a quiet ride home on my bicycle, working at it still in the mind's eye, a sleepless night perhaps, a steady attack all the next morning—and we have things under control again. But it will not be quite what I had hoped.

I am sure it is the same with all our work. We are creatures of God and we are haunted by images of perfection. If all our experience could be summed up in a single phrase, a song, a figure, a sonnet, it would still fall far short of that transfigured summary in the mind which has neither word nor shape nor music, but is a source of perpetual energy like a spring of water in the hills. We store experience as the hills store rain, and deep inside us a great pressure is built up, until out through a crevice of the rocks it comes, not as it fell from the sky in leaden misty drops, but in a leaping crystal stream. With the power of this spouting well of joy we work. We grind away at our material with that peculiar transforming instinct of our kind. And thus from the breaking down of one wholeness into parts, from a separation and a refinement, from a pounding in the press, from an annealing in the furnace, a fresh wholeness is made, something useful for the sustaining of our lives. We cut into the loaf, we taste the wine, and we are disappointed. Something has gone wrong and the stuff is not as good as it should be, it has the musty odour of death about it. We can do nothing to improve it, but we are like children and we desire some sort of assurance that what we have done wrong can eventually be put right. So we take the result of all our pains, we take our imperfect crust and our faulty vintage, and we go into the church with them, and in fear and trembling we offer them to God. And God in his great mercy takes them and has a look at them, and then he gives them back to us again— AS THEY SHOULD BE.

III

CRITICIZING THE ARTS

In this section an attempt was made to examine the different media and to see what is the artistic function of each. This work of criticism was extended, in the last two papers, to the way in which these functions impinge on the human person, physiologically and psychologically.

12. Music

ALEC ROBERTSON

From his long experience of writing, lecturing and broadcasting about music, Alec Robertson contributed this paper on the medium of music.

SCHUMANN had just finished playing a new and as yet untitled composition to a friend. 'What does it mean?' said the friend, rather puzzled by the piece. 'It means this', Schumann replied, and played it again.

This little incident contains, really, the essence of what I want to say. If music is a language, with its own special methods of articulation and expression, it must have meaning: and that meaning can only lie in the ordered sounds of a composition, not, in the final analysis, in anything extra-musical. If, therefore, Schumann afterwards called his piece *Dreaming* he added nothing to the music but merely gave a general description of its prevailing mood and a prod to the imagination of the listener. Richard Strauss also called one of his piano pieces *Dreaming*. What is the difference between the two?[1] If there were two poems about dreams, let us say, 'Come to me in my dreams and then by day I shall be well again' (Matthew Arnold) and 'I dreamt that I dwelt in marble halls' (Alfred Bunn), one could easily describe the difference between the two by paraphrasing the words. But music, as Goethe said, begins where words leave off, and we have to seek the difference in sounds, not in concepts. That difference could be expressed technically—one relies on

---

[1] A number of points in this paper were illustrated by musical examples which unfortunately cannot be reproduced here.

melodic line, the other on harmony—but however expressed it is a difference apprehended by the mind, reported to by the senses: mental activity followed by emotional response.

Now it has been said *ad nauseam* that the expression of emotion is the final end of music and it seems necessary to emphasize that 'the emotional or signal ingredient is practically the only non-artistic material left in music, and so it attracts more attention here than in the other arts, to the detriment of aesthetic considerations'. This last sentence is a quotation from an article by Hans Tischler, in *The Music Review* of August 1956, on 'the aesthetic experience' which itself quotes largely from Susan Langer's remarkable book, *Philosophy in a New Key*. In what I have to say I gratefully acknowledge a debt to both authors.

For the moment I will add this one further quotation: 'In music those that react only to the emotional implications of a composition can be well said to have had hardly any aesthetic appreciation of the work but only of the performance. They are often good judges of performers and conductors but much less successful in criticising a composition.'

One has only to listen for a while to the chatter in the vestibule of a concert hall or to the conversation of gramophone record collectors to discover the truth of this. But it is not a matter for priggish disdain. People must be free to enjoy music in their own way since it eludes verbal description, other than technical, except of a vague kind. One cannot know just what the ordinary listener does experience mentally or intuitively. He cannot express it in words, but it may have been a real communication.

Let us remember that 'Art happens', as Carlyle said, 'in palace or hovel' and the widespread dissemination of music today has made that saying more meaningful than it ever can have been. Its results are often inspiring. Only a few months ago I heard a porter at a small junction station in Sussex say to the woman in the refreshment room, 'I'm saving up for Leonora No. 3', and it was Beethoven, on L.P., he meant, not polygamy!

One often hears people say today, 'I'm going to *see* so-and-so,' referring to this or that artist, conductors especially, the composer only being mentioned thereafter. But music is not primarily artists and concerts. Concert promoters certainly give the idea, in their publicity methods, that the composer exists for the glorification of conductor, singer, or instrumentalist—an idea occasionally shared by these same people—and of course human personality, even if second rate, is a matter of absorbing interest. But every genuine artist knows, with humility, that he is only a means (the only means, in this context) to an end: and the end is the communication of musical ideas by way of symbols, these ideas being produced by an intellectual process. Hence, as Mr. Tischler says, 'to speak of music as the art of feeling or emotion is, therefore, a contradiction in terms, for any work of art, like the solution of a mathematical problem or the presentation of a philosophical idea, is an intellectual attainment'.

This is by no means a new idea. St. Augustine spoke of music, in the well-known phrase, as *Musica est scientia bene modulandi*, that is, a science of shaping music as perfectly as possible to a moral end: which is not a matter of feeling or emotion. Plato, and Aristotle whose outlook was more liberal, had earlier reached the same conclusion. At the same time St. Augustine, though disturbed by his own delight in the sensuous sound of voices singing in church, 'allows full value to the pleasure content of music and never advises the readers of *De Musica* to beware of pleasure as such'.[1]

In *A Composer's World*, Paul Hindemith has usefully summarized St. Augustine's exposition (in *De musica libri sex*) of musical perception and understanding, showing that musical impressions are by no means simple reactions to external stimuli but a complex mixture of diverse occurrences.

First there is the mere physical fact of sound . . . indispensable as a basic experience before the perception and mental absorption of music can take place; second, there is our faculty of hearing, the physiological fact that sound waves act upon our ear and, by muscular and nervous transmission, release reactions in the brain's centre of hearing. Third, there is our ability to imagine music mentally without

[1] Erik Routley: *The Church and Music* (Duckworth, 1950).

the stimulus of music actually sounded or without recollective reference to a definite former impression. Fourth, there is our ability to uncover previous musical experiences, stored in our memory like old keepsakes, to draw them out of their hiding places, revive them mentally, and allow them to impress us with the same intensity as actual music would do, after which they may again be put to rest in the storage chests of our soul. In all these musical happenings both our corporeal and mental nature participate, with the emphasis constantly shifting from one to the other. Fifth, our mental activity must rise to predominance; we must in the moment of actual perception or of soundless concept subject the musical substance to an intellectual examination and judge its musical shape and grade. Thus the mere activity of perceiving or imagining music is combined with the satisfaction we derive from classifying and evaluating it. But we must not become slaves of this enjoyable satisfaction. . . . Musical order, as recognized and evaluated by our mind is not an end in itself. It is an image of a higher order which we are permitted to receive if we proceed one step further to the sixth degree on our scale of musical assimilation if we put our enjoyment of such knowledge (enjoyment, the weight of the soul) into the side of the balance that tends towards the order of the heavens and towards the unification of our soul with the divine principle.[1]

The philosophical approach, thus summarized, may indeed seem formidable and it raises difficult questions in regard to an art of music so much more complex and diverse that St. Augustine could have imagined. At the same time we must remember that he means by *musica* those arts that use sounds as their basis of expression; and so poetry is included, though music itself is obviously the art most prominent in his mind.

After this apparent, though I hope it is a relevant, *détour*, I return to my main thesis. Music is a language, expressing ideas without concepts, and as a language must have meaning, and 'the real business of loving and possessing music (just as of creating it) is done in one's mind if it is done at all'. Everyone who listens, who *really* listens to music, does, even if

1 Paul Hindemith: *A Composer's World* (Oxford University Press, 1952).

intermittently, think with it and follow its logic. To give a simple example. When some obvious vital tune carries us off our feet— let us say the big tune in Tchaikovsky's *Romeo and Juliet* overture— we become airborne with it—up we go with the upward going strings to be carried along each curve of the tune. You do not stop to register your emotional involvement with the tune, or consciously to analyse it—but in listening to the temporal succession of notes, heard in phrases, you have in fact related every note to the next one—or the tune would not make sense; and when, on the way home, you find yourself humming that tune you are *thinking musically*. In this, especially in its wider aspects, lies the whole art of listening, and when we do this we exercise those powers of concentration and recognition through which this chronological art becomes intelligible to us. Music is, there- fore, even at its most sensuous, in some degree an intellectual pleasure.

Music, however, is not all tune: this is what disappointed the charlady who said, elliptically, 'I like classical when it starts, but not when it goes on!' Popular music makes its appeal by depend- ing only on tune and rhythm, often of the most obvious kind, with, indeed, some harmonic decorations derived from serious music; but the actual tune material—in the popular sense—in the extended forms of sonata or symphony—is small. How dis- appointing for the light-minded public that Beethoven should begin the *Eroica* Symphony (if ever they happened to listen to it) with what promises to be a beguiling tune, but which is abruptly halted on a D flat.

Music for the millions, that deceptive phrase, means, in regard to 'good music', cutting chunks from the living body and throwing them, often thoroughly vulgarized, to the people, an operation performed by men with reverence only for material gain, men who, in different ways, may yet destroy Western civilization with the atom bomb of triviality.

It is time now to determine how music, as a language, differs from the language of the other arts. It shares two things with them —form and rhythm—but this most intangible of the arts uses these in a way that renders analysis, very useful up to a point, finally a dead end.

In its temporal succession of material there is of course a correspondence between music and literature. We do not 'see' a play as a whole, or anything read to us, until the end is reached, and so with a piece of music: but whereas, as I have said before, literary material is related to concepts, musical material is not. Hence the art of music has been called, above all, the grand art of reminiscence, and in any complex work repetition or recourse to the printed score is a necessity.

There is no correspondence between the characters in a play and the thematic material of a symphony, as a moment's thought will show. Each follows different laws of development. It would be very odd if the characters in the first act of a drama suddenly began to say, even if in somewhat different terms, what they had said at the start of the act, and even odder if they disappeared and new sets of characters appeared in each of the three subsequent acts; nor has the analogy really any more validity if the symphony be of the cyclic kind, or if it is a matter of theme and variations.

Music articulates form in a way unique to itself. Furthermore, its material is presented horizontally and vertically, in the two dimensions of melody and harmony, and in counter-point arising out of combined horizontal lines, one of music's greatest glories.

We speak, by analogy, of tone-colour in music, the colour of an oboe or a trumpet; Beethoven, and others, have spoken of the colour of different keys. To him D minor was dark brown— but in fact the analogy is no more than a convenient method of allusion, as it is in speaking of the colour of words: the purple passage.

This or that instrument is chosen by a composer because of its tonal characteristics, and a musical idea may be at once conceived as a piano thought or a violin thought or for this or that medium as a whole, orchestra or string quartet. Limitations now appear. It was no use, in the eighteenth century, writing notes for the valveless horn or trumpet that could not be played, or today writing in a key that will take instruments outside their compass.

In this matter composers have often made a virtue of necessity. Thus Mozart, in the first aria of Donna Elvira in *Don Giovanni* writes a certain phrase in the key of the dominant, as the convention of the time required. When this strain is due to re-appear in the tonic, again in accordance with usage, the soprano, had Mozart repeated the pattern, would have been compelled to sing notes which instrumentally would have offered no difficulty, but would be a strain vocally, so Mozart hit on a wonderful subterfuge, and the whole piece gains from the discipline.

I have said that analogies between themes and characters in a play will not hold good, nor will that between the form of a play and that of a symphony, nor that from the metaphorical use of colour for the tone of instruments, nor, to return to form, can we equate form with architecture.

Since musical form is fluid it is absurd to speak of architecture as frozen music. Browning's description of a fugue in 'Master Hugues of Saxe-Gotha' is ingenious, but tells us nothing at all significant; it is merely picturesque and makes one doubt that Browning had ever really *heard* a fugue.

> What with affirming, denying,
> Holding, risposting, subjoining,
> All's like . . . it's like . . . for an instance I'm trying . . .
> There! See our roof, its gilt moulding and groining
> Under those spider-webs lying!

As Ernest Newman has lately said, no poet has ever done more than say how music affects him, and no one could really do more except, to go back to Schumann, by saying 'this is what it means or is', by playing it.

Form and content are identical in music, by which I do not mean formal form—the conventional blue-print of A. B. A., the minuet and trio let us say—but the shape that phrases take therein. Out of such phrases tonal structures are built up from the simplest to the most complex. In this matter form, like rhythm, each according to its medium, is common to all the arts.

▲ 1. Fresco in the catacomb of Domitilla: the deceased, Veneranda, with her patron saint the martyr Petronella. The scrolls in the case and the bound book probably indicate the teaching of the scriptures

◄ 2. Fresco in the catacomb of Priscilla: a bishop in cathedra receiving the vows and bestowing the veil of a consecrated virgin

MVNIFICENTIA LEONIS. XIII. P. M.

3. Sculptured sarcophagus: the instruction of a catechumen.
   An adaption of a pagan theme for a Christian tomb

4. The Dogmatic sarcophagus: so called on account of its
   comprehensive illustration of Catholic doctrine

FAITH AND WORK
IN MEDIAEVAL ART

5. Vezelay Cathedral, looking up
the nave to the High Altar

6. York Minster. View of nave
from West End

13. Saskia as Flora by Rembrandt

13. Saskia as Flora by Rembrandt

▲

11. The Flagellation
by Piero della Francesca

12. The Trinity by Masaccio. Fresco ▶
in Santa Maria Novella

7. The Crown of Otto I, commonly known as 'Charlemagne's Crown'

8. The Imperial State Crown

9. Cameo by the Master of the Crown of Stockholm

10. The Wilton Diptych

5. Vezelay Cathedral, looking up
   the nave to the High Altar

6. York Minster, View of nave
   from West End

14. Rock painting of a magician disguised with antlers and paws in the cavern of the Trois Frères. Mimicry was used to create ritual or magic

15. A child artist in Rome. Inventive variations are sometimes made upon the themes given by other children on the same wall surface

. From the cover of a Japanese lacquer writing box by Shimsho. A method by which black tooth stain is skilfully squirted on to a screen to form a message. Style evolves to some extent according to the laws of chance

17. The Birth of Aphrodite

18. Stone Effigy, Dorchester

*From 'Greek Sculpture' by Lullies and Hirmer,
published by Thames and Hudson*

19. St. Bernard of Clairvaux by Peter Watts

20. Shanta Rao

21. Ulanova

We have now to consider the part of composer, performer, and listener in a piece of music, and follow with a practical demonstration.

The composer, obviously enough, regards his work as an intellectual task, based on technical craftsmanship. I do not know when musical craftsmen first were known as composers, but I suspect that Beethoven, with insistence on the dignity of his craft, stressed the distinction. Anything internal or external may be the starting-point of creation, the waving of a tree in the wind, the song of a bird, any natural phenomenon, any material or spiritual experience. Are the composer's feelings, however inspired, what the music expresses, or are they those of the performer, or the listener himself reacting to the stimulus of music?

Hindemith declares that music cannot express the composer's feelings. In writing, over a space of several months, a funereal piece, are we to imagine, he says, the composer to have been thinking of nothing but funerals, or more absurdly, to have felt grief as a starting-point only. Here, Hindemith says, is what he really does:

> He knows by experience that certain patterns of tone-setting corres-
> pond with certain emotional reactions on the listener's part. Writing
> these patterns frequently and finding his observations confirmed, in
> anticipating the listener's reactions he believes himself to be in the
> same mental situation, and is not only reproducing the feelings of
> other individuals, but is actually having these same feelings, being
> obsessed by them whenever he thinks he needs them, and being
> urged to express them with each stroke of his ever ready pen.
> Consequently he does not express his own feelings in his music.

This analysis obviously needs qualification. Keats said he never wrote a single line of poetry with the least shadow of public thought: Bach would have said the same. Handel, on the other hand, a composer of the theatre, always had a finger on the pulse of the public. Hindemith has certainly described the attitude of the composer who must pay special regard to his public, but he forgets, it seems to me, the instinctive nature of the artist and the despotic nature of art which, as Maritain has said, demands the whole strength and intelligence of the composer's manhood in the service of the thing he is making. Haydn and Mozart, for example, took heed of the conventions of their age, loved them, sometimes laughed at them and sometimes—indeed very often— superbly transcended them.

Musica scientia est bene modulandi; the process of creation is a science, one of continual calculation, a mathematical process; the rhythms, the melody, the harmony, the combination of melodies, the key sequences, the evolving form, all have to be brought into a just relation. A composition, once again, is therefore an intellectual attainment. Let us not worry about what feelings the composer has or has not.

The performer, for his part, has quite simply to try to interpret the composer, not himself. The introduction of his own feelings can only distort a work. And the listener? One can say at once that he must try to approach a work with a mind like a clean slate. The enormously suggestive power of music, emotionally, combined with emotional experiences of the day or of his life, makes this no easy matter. All too easily he may be using the music he overhears as a background to some romantic experience of his life and so he hears, in fact, nothing but stimulating sounds. Every serious listener to music has to work out his technique of listening, with honesty and true humility. There is or is not a cultivatable field of music in individuals that either can be left fallow by those who are content to be emotionally moved by music, or can be cultivated rationally.

The possibilities, so far as they can be systematized, have been stated by a Swiss author, Dr. Odier, as follows:

(1) Those whose pleasure in hearing music depends on their technical knowledge of the art.

(2) Those who, consciously or unconsciously, substitute images for sounds.

(3) Those whose pleasure depends on sentiments or emotions with which they are 'inspired' or which they find in the music.

(4) Those whose pleasure depends on ideas or thoughts suggested by the music.

(5) Those who experience an emotion *sui generis* and not to be compared with any other psychological phenomenon: in other words a purely musical emotion unable to be expressed in other terms.

The best listener, the conclusion is, will be he who has experienced each of these stages.

I would add to this analysis that an intelligent listener might be expected to ascend from sensuous to aesthetic emotion, and finally to spiritual awareness.

The reader may put the matter to practical demonstration, since a bar of music is worth pages of foolscap. First of all let him listen to a piece of music that is concerned with nothing outside itself, the first movement of Haydn's *London* Symphony. It *is* its meaning. Here is articulated form. What should the listener perceive? The musical language of the piece makes it referable to the listener's experience; there is no difficulty here and he should have acquired some awareness of eighteenth-century conventions. Does he follow the *meaning* of the music?

Now let me take a piece of music which though perfectly intelligible in itself yet testifies to something beyond itself, the second movement of Beethoven's 4th Piano Concerto. There is no stated programme, but there is a striking antithesis that calls for explanation by the inquiring mind. Here there is a special call upon the imagination.

Blake said that man's desires are governed by his perceptions, no man can desire what he has not perceived. So he may not desire to receive more than a certain sensuous or emotional satisfaction from these pieces and be content with that. Music for him will not be a language that conveys meaning, and for him the craftsman will have laboured in vain. But in saying this, one must never forget that there are listeners, if few, who in some way that cannot be explained do intuitively reach the heart of the matter.

I cannot take the matter further, but must pass on now to final considerations: the moral and spiritual values of music.

It was, as we saw, an Augustinian precept that our mind absorbs music and transforms it into moral strength. This raises issues too large to be more than touched on here. A work of art may be aesthetically good and morally bad, or the reverse. To take a familiar illustration, aesthetically bad church art, say a Mass by the deplorable Augustus Tozer, or Gounod's Catholicism *sucré*, may bring an access of moral strength to the simple un-aesthetically-minded listener; so can, presumably, one of those commercial ballads the Americans call *religioso*, in which great spiritual themes are nauseatingly vulgarized. But music *itself* can in no way be morally bad—and of no other art can that be said. It should be remembered that the denunciations of the Fathers of the Church were directed against the *associations* of certain instruments as used by the pagans, and against the *words* of their songs, just as Tolstoy's outburst in his celebrated essay *What is Art?* was directed against 'all the filthy operettas, songs and ballads with which our world teems . . . with the object of disseminating vice as widely as possible'. He came to the conclusion that it would be better for the Christian world to be deprived of all then esteemed to be art and, together with the false, to lose all that is good in it; and he called as witnesses Plato, the Fathers of the early Christian Church, and Mohammedan teachers! This condemnation can only be applied to music that is committed to words, or a programme, but it at once raises a difficult question for the Christian moralist. Is a work aesthetically good, but, as he sees it, morally bad in its subject-matter, to be banned to right-living Christians? The Anglican and Nonconformist preachers, and no doubt the Catholics too, thought so when Verdi's opera *La Traviata* came to London. It was hotly denounced, but the faithful yearned to see it. So—and how English this is!—a *concert* performance was given at that home of Nonconformity, Exeter Hall in the Strand, thereby inspiring a lampoon that ended:

> God bless our happy land
> What's sin in the Haymarket is religion in the Strand.

And what of Wagner's *Tristan* or Strauss's *Salome*, which hardly exhibit virtue triumphant.

I once found myself sitting next to two nuns at a performance of *Tristan und Isolde* in the Prinzregenten Theatre at Munich and could not refrain from asking them, when we were chatting in the interval, how they came to be present at this particular opera. They fluttered their eyelids and murmured that it was educational! As a matter of fact they were right. It is a great masterpiece and like all such is not to be placed on an *index expurgatorius*.

This brings me to the point of these present reflections. There is always between the listener and the work a certain 'psychical distance' separating the object and its appeal from one's own self. 'This does not imply an impersonal, purely intellectually interested relationship; on the contrary, it describes a personal reaction, often highly emotionally coloured—its peculiarity lies in that it has been cleared of the practical concrete nature of its appeal. The content has been symbolized for us, what it invites is not emotional response, but insight.' That goodness inhabits great music is a fact thousands have experienced, and from it many have found an access of moral strength. I heard recently of a man who said, after listening to Beethoven's C sharp minor String Quartet, 'Well, if it's like that, everything is all right.' In its humble way this was no less a revelation than that received from a divine source by Mother Julian of Norwich: 'all will be well, and all manner of thing will be well.' I conclude that music in itself cannot be evil—Salome's possession of the head of John the Baptist calls forth merely romantic lyricism from Strauss—unless *deliberately* prostituted to evil ends by extra-musical additions: words and gestures and so forth.

Music is therefore the most spiritual of the arts. In this very fact lies a danger. Cardinal Newman, in a sermon recently printed, said the great danger Christianity might have to face was of a world purely irreligious. The danger is with us now. We are indeed the children of the Renaissance. 'Medieval art', it has been said, 'aimed at interpreting life and elevating man. Renaissance art aimed at enriching life and delighting man.' And, as St. Thomas Aquinas said, if man deprives himself of the things of the spirit he will go over to the things of the flesh. With a cynical contempt for the soul, evil men today do everything in their power to accelerate this process.

At the same time thousands hungering for a religion of some sort turn to music. Tchaikovsky, living without faith or hope, had a clear vision of what this meant: 'that sadness, that dissatisfaction, that undefined aspiration towards an undefined ideal . . . that capacity for finding only in music the answer to vital problems—we swim on the shoreless sea of scepticism, looking for a harbour we never find.'

No, that is not wholly true. Art is not religion, but it is one of God's most wonderful gifts to man and it can most certainly be a help on the way to him if rightly used.

Made into an idol it will perhaps end by betraying its worshipper. Michelangelo spoke of 'the illusion that made me turn art into a monarch and an idol: neither painting nor sculpture is any longer capable of calming the soul turned towards that divine love that opens its arms upon the Cross to take us.' These were the words of an old man broken by sorrow and ill-health. But the experience of great art in the life of the ordinary man is also a glimpse of the divine beauty, little as he may realize or want to realize it; for if the expression of beauty is the highest attainment of existence in the aesthetic and metaphysical categories, it is only because of God's creation of the world as an act of love. He created it, and man, in freedom, love, and truth, and saw that it was good.

Music, more than any other art, speaks of a harmonious world, that heaven for which we are homesick.

It is the instinct for beauty which makes us consider the world and its pageants as a glimpse of, a *correspondence* with, Heaven. . . . It is at once by poetry and through poetry, by music and through music, that the soul divines what splendours shine behind the tomb; and when an exquisite poem brings tears to the eyes, such tears are not the sign of an excess of joy, they are rather a witness to an irritated melancholy, an exigency of the nerves, a nature ended in the imperfect world which would possess immediately on this very earth, a paradise revealed.

The quotation is from Baudelaire's gloss on some words in Poe's *The Poetic Principle*. And Stravinsky has said 'Music comes to reveal itself as a form of communion with our fellow men, and with the Supreme Being.'

I am led, for my coda, back to St. Augustine and *De Musica*. In his book on *The Church and Music*, Dr. Erik Routley writes, 'Music for him [Augustine] brings the truth down from heaven and those who regard music as a means of sending up thoughts from the human mind would do well to mark his words.'

13. Language

J. M. CAMERON

Mr. James Cameron, who teaches Philosophy in the University of Leeds, presented this analysis of language as a medium of communication for the artist and the critic of the arts.

RECENT English philosophy has become more self-conscious about language than perhaps philosophy has ever been before. The technical and 'scholastic' character of most contemporary writing has produced wild accusations that philosophers are guilty of a blameworthy *trahison des clercs*; that they have abandoned consideration of the great questions of philosophy and have retreated into a Byzantine hair-splitting; that they do not provide the guidance that a failing civilization needs. These accusations betray a radical misunderstanding of the rôle of philosophy, for they ask of philosophy what can be provided only by religion. It is true that, historically, philosophy and religion have often been so intimately connected that in any given case it was hard to separate the philosopher from the theologian and the believer. Further, many philosophical problems, especially those of a metaphysical character, have been given point and interest by the religious concerns of the philosophers. It may even be true, as Dr. Etienne Gilson has often argued, that the Christian revelation has furnished the data for the solution of purely philosophical problems; e.g. the concept of creation, it can be argued, enables us to solve metaphysical problems that are raised but not solved by Aristotle. However this may be, the complaints advanced about modern English philosophy are in general misconceived, and seem to be in part founded upon impatience with the professional and technical character of contemporary work. This character philosophy shares with the whole of modern intellectual culture.[1]

Philosophical reflection upon language is not a duty to be imposed upon those who wish to use language for critical or creative purposes. Poets, critics, not to speak of philologists and lexicographers, are commonly quite unsophisticated in philosophical matters, but this is no hindrance to them in their own fields. Of course, there is no reason why poets and critics should not also be philosophers, or philosophers poets and critics; and no doubt philosophical poets and poetical philosophers would choose peculiar themes. But this might be just as true of soldiers or farm labourers or civil servants who took to writing verse. What, then, is the rôle of the philosopher in relation to the use of language—critical or creative or just ordinary—by others? How does his work differ from that of the lexicographer or the student of comparative linguistics? Perhaps we ought to begin by asking what it is that makes a problem a philosophical one; then go on to ask in what sense reflection upon language presents us with philosophical problems; and lastly to ask in what way, if any, the work of the philosopher can give help or illumination to the creative or critical user of language.

I

I shall say that a philosophical problem is a second-order problem. (I do not say or wish to imply that *all* philosophical problems are of this sort; merely that a great many are; and that perhaps all the philosophical problems connected with language are.)

A first-order problem is, for example, a scientific or a technical problem. Such a problem is solved, where it is solved, by a combination of hypothesis and information. For example, an educational psychologist may want to know if learning skills acquired in the course of the study of Latin are transferable to the study of military strategy. This question cannot be answered by

[1] This point is well put in John Holloway: 'The "New Philosophy of Language" in England' (*The Hudson Review*, Vol. IV, No. 3, Autumn 1951).

reflection. We have to ask ourselves if we are using the right hypothesis: e.g. it is true that learning skills are *acquired*? Or we may ask if we have enough *information* about those who go from the study of Latin to the study of military strategy. A first-order problem may be very puzzling; and we may even be in doubt as to whether a particular first-order problem—e.g. is the physical universe expanding?—is soluble by us; but we always have a good notion of the kind of conditions that have to be satisfied if we are to be in a position to solve the problem. Indeed, the way in which we set out the elements of a first-order problem is itself a specifying of the conditions which a solution would have to satisfy.

In order to solve second-order problems we do not need to get any more information than we already have. I will take as my examples a set of cognate philosophical problems as old as philosophy itself, or very nearly: namely, problems concerning the concept of mind and kindred concepts. Have we minds as well as bodies? Are there 'acts of will'? Is 'knowing' an act or a dis-position or an achievement or now one and now another? And so on. Now, these are very peculiar questions. It is plain that we do not need any more information than we now have in order to answer these questions, nor is the difficulty one of finding the right hypothesis. It would be odd to say: I will proceed upon the hypothesis that I have (not) a mind as well as a body; for the second-order, philosophical question is about what such a hypothesis would mean. We have more information of a physio-logical and psychological kind, and more fruitful hypotheses, than Aristotle had; but his discussions of the concept of mind are relevant to the answering of the philosophical questions in the same way as those of Wittgenstein and Professor Gilbert Ryle. That he may have believed the seat of thought was the heart does not deprive his philosophical remarks of their point.

To show all this I take the following expressions: 'I will bear it in mind.' 'He has a good mind.' 'I have a thought at the back of my mind.' 'He lacks the will to live.' 'He is in pain.' 'He fails to understand the first principles of trigonometry.' These are all instances of the use of the concept of mind or kindred concepts; and it would be false to say that if I were to use these expressions on suitable occasions I should not know what I was talking about and that you would not understand what I was talking about. These are the very paradigm cases of expressions (making use of the concept of mind) which are understandable. In one sense of 'meaning', then, no question arises as to what I *mean* when I utter these sentences. In what circumstances, then, can a second-order problem arise about the concept of mind? In the following circumstances.

I may bring together the following pairs of sentences: 'He has a well-stored mind'; 'He has a well-stored cupboard' *or* 'I will bear what you say in mind and use it at the next committee meeting'; 'I will keep the chocolate in the rucksack and only give it to the children when I see they're getting tired.' As we reflect upon these collocations of sentences, the second sentence of each pair continues to be clear, but the first gets more perplexing and even menacing. We try without success to assimilate the first sentence to the second (never, I think, the second to the first); and we have the idea that because we cannot assimilate the first to the second, there is something wrong with the first. The meaning of the first seems to become obscure and doubtful. What do we mean, if anything, when we use the expressions 'well-stored' and 'in' of the mind? We seem not to know the meaning of sentences of which in the most obvious sense we very well know the meaning. Questions of this kind cannot be settled by getting more psychological or other information. Information and hypothesis are only relevent to the answering of questions about the meaning of such sentences when the questions are put by one who does not know, or does not know well, the English language; and then such questions would be as much first-order questions as questions about the meaning of the Minoan script. But if the questions about meaning are put by one who knows English well, then it is clear that 'meaning' has here a strange, that is, philosophical sense; and that we already have all the information we need to have in order to answer the questions.

We may say that philosophical questions of this kind arise through our becoming perplexed about the use of our language This perplexity comes about through our seeing that sentences of the same grammatical type may have logically very different functions, as for example when we discover that sentences which mention minds do not *refer* in the same way as sentences which mention bodies, or parts of bodies such as brains. When we speak of minds as *things*, but strange things in that they are not visible, tangible, and so on, we may be, and sometimes we are, advancing a philosophical theory which springs out of the effort to assimilate sentences using the concept of mind to sentences using the concept of body. A ghostly referent seems, so to speak, to save the bacon of meaning.

Once we see that philosophical questions, or at least a great many of them, have this strange character, we see why in one sense philosophy never 'gets anywhere'. Extended reflection upon a philosophical problem *is* the solution, and the only one, of the problem. The path of reflection is long, circuitous, and hard; and of necessity its returns to its starting-point: the puzzle, which is in a sense no puzzle, by which we were in the first place moved to the activity of reflection. This is why ancient writers on philosophy are not always 'out of date'; whereas ancient writers on the sciences are almost always out of date and studied, when they are studied, for purposes other than scientific.

The point of the activity of the philosopher is to exhibit what in a confused way we already know. (This is even true of such an exalted form of philosophical discourse as that which is concerned with the relations between God and the world.) Such was the presupposition of the Socratic method and of the inquiries of the scholastic philosophers (those of the Middle Ages, that is, not— not uniformly, at least—those of the period since Descartes). Of course, philosophers, especially the philosophers of the last three centuries, are not exempt from the temptation to megalomania; and they have on occasion put about the view that the philosopher has a privileged access to REALITY. (This view has been shared by philosophers as remote from each other in standpoint as the

Idealists and the members of the Vienna Circle.) They are professionally predisposed to certain aberrations. For example, they sometimes say in portentous tones that, e.g. 'Time is unreal' or 'Material objects are families of sense-data' in such a way as to imply that it is false to say that I ate my breakfast after I got up or that in untenanted rooms there are tables and chairs. Upon all this the best comment is that of Wittgenstein: 'Philosophers who have denied the existence of matter have not wished to deny that under my trousers I wear pants.'

2

It is easy to see in what way reflection upon particular *expressions* may give rise to philosophical problems. We have just seen how collections of expressions making use of the concept of mind may provoke philosophical wonder. But in what way is *language*, in the sense in which English, Swahili, and Serbo-Croat are specific forms of it, philosophically interesting?

No answer which is both general and profitable can perhaps be given to this question, except to say—overcoming the fear of being obvious—that language provides the philosopher with his tools; and that since he is concerned with questions of meaning, language is also in one sense his subject-matter; for it is what we say that has meaning and is true or false. But the sense in which language is his subject-matter must be carefully distinguished from the sense in which language is the subject-matter of the lexicographer, the grammarian, the philologist, and the rest. The sense in which language is the subject-matter of the philosopher may be explained in the following way, though, as we shall see, there is something not quite right about this explanation.

The philosopher is interested in determining the meaning and implications of our uses of such concepts as *cause*, *mind*, *body*, *good*, *obligation*, *justice*, *et al*. This is not the same as being interested in 'cause', 'mind', 'body', 'good', 'obligation', 'justice', *et al*. If it is said, for example, that every event must have a cause, the sentence 'Every event must have a cause' presents the lexicographer with a set of constitutent parts each of which has a history and a rôle in the language, and these can be set out under the appropriate articles in a dictionary. The grammarian can show that the sentence is well-formed and can explain why this is so by reference to the received rules of English grammar. But when the philosopher discusses whether 'Every event must have a cause' is *analytic* or *synthetic* he is raising questions which do not interest the other students of language as such; for this question is not about 'Every event must have a cause' as a sentence in the English language, but about what the sentence *means*, and what the sentence means can, more or less, be said in French or German or some other language.

This is not quite satisfactory for various reasons. While language is certainly a lens through which we see the world, or a mirror which reflects it, each natural language is different from every other natural language; and within each natural language there are many linguistic strata, to use Dr. Waismann's phrase. That current in modern philosophical analysis which flows from the work of G. E. Moore now admits that the analysis of any given expression can never be quite satisfactory in the sense of being quite complete. In technical jargon, the *analysans* is never substitutable for the *analysandum*. What the sentence means can only be said by the sentence; and what it means it means within the language in which it is said and within the situation in which it is used. This has often been hidden from philosophers through their habit of taking single expressions and presupposing that they have a standard use. There is, of course, nothing vicious in this method provided its limitations are recognized, and such early models of analysis as 'A brother is a male sibling' did no harm except in so far as they encouraged excessive expectations as to the scope of the method. While no expression taken as an analysandum can be given a wholly satisfactory analysans, it would be absurd to suppose that an expression cannot be *explained*. That is, we can give an extended description which at some point or other will enable the inquirer to 'catch on'. In principle, this can be done both within languages and between languages. In so far as it is done *between* languages we are almost irresistibly im-

pelled to suppose with the early Bertrand Russell that what a
sentence and its translation have in common is a third entity, the
proposition which both sentences express; but there is reason to
suppose, as I shall try to show, that this way of speaking presupposes a misleading model of language. How tempting it is to
say that if two expressions share the same proposition, there
could be a language, free from the untidiness and ambiguities of
the natural languages, in which the proposition, which now lies
hidden in the depths of the two expressions, could be expressed
with perfect lucidity?

An old philosophical dream is that of a perfect language in
which everything that is the case about the world could be said
without ambiguity. Behind this dream there lie two models of
language.

One model sees descriptive uses in the indicative mood as the
normal or standard uses of language, with other uses eccentric to
this norm or standard. Such language is *referential* in a checkable
sense. Other uses of language are either reducible by analysis to
descriptive uses or are inherently trivial (emotive, decorative,
metaphysical in the pejorative sense, nonsense, and what have
you). The influence of this model is to be seen in the way in which
discussion of moral judgments (e.g. '*x* is good') has staggered
between the view that 'good' is descriptive of a simple, un-
analysable, non-natural quality and the view that it merely
expresses feelings of approval. In the former case the model for
'*x* is good' is '*x* is yellow'; in the latter, it is held that '*x* is good'
must be expressive of feelings if it can be shown, as of course it
can, that '*x* is yellow' is not the right model for '*x* is good'; for if
it is not descriptive—the standard thing for sense-making
expressions to be—the only thing left for it to do is to express—
or evoke—feelings. (The influence of this model is very plain in
the distinction, drawn by C. K. Ogden and I. A. Richards, in
such enormously influential works as *The Meaning of Meaning* and
Principles of Literary Criticism, between 'referential' and 'emotive'
uses of language. This crude distinction, and with it the misleading model of language presupposed, has largely been transcended

by I. A. Richards in his later work; but the initial crudity, because it is easily grasped and expressible in terms of slogans, continues to be influential, most deplorably, perhaps, in the teaching of English literature to children.)

The other model is that of a logical or mathematical calculus. It is more plausible to take this as the fundamental model; for while it is pure prejudice to favour one mode of discourse against another, it is in fact true that in a very rough way much of our language does function as a calculus. This was noticed long before the appearance of the *Principia Mathematica* of Bertrand Russell and A. N. Whitehead. Berkeley, for example, remarked

> that it is not necessary (even in the strictest reasonings) significant names which stand for ideas shou'd, every time they are us'd, excite in the understanding the ideas they are made to stand for: in reading and discoursing names being for the most part used as letters are in *algebra*, in which tho a particular quantity be mark'd by each letter, yet to proceed right it is not requisite that in every step each letter suggest to your thoughts, that particular quantity it was appointed to stand for.[1]

But even though it is true that language is often used as a calculus, it is plain that there are many uses of language which do not in the least conform to this particular model. This is especially plain in poetic uses of language, where what is said is not 'cashable' in the way that the operations of a calculus must be. Every poetic utterance is what it is and not another utterance. But, as we have seen, this is true, though not so plainly, of every expression in a natural language.

The inadequacy of such models for the interpretation of language can perhaps most readily be seen if we examine the problem of metaphor. (This problem is of special interest in connexion with the critical discussion of poetry and other forms of imaginative writing and consideration of it is thus peculiarly appropriate to the present occasion.)

There is a long tradition in philosophy which sees in the un-

---

[1] George Berkeley: *Principles of Human Knowledge* (1710), Introduction, para. 19.

guarded use of metaphor one of the principal sources of philosophical error. Equally, there is a long tradition—related to the philosophical tradition—among writers on rhetoric and literary critics which sees metaphorical uses as merely optional and decorative. This tradition is enshrined in such canonized expressions as 'figure of speech', 'poetic licence', 'metaphorically speaking'. It strengthens philosophical suspicion of metaphor, since it seems to imply that for a philosopher to make a metaphorical use central in his discourse, or to take metaphorical expressions as more than expressions always reducible to expressions in the literal mode, is to forsake what is central in language for what is peripheral, appropriate in the higher flights of poetry and oratory, inappropriate in discourse about what is the case.

It is simply false that metaphorical uses are peripheral in the natural languages. The natural languages are in substance so metaphorical that to prune a natural language of its metaphorical uses, dead, fading, living, and not yet born, would be to abolish it rather than mutilate it. This can be verified by examining pretty well any prose passage of more than two or three sentences. It is even plausible to say with I. A. Richards (in his *Philosophy of Rhetoric*—Lectures V and VI are especially relevant) that metaphor is 'the constitutive form of language'; and there is some support for this from historical linguistics. That metaphor has a rôle in producing second-order problems of a philosophical kind is evident if we ask ourselves why sentences, such as those discussed above, which make use of the concept of mind are puzzling. They are puzzling because as a matter of fact our language is such that some uses of the concept of mind are ineradicably metaphorical. 'In the mind', 'a deep mind', 'hidden motives'—there is no literal mode into which these expressions can be analysed without loss. We understand what is said *through* the metaphor; and there are no alternative non-metaphorical expressions which will do the same job. What is true of ordinary discourse is just as true of the discourse of philosophers. The Wittgenstein of the *Tractatus*, for example, places a metaphor at the centre of his discourse. Of the framing of propositions he says: 'We make to ourselves pictures of facts. The picture presents the facts in *logical space*' [my italics]. The same thing could be shown in connexion with other philosophical terminologies (e.g. 'substance', 'impression', 'dialectic', etc.).

All this is so clear that it seems plain that the power of the traditional models of language to mislead must be very great. Almost all writing on rhetoric in recent centuries (Hobbes, Johnson, and George Campbell may be instanced) flies in the face of the facts; and the tradition is still influential.

We may conjecture that one at least of the motives for a radical suspicion of metaphor is the dream of an ideal or logically perfect language freed of the ambiguities which infect all natural languages. In such a language every simple would have a name and no two simples would have the same name; and this would suffice to rule out metaphor; for whether or not there are simples to be named (this is, after all, a metaphysical assumption), whatever can be named in a natural language can be named otherwise in the same language by that shift of meaning which occurs every time a new metaphorical usage is coined.

It may be important to emphasize once again that this approach to the problem of metaphor is philosophical and not linguistic. Metaphorical uses are commonly understood without difficulty, even in the case of newly coined instances. A philosophical inquiry into metaphor is not, therefore, an inquiry into an as yet unexplored symbolic system, nor is it an inquiry into a class of expressions eccentric to the canons of ordinary usage. We can in one sense be said not to understand what we do when we employ metaphor; but this is the sense in which we may be said not to understand, if we are not philosophers, the distinction between, say, 'syntactical' and 'semantic' rules, though in another sense those who in the former sense do not understand this distinction may be said to understand the distinction perfectly since they are able, for example, to use correctly, and to make the correct inferences from, such expressions as 'the whole is greater than the part' and 'John has red hair'.

3

Enough has now been said to show that the philosopher is not fitted to be a censor of anybody's language, and that the notion of the philosopher as linguistic legislator—one who tells us how to talk about cats and dogs, protons and electrons, right and wrong, God and the world—is a superstition rooted in the confounding of first-order with second-order questions; and in the ungrounded view that certain modes of discourse are standard, proper and central. If we make a question about the meaning of these expressions which use the concept of mind (a second-order question) into a question about whether there are or are not minds (understood as a first-order question), we find ourselves in the absurd position of asserting that sentences the meaning of which everyone understands are without meaning and absurd. If we argue that descriptive expressions in the indicative mood are central or standard, then we become entangled in impossibly elaborated theories which either reduce expressions of other types—commands, exhortations, value judgments, assertions of rules, and what have you—to the required standard, or decree that expressions everyone makes use of and the function of which everyone understands are improper or meaningless.

The first and chief gain, then, of philosophical reflection upon the problems of language is to show that the creative or critical writer is autonomous in his own field. There are, so far as I know, no convincing philosophical arguments calculated to show that the philosopher has any title to instruct the poet, the novelist or the critic, or that these writers need an elaborate training in philosophy before they can talk sense in their own fields. Indeed, the greatest critics since the rise of the vernacular literatures in Europe are in no sense philosophers of any strict definition of the term. Johnson, Matthew Arnold, or Dr. Leavis and Mr. Lionel Trilling in our own period, are superb critics without ever feeling called upon to philosophize. Coleridge appears to be an exception, and he is perhaps the most remarkable of our philosophical critics; but he is remarkable, not as one who sees clearly the connexions between critical and philosophical questions, but as one who combines in himself the two rôles of philosopher— reckless, disorderly and intuitive—and of literary critic.

I should not be taken as saying more than I am saying. *Of course*, in one sense criticism is a part of philosophy: that is, the theory of criticism is as much a part of philosophy as the theory of politics or the theory of science (not to be confused with scientific theories, e.g. the General Theory of Relativity). This is to say that the terminology of criticism, the arguments of critics, the implicit standards of critics, all of them generate a variety of philosophical problems; and of course sensitive critics are very often aware of these problems, talk about them, take up positions in relation to them; and do all this without being clear about the precise moment when they leap from critical questions of the first order to second-order questions about criticism. Such leaps occasionally provoke philosophers to humourless knuckle- rapping. This is sometimes in place; but one has to remark that the good critic, precisely because of his insight into his own practice, may produce excellent philosophizing, no doubt open to technical criticism, but sharper and more original than the performances of philosophers in the same field. An impressive example of what I have in mind is Mr. Allen Tate's brilliant essay on 'Literature as Knowledge'.[1]

An important example of the kind of philosophical problem which is prompted by the practice of criticism is that of 'poetic truth'. Such a problem is not to be bottomed in the closing para- graphs of this essay.[2] But something may be said by way of show- ing that the philosopher may be of service to the literary critic— perhaps even, though about this I am more doubtful, to such creative users of language as the poet and the novelist—without usurping the proper function of the critic.

Poems, novels, and plays are composed of statements and utterances of other kinds which seem to make the same sort of

[1] In *The Man of Letters in the Modern World* (New York, 1955).
[2] I have tried to say something on this question in my three articles on 'Words and Meaning in Poetry and Philosophy', *The Downside Review*, Spring and Summer 1952, Summer 1953. I am not now very happy about much of what is said in those articles.

claim to be judged as being true or false, appropriate or in-appropriate, wise or foolish, and so on, as the utterances of historians, natural scientists, and witnesses on oath. This seems, *prima facie*, to be the case with 'Mr. Pickwick slept', 'There lived a wife at Usher's Well', 'Ripeness is all', 'Gather ye rosebuds, while ye may'. Indeed, Bentham said that all poetry was mis-representation and for Hume poets are 'liars by profession [who] always endeavour to give an air of truth to their fictions'. There seems to be something very odd about this view. Crudely, it is strange to say that 'Mr. Pickwick slept' is false because to say that it is false seems to imply that it might have been true but wasn't, like 'Napoleon won the battle of Waterloo'. It seems safer to say that poems, novels, and plays are neither true nor false. 'There are unicorns in Mesopotamia' is (I suppose) false; but 'Unicorns can be captured only by virgins' is neither true nor false, simply because there are no unicorns to be captured. Because works of imaginative literature are composed of words and sentences that we are familiar with in other contexts, and feign to treat of matters that really are so, we commonly fail to see that there is a very strong case for stressing the resemblance between such works and work in the plastic arts or in music, rather than between such works and histories or scientific theories. This is only to say where approximately literature should be placed in the chart of discourse in relation to history and science on the one hand, painting and music on the other; it is *not* to say that, for example, poetry *is* 'fundamentally' or 'basically' music or painting or anything else; but to suggest that if we are worried about the paradoxes generated by supposing that poetic or fictional utterances are false because they seem to say what is not the case, we may lessen the worry by noting that this mode of discourse may in some respects, at least, have affinities with music and painting. About symphonies and pictures, at least, it would be absurd to suggest that they are true or false in the way factual statements are true or false.[1]

[1] On the whole question raised in this paragraph, see the brilliant paper by the late Margaret Macdonald, 'The Language of Fiction', in *Proceedings of the Aristotelian Society*: Supplementary volume XXVIII, 1954.

So far, so good. But good critics do nevertheless use 'true' and 'false' of works of imaginative literature; and it is not the business of the philosopher to tell him that he mustn't talk like this. Here is Mr. D. G. James, for example:

A play such as *King Lear* exhibits human life as it is known by its author; our judgment on it is necessarily a judgment on its veracity, on its rendering of the features of things. It is not a matter of submitting the shows of things to the desires of the mind [the reference is to *The Advancement of Learning*, II, iv, 2]; it is a matter of seeing things as they really are; and if things are not conveyed as they really are by the poet, the play, whatever else it may be, is a bad play.[1]

Here, then, is a task for the philosopher. He cannot, for reasons I have already given, say that whereas 'true' is properly used of 'Napoleon was the husband of Josephine at a given time', it is improperly used by Mr. D. G. James of the complex of expressions which is the play *King Lear*. His task is rather to explore the logical relations between these different uses in the hope that those who are seized by logical cramps when they read Mr. James on *Lear* (just as we envisaged one who was seized by cramps when reflecting upon 'he has a well-stored mind') may be freed from them. This the philosopher will do, not to explain to Mr. James and his readers what Mr. James is *really* saying, what he *must* be saying *if* he means anything at all—this would be fatuous and insolent—but to enable us to give our undivided attention to what is said.

In the end this will probably involve a long excursion in the field of symbolism. Poetic wholes (such as *King Lear*) are symbols or groups of symbols. The word 'symbol' is here used in a sense analogous to, not identical with, the sense in which 'red', 'triangular', 'furtive' and 'holy' are symbols. The latter are symbols because, in accordance with certain rules, they can be used to characterize an indefinite number of things, real and imaginary. A complex of poetic symbols, such as *King Lear*, is not symbolic in the same sense, for it lacks the availability of verbal

[1] D. G. James: *The Dream of Learning* (Clarendon Press, 1951), p. 79.

symbols. It can no more be *used* to say something than can the *Eroica* Symphony or one of Mr. Henry Moore's reclining figures. But it does say something, or a critic of Mr. James's percipience would have no inclination to say what he does about it. Indeed, if anyone, philosopher or not, were to be astonished that one should say of *King Lear*: 'How true it is!', this would be a ground for thinking that he was unacquainted with the play or was deaf to poetry as the tone-deaf are deaf to music. We can talk about and round *King Lear*—this is what Mr. James is doing—in the hope that in the end this talking about and round will enable us to listen to *King Lear* more faithfully. But what *King Lear* says is said only in and through *King Lear*.

14. The Visual Arts

LANCE WRIGHT

Mr. Lance Wright, Technical Editor of The Architectural
Review *and of* The Architects' Journal, *presented this
analysis of the visual arts as media.*

BEFORE we can say what is the effect of the visual arts upon us—
what they do *for* us, what they do *to* us—something must be said
about the general purpose of all art. What is art for? This will be
answered very differently by different generations. Casting round
for an answer, it seems to me that there are four main uses
which all arts serve in some way or other. The first and primary
use is a very simple one: namely, to arouse and exercise the
faculty to which each corresponds. It is, I think, this use which
people have chiefly in mind when they speak of 'art for art's sake'.
It is a use of great importance and dignity since, of course, the
awakened faculties are ordinary means whereby we see God. The
next use is to make comprehensible the external world. Seen in
this way, art is a function which we all use all of the time, though
when left to ourselves we may use it very ineffectively; the mind
is perpetually groping with the external world and art shows it
how. Art gathers phenomena for us, puts them together in a way
we can understand, signposts reality. The third use is very similar
to this and perhaps hardly distinguishable from it: it is to bring a
physical human order into as much of the external world as is
susceptible to it. This is a global function of art to which
individual works of art contribute but which they seldom realize
in themselves. It is this function which we have in mind when we
think of the sum of a whole mass of diverse but related works of
art and speak of 'culture': for together they have made their time

and their part of the world different from what it would otherwise have been. Lastly there is the most modest of all uses and the most common: simply to make an object, a salt-cellar or a carol or a detective story.

It is possible to see all four of these 'uses' in any work of art in any medium, though in many one or other use will be so vestigial as to be not worth noticing: all are capable of awakening in someone the faculty to which they appeal (though they may not awaken yours or mine), all can serve as a signpost, all contribute to an order, all are (or have been) useful objects.

WHAT IS THE SCOPE OF VISUAL ART?

When we apply these criteria to the group of arts which we call 'visual' we come against two difficulties. The first is that of deciding which are the visual arts? The Classical tradition confined the term effectively to architecture, painting, and sculpture, though this same tradition went on to distinguish between these three 'major' arts and an undefined number of 'minor' or 'decorative' arts. This latter definition corresponded to the age-old distinction between the 'liberal' and the 'useful' (or 'mechanical') arts, a distinction which has so close an analogy with that other distinction between 'sacred' and 'profane'. This is a more important matter than it looks because the tendency of the present age to blur, if not formally to reject, both of these distinctions is an exceedingly important phenomenon which in the long run is going to make a profound difference to our artistic as to our devotional ideas.

This blurring or rejection is due not to any inability to distinguish between the motives which have given rise to these ideas, but to our practical realization that in life itself the two categories are commonly mixed up. At the religious level we Christians speak of this as 'the incarnational idea', meaning thereby that common everyday acts are transformable by the will of him who makes them to play the part of Christ and that in the end religious ideas are normally best conveyed by acts which also have a temporal end in view. Something analogous to this has taken place with our notions of art and utility. We recognize that art is an end in itself which owes nothing to utilitarianism, but we go on to point out that art can inhere (if that is the right word) in any object made by man and that as all such objects are useful in some way or other it is generally a meaningless task to sort out objects in which the 'will to art' was greater than the 'will to usefulness'. This is not to say, of course, that all man-made objects are works of art, but only that they are capable of being such; also, though we speak of 'the will to art' it is not suggested that the making of works of art is a matter of the will, for in the end important works are made only by those who possess a certain, comparatively rare charism.

This notion of the interdependence of art and utility and the consequent fallacy of the academic delimitation of art has been brought home to us by a great number of facts of experience; and as these bear directly on the way works of art affect us, it seems worth citing some of them here. Perhaps the most startling case and the one which has most caused people to think, is the celebrated division which has occurred between architecture and engineering. Almost imperceptible at first, in its beginnings at the end of the eighteenth century, the open nature and hence the scandal of this division has grown with the advance of applied science. For architecture, being a 'pure' art and therefore governed by unchanging principles, has tended to be static and to enforce its 'other worldly' quality with a long series of period revivals; while engineering, being pure utility, has made it a point to make instant use of as much new knowledge as her practitioners could digest. The curious separation between sensibility and entrepreneural skill to which this gave rise was aided by the formation of the separate profession of engineer; if you were artistic you became an architect, if you were good at mathematics you became an engineer. From the point of view of the man in the street, the architect was the chief loser by this, becoming first a sort of social luxury, to be used only when money was no object, and latterly—when money is always an object—something akin to an incubus; but now a number of facts have come to light which show that this kind of evaluation has little meaning and that engineering has been equally impoverished by the absence of the kind of ability which the architect has to bring. The moral of this seems to be that great structural artefacts are capable of making the same order of imprint on the mind of the observer as buildings which have been designed particularly with the object of making such an imprint.

This is certainly one of the cardinal principles of the newly rediscovered art of Town Planning. Here it is recognized that the 'work of art' is not the isolated building but the environment in which it stands. There is always some doubt about what environment is, how far it extends. Those who manipulate these things say that environment is a visual thing and extends as far as the eye can see: it is, in other words, a personification of the *genius loci*. It is an important admission that places affect us in the same way as formal works of art; and in fact the changes in our ideas about environment which have taken place in the short forty years or so that we have been giving the matter thought are in themselves evidence of our persistent broadening of what we mean by 'art'. At first the only environments worth worrying about were those which possessed an unbroken screen of buildings which were both old and possessed a good architectural quality: they were the places where people went in charabancs to gowp. In those days the only permissible way to intrude a new building into this environment was to build it in the same architectural style as the remainder. This concept has been progressively broadened in two ways. On the one hand the number of types of environment which are approved has been continually extended until it is now conceded that every locus has a genius of some sort which requires fostering; and on the other the doctrine of how to intrude new elements has been liberalized. The most recent expression of the theory is the issue of the *Architectural Review* entitled 'Outrage. Counter attack' (December 1956). In this, all environments are classified under five heads and a grammar of visual effects appropriate to each is proposed. We are not here concerned with the inherent weakness of this theory so much as with its recognition that all things seen are capable of producing an effect on the observer and that this effect matters.

Passing to figurative art, we find a similar revaluation caused, this time, by the growing importance of all forms of reproduction. Gone are the days when works of art are only 'one off', to be seen only in one place. There are two manifestations of this change: there is the use of methods of reproduction—mostly photographic—to publicize original works of art (we think particularly of the use of photography to illuminate sculpture and to show it in new and unexpected lights); and there is also the growing importance of work which is actually designed for reproduction, and where the finished work is therefore not the artist's drawing but each copy of the published work. There is little doubt that the techniques of reproduction have great influence on the way in which we regard visual art and on the effect it has upon us: they are becoming an integral part of our artistic dispensation to the extent that works which have been through the mill of reproduction tend to have a greater impact upon us than those which have not. How many pictures in our galleries are more effective as coloured postcards than as originals! The dignity and importance of this event has to some extent been masked by the fact that the poster, which is the most important art-form to undergo reproduction, has tended to be used mostly by those whose visual sense is undeveloped. Nevertheless the cult of the good poster is evidence that a humble (or even suspect) motivation—i.e. to persuade someone to buy something—may still give rise to an authentic work of art.

THE LITERARY USURPATION

I have been concerned up to now to show how the scope of what we mean by visual art has been widened far beyond the traditional categories, so that we are rapidly approaching a situation in which it will be generally accepted that since all things which are seen are capable of affecting man, all are potential media for art. The second complication which has to be faced before we can give any account of what the visual arts do to us arises from our own educational background and may be described as 'the literary usurpation'. Our civilization is incurably literary: the printed word is our instinctive means of conveying all but the simplest ideas. Even a Member of Parliament, as Mr. Evelyn Waugh has pointed out, can write a book, but how many can make or read a symbol? In England this literary bias is even more developed than in other countries, to the extent that even urgent signs like 'Keep left' or 'Major Road Ahead' are written out because authority dare not rely on the simple visual symbol even though this, when understood, would register more rapidly. In fact the visual faculty has been partially atrophied through disuse. This is in itself unfortunate, but what concerns us here is that we tend to see works of art through literary glasses: in other words we don't *see* them at all—we read literary associations into them. The strongest evidence for this can be found in the response of ordinary people to architecture. When they are confronted by a building they are not impressed by whether it is a good shape, has a good colour, is a good symbol of what goes on inside it. Instead they cast round to think what it reminds them of: if this memory is a gracious one—as an historical memory usually is—they will take some sort of pleasure in it, if the memory is disagreeable ('it reminds me of a factory') they will dislike it: their reaction will always be at one remove from the thing they are actually seeing. The great majority therefore are immunized against visual art: they don't see it at all and their reaction to it is not a visual reaction. For this reason we are probably justified in disregarding the characteristic response of today's people to works of visual art and in passing on to the question of what that response ought to be—to the inherent nature of visual communication.

ART AS A VISUAL THERAPY

The best way of doing this seems to be to revert to the four purposes of art at the beginning of this paper and to set down in what sense the group of visual arts fulfils them.

The first of these is simply to exercise the faculty to which they correspond, here the faculty of sight. Art is a sort of therapy for the human person. The eyes are windows through which God's reality penetrates to the soul. But in so many cases, as we have seen, it doesn't because the soul has not looked through the window for so long, but has sat indoors instead looking-in to the television set provided by literature. It would be interesting to know how much people do in fact 'see': how much of the reality which flashes past in fact strikes home. It seems that there is a sort of 'law of familiarity' with this kind of seeing: in general we don't 'see' anything at all unless it is pointed out to us in the first place or unless we are in a particularly receptive mood when it flashes into view: that thereafter our perception of it becomes more acute each time we see it—but only up to a certain point: beyond that point the object becomes familiar and gradually fades before our real vision. Curiously enough this fading is often accompanied by a certain distaste, so that we are surprised and rather impatient when someone else sees this same thing for the first time and finds it fresh and interesting. This is something which happens very noticeably in architectural fashions: nothing is more intensely annoying to the few who 'follow' architecture than to hear of the delight which others express for architectural habits which to them are stale. On this question of visual impressions it is interesting to notice the extraordinary transformation wrought by repainting a building or by redecorating a room. This is caused not by the mere consideration that what before was dirty is now clean but by the fact that the changed reflectance of the surface compels you to 'see' the old forms afresh.

It seems probable that the desire to make people see plays a more important part in the present development of the visual arts than we think. One of the formal purposes of abstract art was, of course, to give the onlooker no chance to search round for associations and thence to appreciate forms and colours for their own sakes; but apart from this it seems probable that a certain coarsening of effects which can be noticed over the whole field of contemporary art is due to a sense that it is more important to re-establish communication with people, to ensure that a work is *seen* than to ensure that it is lastingly acceptable.

Again architecture has embarked on the difficult venture of making people 'see space differently', removing as far as possible the sense of enclosure and emphasizing instead the space continuum. A wall is no longer an element enclosing a compartment, it is a plane set up in space. This experiment aims at producing a profound psychological change in man by visual means, by little more than a sustained visual trick: for man will in fact be enclosed as before.

Visual Art as Interpretation

This same example might be used to illustrate the second purpose of visual art, namely 'to make comprehensible the external world', though it is more commonly described as offering a new interpretation of the external world. 'You may think that you are fenced off from the external world, that you have built for yourself a little haven, a lasting abode: but in fact you have done none of these things: you are living in space and in time and are conditioned by both of these; is it not better that the places you live and work in should express this truth?' This is not intended as a quotation but as the sort of argument which this architectural ideology poses. 'In time' as well as 'in space' because it is also concerned to point the moral of the ephemeral nature of all human building. Though some buildings may prove even more ephemeral than their architects intended, it is very significant that—perhaps for the first time since the beginning of history—the time-dimension enters into our calculations. Particularly is this true in big cities where it is formally recognized that change is inherent in life, that buildings should be designed to last a certain span of years and the cost of their demolition and rebuilding at the end of it covered by a sinking fund. Once more I am not concerned to say whether this is right or wrong but only to point out the link between visual forms on the one hand and fundamental human arrangements on the other.

Nevertheless the 'making comprehensible the external world', in our civilization at least, is more properly one of the purposes of painting than of architecture. In a sense this is no more than a

by-product of the figurative artist's constant effort to make people
see. He wanders round the world seeing what is there and what of
human value is to be found. Once more it is an important
purpose, for it teaches people to take as much pleasure as they
can from what they have got. This purpose has been particularly
noticeable during the last three or four generations or so when
more and more of the visual scene has been rendered unfamiliar
(and usually horrific) by unconsidered technology. Here the
figurative artist has followed in the wake of devastation, recording
its effects (its dumps, its dreary wastes, its slums) and picking out
the elements (machine forms, for instance) from which a new
order of symbols may be built. It is the first of these two services
which comes most properly under this head. Generations who
begin by seeing environmental beauty only in unspoilt country-
side are slowly taught to accept such things as viaducts and
dockyard cranes; and gradually through the effort of figurative
artists, to see and accept more and more. It is a curious fact that
what is strange and new in life has no meaning, no resonance until
painters (and indeed writers) have drawn a meaning out of it.
Theirs is a sort of digestive function, making new and unfamiliar
things a part of ourselves. The figurative artist acting as interpreter
sees what is, and makes the best of it.

VISUAL ART AS A PRINCIPLE OF ORDER

Once more it is difficult to see the dividing line between this
function of interpretation and the next function, that of reform:
or as we put it earlier 'bringing a physical human order into as
much of the external world as is susceptible to it'. Yet it is an
essentially different function and the most important of all. It is
indeed this creative, prophetic function which people mostly
have in mind when they think of the artist as a man: it is the
possession of this charism which makes him a social oddity, a man
apart. The trouble is that this charism is exceedingly rare, the
possession of it is not at all easy to detect, either by the possessor
himself or by other people, and that all who make their living by
one or other of the arts are obliged to lay claim to it. The possi-

bility that he has this charism gives the artist an absolute right to
carry on his work unmolested by the laity. That is why it is at
best exceedingly inadvisable for those who have commissioned a
painter or a sculptor to make a nuisance of themselves by demanding adjustments to what he has done.

It is a curious fact that this prophetic quality seems to inhere in
the group of visual arts in a more positive and definite manner
than in any of the others and that it is able to operate in a society
which as a whole has no appreciation whatever of visual things.
Few facts of recent cultural development are more impressive
than the way in which ideas conceived wholly in the visual order
thirty and forty years ago by men like Mondrian and Picasso and
unleashed by them have been persistently working in the world
and have been used to solve technical problems which themselves
are unrelated to figurative art. In this matter of prophecy there
seems to be a clear line of development: for it begins in figurative
art, passing from there to architecture and passing from architecture to town planning. Thus it is that those of us who are now
about half-way through our lives may live to see the idea of
simultaneous vision (which was proposed by the cubists round
about the time of the first World War) being used to solve the
complex spatial problems which we must soon face in our city
centres. It is this sort of prophecy which we have in mind when
we say that the broad effect of visual art is humanization. Man
without visual art invents, creates, changes; but the outward
effect of all this effort lacks humanity. This is a truth which we are
particularly aware of at the present time. We agree that modern
developments affecting the visual world have been worth while,
that they 'work': developments in transport, the industrialization
of building, etc., etc. We are glad of them and do not want the
clock turned back; but we are also agreed that they are mostly
ugly and incoherent, that they do not in the aggregate give us the
kind of pleasure that we get from the finished works of past
periods, even though we recognize that they are 'ours' and the
works of the past are not. This is because of the visual artist's
absence from the *milieux* where these great developments were

12

taking place. It seems strange to keep reverting to the analogy
with religion, but it seems that the sense in which the artist's
'presence' in this world is necessary is very similar to that in
which the Christian's presence is necessary. One is concerned
with persons, societies, and institutions and the other is concerned with signs, things, and places. Both work through other
people and require intimate association with them, both generate
ideas which illuminate and heal. Above all, there is a certain
mystery about the propagation of visual ideas which is analogous
to the mystery of the propagation of faith: both work a direct
and indefinable 'illumination'.

The fourth and last purpose of art and therefore the fourth and
last criterion of the manner in which works of art strike us, is
that of making an object. I described this as 'the most modest of
all uses and the most common; but it is evident that there is no
scale of values in these purposes. The old phrase 'the arts of man'
was made to include precisely this making of things for use—for
common use as well as for representational use—and it seems that
we are getting back to this primary meaning. We are coming to
realize once more that a thing made and which you can see is in
fact a symbol, a very complex symbol of the purpose which it
serves, of the materials of which it is made and indeed of the
outlook of those who shared in its making and in its use. It is for
this reason that to exceptionally sensitive and well-informed
people the sight of a common object calls a whole civilization to
memory. When things were relatively few and hard and expensive
to make, their symbolic value seems to have been more easily
recognized: at least we have the impression that people cared
more about them and were more successful in endowing them
with the mark of their human origin. With the beginnings of mass
production, 'things' lost this kind of respect and there followed
what is often referred to as 'the devaluation of the symbol'—a
devaluation which did not only affect small and common objects.
Symbols are devalued when things are no longer prized, but they
are also devalued when people no longer reflect upon them. It is
necessary for the onlooker to reflect before things seen can com-

municate their symbolism. It may well be, therefore, that while we have been so ready to attribute devaluation to the lack of hand craftsmanship, another and more decisive cause has been our own loss of the power of reflection.

We have been speaking in this context only of small and common objects because it is the particular success of the last generation to rediscover the dignity of small and common objects. But the branch of art which is traditionally concerned with this idea of the work of art as a thing or an object is sculpture. For a piece of sculpture, one might almost say, is a thing of the highest order, it is a 'presence' which enforces reflection on all but the most distrait, and it is no accident that it has come down to us as the medium best suited for making an image of God.

Conclusion

If these, then, are the 'uses' of art, there is still something to be said about the place of art in everyday life; and there is a moral to be drawn from a comparison between what that place should be and what it actually is.

When we come to consider the place which visual art actually holds, we are aware of three different facts of experience which seem to tell against each other. First we have the impression that, so far as the business of everyday life is concerned, visual art is virtually written off: people give the impression that they get on very well without it. We hear for instance that odd and interesting phrase—on a bus perhaps—in which someone is described as being 'ever so artistic' (as he or she might just as well be described as 'ever so religious'). Though we are usually left in doubt about whether this description is intended to be approving or not, we are left in no doubt that it is something which the speaker does not consider as applying equally to herself. It is a distinguishing mark, something which you need not be.

The next fact of experience is that in those comparatively remote quarters where visual art *is* esteemed, it appears to be esteemed chiefly for the wrong reasons. There are, of course, an infinite number of wrong reasons for thinking highly of the visual arts, and each generation has its own. The most common is to think of it not as a normal function of life and of the intelligence, but in terms of its products, which they see as a necessary part of culture. To these people, 'culture' is something which has a value of its own; it is an immense superstructure which must at all cost be maintained. Such people become easily worried about 'the future of European Culture' and when some particular art seems likely to die out, they will go to extreme lengths to preserve it, even to the length of practising it themselves.

The third fact of experience tells us that visual art represents an activity which is basic to man and which keeps cropping up in unexpected places. This is the age of what I would call 'un-registered' art: of the dispersion of this symbol-making activity into all sorts of fields where no one up to now has thought of look-ing for it. I am thinking particularly of ephemeral printing, of the design of mass-produced components, of humble back-yard hobbies.

Nevertheless, this sporadic evidence of visual art in unexpected quarters must not be mistaken for evidence of widespread practice. The fact remains that, for the overwhelming majority, the twin faculty of symbol-making and symbol-recognizing is nine-tenths atrophied—as is also true of the faculty for believing. The natural outcome of these two long-standing defects is that life is not valued as it should be, and that the privilege of mere *being* is not valued in the least. There is little or no *reflection*: life is a routine, the world a place we have stumbled into by accident.

This deplorable *insouciance* is the aspect of modern society which concerns us most and which it is the particular function of visual art to dispel. It is the antithesis—to quote deliberately a non-European example—of that extraordinary awareness of the miraculous nature of life which we see in the classical civilization of Japan.

Clearly this restoration of the faculty of visual art demands a certain programme, a missionary effort. It is beyond the scope of this paper to outline such a programme, but a few points can be made.

The first point is that visual art, like belief, seems to require a certain preparation in the subject: its truths are not universally self-evident. This is a fact of which we have become painfully aware recently, when the language of art has been changing so rapidly. But apart from this there is a simple law which lays down that the more you know about a thing the more it means to you and the greater its effect upon you. In order to appreciate the complexity of a work of art you have to be able to differentiate the parts. There is, in a sense, almost as much effort required in reading a symbol as there is in making one: for the two activities are complementary. There is thus a great effort to be made by everyone if we are to create a society and an environment in which symbols can live and be recognized and vivify all who share them. How are people to be persuaded to make this effort?

Up to now it seems that we have been merely making an appeal to the prestige of visual art, have held it up as the sort of thing that really cultured people delight in. We wonder if this is the right approach.

Considering the other atrophied human faculty, that of belief, it has been our experience that the best way to bring about authentic revival is to get people to ask the fundamental questions: 'What am I?' 'Why was I made?' 'Where am I going?' The point arises whether there might not be some analogous way of restoring the atrophied faculty of sight. It was with this end in view that I tried to set down at the beginning of this paper what were the purposes of Art. It is a matter—is it not?—of seeing the human person anchored in time and place and *dependent* on visual art for primary help and support. We need it to egg us on to see; we need it to help us to understand what is going on about us, to pin visible tickets on to facts; we need it to show us how to reorganize our physical surroundings so that they are a real home to us—the function of that exiled queen, Architecture; and we need it to show us how to make things, smallish things, which we want and which will symbolize for us the magic which inheres in the humblest artefacts serving human life.

15. The Dance

ARNOLD HASKELL

Mr. Haskell, the director of the Royal Ballet (Sadlers Wells) School, has had a lifetime of experience of ballet. He writes here of dancing as a spectator.

THE dance is so vast a subject—in some of its aspects it embraces a social history of mankind—that I must make clear from the start what are to be the narrow confines of this talk. I am on the other side of the footlights from Mary Drage and my point of view throughout is that of the trained watcher. She tells us what dancing can mean to the performer while I will try to set out what the watching of dancing has given to one particular spectator. I am concerned with dancing and not with the composite art of ballet of which dancing forms a part. I must stress that I am very much concerned with my individual reactions, not only because they happen to interest me intensely, and they do, but mainly because I can see no other way of dealing with the subject. During the past forty years or so I have watched hundreds of dancers all over the world in hundreds of performances, I have met and discussed their art with them and during the past ten years I have been intimately concerned in their creation. Inevitably I have come to certain conclusions.

Paradoxically it is more modest by far to talk in personal terms than to lay down the law about dancers in general. Moreover, there is in the criticism of dancing a wider diversity of opinion than with any other art. There is no script, no score, and no illustration through which one can refresh the memory. So much of one's point of view therefore depends upon the exact period at which one started watching and what opportunities one has had.

It is quite certain that anyone familiar with Pavlova, Karsavina, and Ulanova will judge not only dancers but the whole art of dancing differently from those who have not been so fortunate, just as one's views on the art of ballet in general will have been coloured by the golden years of Diaghileff. It is quite impossible therefore to be objective, and dishonest to maintain the pretence.

I must, however, start with certain basic ideas about the dance in general. I can best begin with the charmingly revealing parable that Degas was fond of quoting. After the Muses have had a busy day, each as the inspirer of her particular art, they refresh themselves by joining Terpsichore in the dance.

Dancing, expression in rhythmic movement, is something that is a basic part of everyone's make-up, though, like so many other things, this is largely obscured in the civilized city-dwelling man (perhaps after all not so disguised when one thinks of 'rock 'n' roll' and the Palais on a Saturday night!). Animals have elaborate courtship dances and man danced long before he had coherent speech. The origin of music doubtless lay in the clapped hand, the stamped foot, and the rhythmic chant in some jungle clearing. The very first dance was used for some magic purpose connected with fertility or the hunt, and the body was also used for acts of worship. 'The Dance was developed among men under the direct guidance of the gods', wrote Plato. Much of the rich Hindu dance consists of danced hymns that are deeply moving when performed by artists of such integrity as Shanta Rao.[1] Their sacred nature is unmistakable. For the first time I understood the religious nature of the Song of Solomon when watching Shanta Rao. This oriental dancer could make one feel the expression of religious emotion in sensual symbols in a way that no reasoned commentary could achieve. Shanta Rao using the oldest surviving dance technique gave me a major dance experience.

In Christianity what exquisite beauty lies in the movement of the mass, which Ronald Knox has compared to a ballet, and a true danced performance still survives at Easter at Seville where boys dance and play their castanets in front of the altar.

[1] See Plate 20.

At a later date people began to dance for social purposes, for their own recreation and enjoyment. Such dances could be simple capers round a maypole or elaborate performances at court that took time, money, and the skill of the greatest artists of the day to produce. Such performances were essentially a product of the High Renaissance and it is from them that the Western European dance form of ballet was born.

With the Renaissance and the birth of ballet the dance became divorced from religion or from the expression of anything mystic, but the exercises and. rigid discipline required maintain a close link with religious training—this is of course unsuspected by most dancers though some of my Catholic and oriental pupils have shown their awareness of it—and of all artists the dancer is the most subjected to a continuous discipline and to the maintenance of an attitude of humility throughout her career. Even when at the top of the tree she takes a daily lesson, she is always the pupil, corrected and criticized, and can avoid none of the long series of exercises that are a veritable rosary of movement. It is, I am sure, this intense discipline that makes possible those rare performances which are the culminating achievement of the dance and that shows that the once strong link between mysticism and dancing is not entirely severed.

The attitude of humility that I have mentioned is an indispensable attribute of the great dancer. It is not modesty; the dancer may be well aware that she is ahead of her nearest rival and may express this awareness in no uncertain manner, but she is humble about her own gift. She never talks of it as if it were something that she had created. She regards herself rather as the guardian of something that is bigger than herself. I have noticed this attitude particularly in many talks with the Russian dancers Pavlova, Karsavina, and Ulanova. I think that it is implicit in their dancing. It is a commonplace for Russians to talk of *doucha* (soul) in an artist where with us it would sound affected.

Just a few words about this arduous technique of ballet. It is so often misunderstood, particularly by the sentimental who imagine that the highest form of dancing is an improvised skipping around

in flowing draperies, a view they borrowed from a misunderstanding of Isadora Duncan, an artist who completely misunderstood her own great gifts.

Ballet technique is nothing more nor less than the grammar of
language. It has grown up all over Europe just as language did,
steps (words) being gathered in from village green, fairground,
and court ballroom. It has travelled extensively, enriching its
vocabulary in Italy, France and Russia, and recently in Britain
and the United States. This is not therefore something created
artificially like Esperanto or Volapuk and incapable of producing a
literature. It is a perfect system of physical training, and when it
has been assimilated by the dancer and is completely at his command he can use it to express anything that can be expressed
through his body. It is also, as I have come to realize more and
more through experience, of the very greatest value in general
education. There are many, particularly in the U.S.A. today, who
have completely misunderstood the nature of ballet technique.
They have invented an esperanto-movement of their own in order
to express certain ideas; incidentally ideas usually totally unsuited
to movement but which they say can only be expressed through
this new technique. They forget that Picasso learnt painting in the
orthodox manner and not through some freshly evolved *ad hoc*
technique. They are also inclined to assert that the discipline of
ballet is so rigorous that it kills personality. That too is nonsense.
Personality may be rare but it is certainly not something that is
delicate, and it can only be developed to the full when it makes
use of a disciplined technique. The free-lance or 'modern' dancer
may have something to express; she may in fact have a positive
contribution to make to choreography, but she will never have
the full means of self expression because she will never have truly
conquered her body. I can think of nothing more earth-bound than
the 'modern dancers' of the U.S.A. or of Germany in the 1920s.
This dance is not even a glorification of the body; the body
becomes a burden. I believe that this 'modern dance', still so
popular in some educational circles, because it can be taught by
the gym mistress, is as definitely harmful to the pupil as it is

unpleasant to the spectator; and that is putting it strongly! Even Isadora Duncan, an exception to so many of the rules, came to her full development in the person of the ballet dancer Galina Ulanova,[1] in so many ways the spiritual child of Pavlova and Duncan.

I hope these generalizations will have cleared the way for the main theme of my talk: the pleasure and the experience that I personally have gained through watching dancing for over forty years.

At the very lowest level an audience gains pleasure, which it shows through noisy and instantaneous applause, from the performance of an obviously difficult feat. An example of this is the notorious thirty-two *fouettés* in the ballroom act of *Swan Lake*. The dance of which this is a part is often put into a programme alone and out of context under the title *The Black Swan*, definitely to inspire the reaction, 'Isn't it difficult, isn't she clever. I could never do that.' Here dancing and acrobatics overlap; there are, after all, musical acrobats and unmusical dancers!

At quite another level the performer can match the brilliance of the steps with the brilliance of her presentation. The effect is to show that such dazzling technical feats are natural and easy to a person of dazzling personality. The audience does not feel any anxiety; on the contrary, it identifies itself with the performer and is uplifted, 'we are experiencing this with her'.

A superb example of this is the shining and glowing Fonteyn in the famous *Rose Adagio* from *The Sleeping Beauty*. Taken out of context and done as a separate item it is a stunt, but as a part of the development of the little Princess Aurora coming after her charmingly gay entrance and before the finger pricking episode it is truly romantic. Its difficulties, though obvious to the specialist, are of secondary importance. Fonteyn in this rôle justifies the heroine's name of Aurora.

At yet another level there is the immense pleasure to be gained from the sheer beauty of line, both static and in motion. Take the *arabesque* for instance. Here the eye travels slowly down the line of the back and then, in contrast to this gentle slope, there is the triangle formed by the legs. It is in a sense a physical

1 See Plate 21.

pleasure akin to the feeling of a statue with the fingers; an important element of appreciation in sculpture.

When the dancer is in motion very much the same thing applies. We rely on our memory of a whole sequence of movements. We ask ourselves how harmonious is the single dancer, transformed by our kino-aesthetic memory into a frieze? To put it more clearly: imagine all the movements of a solo dance exposed on a single long strip of photographic plate; is the composition formed a harmonious one?

Hitherto I have talked as if this were purely a question of sculpture, but remember that the movement is conditioned by music. At this level therefore we are at the same time enchanted by harmony of composition and by the fact that, because of the dancer's feeling for musical line and phrasing, we are actually watching music. A supreme example of this is the *prélude* from *Les Sylphides*. Here is a magnificent composition that not only follows the musical line but that interprets the spirit of the music. Fokine believed it to be a supreme test of musical-dramatic interpretation. I have seen very few really moving performances of this dance; to be adequate is to fail.

At yet another level is the pleasure to be gained from the dramatic interpretation of a rôle; and to this are added the pleasure in composition and in musical interpretation already mentioned. The important thing is that the body must be able to express to perfection something that cannot be expressed in words. Movement is in no sense a substitute for words.

I can best give an example or two of such unforgettable moments of complete poetic expression in ballet.

The first was Karsavina in *Le Spectre de la Rose*.

> Soulève ta paupière close
>   qu'effleure un songe virginal
> Je suis le spectre de la rose
>   que tu portais hier au bal

A young girl has just returned from her first ball. We see her standing in the beam of moonlight that floods through the french window of her bedroom. She is looking at a rose that has been given her at the ball. She sinks down into a chair and dreams. The spirit of the rose (Nijinsky) floats through the window and dances with her. In her dreams she lives through all the excitement of the dance. And then once again she is sitting in her chair; the spirit of the rose has leapt through the window; and what a sensational leap it was, one of the legends of ballet. It was not, however, the most memorable part of the ballet; that, for me, was the awakening of Karsavina. In those few moments, moments with no dancing in them at all, you had the moving picture of adolescence with all its pathos, its problems and its beauty. She had gone to sleep a child and awoken a woman.

Another unforgettable moment, very similar in theme, was that given by Ulanova in *Romeo and Juliet*. It is the moment when she suddenly sees in the mirror that she is growing into a woman and is half pleased and half frightened. It is interesting to note that here is an episode that Shakespeare has not recorded, though the ballet interprets the text very closely. This dancer, no longer young, transformed herself completely into the child-woman Juliet; but more of Ulanova later.

To fulfil itself in this way the dance requires simple music and technically simple movement. On the whole, modern choreography, outside Russia, gives very little opportunity to the dancer to provide such moments of poetic truth. The choreographer tends to exploit his own personality through the use of difficult steps and acrobatic lifts and the accent is on a technique that cannot be hidden. This may make for excellent ballet, but here I am not talking of ballet as a whole but of dancing and the impact created by the dancer. I will say, however, that for my taste the great ballet is the one that affords the dancer the greatest opportunities of developing her personality and her stature as a medium for poetry. More and more I have come to prefer watching the ballet that is already so familiar that nothing distracts me from the dancing. I am beginning to find the 'clever' choreographers a bore. Were I to relive moments spent in the theatre, I would, I believe, choose to see Pavlova in *The Dying*

Swan rather than many of the brilliant ballets that Diaghileff produced in collaboration with the greatest artists of the day. In *The Dying Swan*, using a simple *pas de bourrée* within the reach of thousands if considered purely as a technical feat, she created in the space of two or three minutes a tremendous tragedy of life and death.[1] It is a commonplace to comment on the ephemeral nature of ballet. I cannot, however, over a quarter of a century after, hear that music of Saint Saens without seeing every movement and feeling the same emotions. Pavlova has left a stage full of ghosts that will dance as long as anyone remains alive who saw her.

Dancing can on rare occasions rise to a still higher level than the perfect line, plus perfect musical phrasing, plus the interpretation of a character and the conveying of an atmosphere. It can rise to such heights that one is compelled to use the language of mysticism, for nothing in the theatre vocabulary will describe what has taken place. The dancer expresses a universal truth, watching her is an *experience* of which we are conscious but that we cannot put into words.

To me the supreme example of this has been the Russian ballerina Galina Ulanova. Until I saw her I had no conception to what heights the dance (or for that matter the theatre) could rise. I am well aware that I cannot express this emotion in words. It is possible of course to write a reasoned appreciation of her interpretation of Giselle, to say why I considered it by far the best of the many Giselles I have seen. It is possible to examine in detail the wonderful touches that made her Juliet so remarkable an achievement. I have done so at length, elsewhere. It is the something extra added to the Ulanova-Giselle and Ulanova-Juliet that defies reasoned analysis. Ulanova's concentration on the character she is portraying is so intense that her identification with the character is complete. She deliberately surrenders the 'ballerina-personality' always present even in the best Giselles. She rises above the banality of Gautier's story and Adam's music to confront us with the soul of a woman who loves. In this

1 Ulanova used the same choreography to convey an entirely different emotion; not one of pathos but of the triumph of humanity over death.

surrender of personality we come once again to the humility I
have already stressed. It comes from the surrender known to
mystics in art and religion. 'Aesthetic experience is the twin
brother of mystic experience.' The Indian writer on aesthetics,
the late Ananda Coomaraswamy, in his fine collection of essays
The Dance of Shiva, has many illuminating things to say on this
subject. He talks of 'a state of grace that cannot be achieved by
deliberate effort'. By this he does not, of course, mean that no
effort is required in attaining craftsmanship. In other words the
artist aims at perfection of craftsmanship but the resultant work of
art is independent of the will.

Ulanova's curtain-call confirmed the full extent of her surrender. It was an awkward almost gawky bob with none of the
customary dignity of the prima ballerina who is graciously pleased
to acknowledge the plaudits of her audience. She had been
recalled from afar and was not quite sure whether the noisy
intrusion was really welcome.

It is interesting to note, when dealing with an artist of genius
such as this, how completely unanimous was opinion at every
level; from the hardened *balletomane* to the theatregoer who had
started out rather shocked at the idea of a dancing Juliet, from the
stage hand (always a level-headed critic) to the painter and the
writer. And it was quite astonishing how many mentioned the
words 'a religious experience'. When I told Ulanova she was
delighted. She said that her aim was to 'move people and make
them feel better'. In any other dancer this might have sounded a
pose, to her it came perfectly naturally. She had broken the
barrier of technique and come out on the other side.

To me Ulanova is not only incomparably the greatest dancer I
have ever seen: she is the Dance. Although I can scarcely hope to
see such perfection again, the quality that Stanislavsky called 'the
dancer's separation from the materiality of the body', my faith in
the dance as a medium of expression has been increased.

Today I go to the ballet in a spirit of exploration, in the hope
that at one particular performance I will witness a theatrical
miracle and be moved; so deeply moved that the impressions of

what I have seen is a lasting one. That supreme experience may
only fall to one's lot once or twice in a lifetime. I can however
find pleasure at all the levels save the lowest, that of the technical
feat well performed from the purely mechanical point of view.
Technique for its own sake bores and irritates me for the same
reason that it bored and irritated Noverre two hundred years ago
when he said:

> We must be prepared to sacrifice all the more complicated steps;
> what we shall lose in movements of the feet we shall gain from the
> expressiveness of the arms. . . . However, it would be a misunder-
> standing of my aims to think that all I am looking for is to eliminate
> difficult and brilliant steps. . . . All those things are pure gold, but
> only if the mind makes them so.

Just a few words about the words, 'if the mind makes them so'.
Sometimes for a very brief moment in a dancer's career when she
is dancing from the sheer joy of it, before she realizes that it is
intensely difficult and before turning up nightly at the theatre has
made her into a hardbitten professional, one might substitute the
word *instinct* for *mind*. The young and unformed ballerinas
launched by Colonel de Basil in 1933, the year of the 'baby
ballerinas', gave enchanting performances with flashes of genuine
inspiration that they were unable to reproduce later when mind
took the place of instinct. That most beautiful of dancers, the
late Pearl Argyle, has also left behind memories of many inspired
performances. Many dancers well below the top rank can on some
special occasion give us such rare moments of truth, and it is for
these brief moments of truth that one waits in hope. And it is for
that very reason that the filmed performance of a dance has so
little to give. Not only do the conditions make it impossible for
the dancers to achieve a miracle, but all too often one is watching
a purely synthetic performance, a scissors-and-paste affair of a
week's shooting.

We have started with eight or nine years of strenuous work
before the public sees the dancer, with daily exercises throughout the dancer's career, with hours of rehearsal, with much

reprimand, and with very little praise. In fact 'with blood, sweat and tears'. The dancer has achieved the ability to perform the most amazing and apparently gravity-defying feats, she has complete command over her body. Yet to me in the audience the supreme moment, the very essence of it all, may be a brief run across the stage or some fleeting passage in which the dancer is almost motionless. Then I know that my years of training as a spectator have been worthwhile and that I have received my reward. I am deeply grateful to the dancer who gives me that supreme thrill and to all the dancers who are striving.

16. The Mass Media

ROBERT WALLER

It is possible to stand serenely aside from the practice of radio, television, and the film and to discuss their potentialities as art forms. It is equally possible to stand aside and denounce these media from a position of high snobbery. The author of this paper was invited because he had been intimately connected with Radio. For many years, he was a producer in London, where he often worked for the B.B.C.'s Third Programme; later he was senior Talks Producer in the West Region. From this experience Mr. Waller has committed himself to a fairly extreme position of which it can at least be said that no one can demolish it by saying that he does not know what he is talking about. What was said against his thesis at the symposium may be read in the record of the discussion at the end of the paper.

SOMETIMES you hear a radio Producer say: 'It's no use asking old So-and-So to write a script; he's an intelligent chap, but he won't accept the medium.' I've said this myself—and with justification; but it is nevertheless an observation that often makes me shudder. Frequently it means only that the broadcaster won't reduce his ideas to the level of expression demanded by a mass audience. But the medium and the audience are two different things. In discussing the influence on the arts of the mass media, it is essential to keep this distinction between the medium and the audience clearly in mind. I don't wish to imply that the artist need not take account of his audience; very far from it. Communicating a vision of life to other people demands an objective understanding of other people as well as an immersion in a personal vision. The parables of the New Testament are a supreme

13

example of a technique of communication. Nevertheless Jesus communicated his deepest secrets to the few and had something to say about casting pearls before swine. The artist cannot always communicate to a mass audience; some of the finest arts must essentially be for a limited and particular audience. If we are reduced to a condition in which there is only a mass audience, high art will disappear unless our civilization undergoes a radical change. Yet, but for the fact that certain media of communication such as film and radio can reach mass audiences, these media would not differ very much from other traditional means of artistic expression. Speech, paint, print, stone, pencil are all material used by man as artist to express himself: so is the voice, come to that, or, in acting, all the human body. Any of these can be, then, raw material of artistic expression; so can film, camera, or microphone. Unfortunately, we have almost reached a stage where it no longer occurs to cultivated people that a medium of mass communication can be a medium of ART.

We don't talk of non-mass media as 'personal' media (or whatever the opposite of 'mass' is): we just think of it as art. Yet the Talks Producer will always tell you: 'You must think of the listener sitting by himself by the fire; you must talk to him personally.' But you can't talk personally to such a large audience, except by using the arts of demagogy. If you talk personally to a dear friend you will be unhappily conscious that you're being overheard by people who have no sympathy with you at all—to whom you wouldn't dream of talking in this way: so you will talk in a pseudo-intimate way to an imaginary ordinary man. The radio set has created a unique psychological situation: it puts a personal 'presence' into innumerable homes as a guest who has invited himself: so he is judged according to the character of the host and his friends. Unless this professional guest has acquired a technique of good manners for such an occasion, his presence is going to give offence; and this applies, in a way, not only to the personal talk, but to the play or poem or feature which is a self-projection of the artist. One may remember the rumpus over George Orwell's 1984. It's no use saying, 'Well, if he doesn't like me and my work, he shouldn't switch on.' The wireless licensee has his set there and as a matter of common justice feels entitled to enjoy everything broadcast. He feels swindled if any programme is not to his taste. This irrational attitude to radio is, perhaps, due to the fact that all programmes issue from the same instrument, which is the owner's personal possession and which cost him a good deal of money.

Each newspaper programme, so to speak, has its own news-paper. The 'Light Programme' newspaper reader need not tor-ment himself with *The Times* or the *Manchester Guardian* if he does not wish to: the book reader need not exasperate himself with the sight of books he'll never read. But the radio set is for ever his, staring at him. I cannot think of any comparable psychological situation in history. Broadcasting is, therefore, confronted by the problem of whether it is to be an art in which each programme has either its special audience—as it pretends—or one mass audience. It can't have both. Every listener is not the same listener. But we are reaching a stage in our thinking in which we do not see the public as millions of different individuals who divide roughly into groups with special tastes, but as the common denominator, as one 'ordinary man'. Just as economists talk of the economic man, we must now talk of the Entertained Man; and a vast set-up has been organized to discover what entertains him and to lay down the rules of success. Entertainment is becoming another sphere of automation, and machines could perhaps be invented in due course to write programmes—the slang term for feeding an automatic machine is already 'program-ming it'. This is interesting, for the audience and the entertainer make robots of each other. Commercial Correspondence Schools flourish that teach the mechanical rules of success that anyone can master. We are moving towards a machine substitute for consciousness.

Printing was, I suppose, the first of the mass media and has a lot in common with radio considered purely as a medium. For example, when you print a poem you are only using print as a means of conveying the poem to other people. The poem is not written for reading silently from print, and should not be influenced by print. A poem is written for the voice.

The medium of print does not make its own artistic demands so far as poetry is concerned, just as it should not so far as music is concerned. I don't know if there is any music yet written simply to be read in the score. The true medium of music is the instrument for which it is written. I don't deny that there are poets who, knowing their work will be read and not heard, say to themselves, 'This can be more difficult, as it is written for a book, and the reader can keep reading it over and over again.' If a poet writes for radio (for the 'medium' as the producer says), then he must say to himself: 'I must make this poem very simple; I must try to keep to words of one syllable, for the listener will not be able to turn back the page; he must understand the poem *at once*.' Neither of these considerations is a true artistic consideration in my view; they are distortions of inspiration resulting from a misconception of the nature of media. If a poet does not write for the voice and an intelligent audience, but for some imagined universal print or radio audience, he is betraying himself as a poet. There is therefore this double use of the mass media: to convey to a large audience some other art in a form as little distorted as possible; and to serve as the material of art itself. Both are legitimate uses. One is so accustomed to print that one forgets that here, too, this applies. Though the printed word is an impersonal vehicle for poetry, it is the very condition of the novel. The novel is written to be read; the novelist knows he cannot get effects on the printed page in the same way as he could on the stage. He assumes, though, that his reader will not throw his novel away if he can't finish it in two hours, which is the time that a dramatist must hold his audience.

The printed word is a medium making its own intrinsic artistic demands; but when print becomes a mass medium, when the best-seller and the newspaper come on the scene, then it is not the exigencies of the word to be read that determines treatment, it is the taste of the mass reading public. We are now back with the 'common man', or perhaps we should say the 'lowest common man'. Printing is a particularly interesting example of mass media because it existed before the mass civilization of today: when those civilizations developed it then became a mass medium. It is not the nature of the medium that determines its influence on the arts, but the civilization in which it is used. Perhaps the pressure of mass demand will in time make all arts mass-arts and invent means of mass distribution for them all. A time may come when even a painting will be assessed by its marketability as a printed reproduction. Music and poetry can both reach mass publics through radio; most orchestras can only survive through the direct or indirect subsidies of broadcasting: and the broadcasting authorities have a say in programme choice. Even the theatre now tends to be dominated by the play that will run for years and cover the high costs of production.

In spite of all this, the microphone and the loudspeaker do provide a means of a highly refined art, because they exclude the visual; arts are arts because of their chosen limitations. Marvellous things can be done with the spoken word, and with sounds of all kinds, within the framework of the loudspeaker, within this arena of pure sound. In a love scene you cannot see the lovers; you must evoke their feelings poetically with speech and with background effects of music, the sea or whatever is suitable. As everyone knows, a solitary seagull's call will evoke seaports, ships, and shores. That's a trite example; the artist in sound radio will conceive subtler ones, if he's given the chance. But severe limits are put on his subtlety, because the audience are not interested in any medium as art. They are interested in REALISM— that is, fundamentally, in themselves, their egos. They want to feel, as quickly as possible, familiar patterns of emotion without the mediation of high art, without the distortions of contempla-tion, without metaphor and symbol to which they are not accustomed. Thus, when television brings before their eyes a couple of real lovers slobbering all over each other and hardly needing to say anything, just gazing lovelorn-like into each other's eyes, well, sound radio can't compete. You have only to look on a station bookstall to see what the mass want to entertain them, real life stories of erotic passion opening the way to social success. They like their natural being presented to them in such a form as to sanction it: jealousy, envy, hatred, and lust, what is called LIFE, is to the taste of the lowest common man and woman. Providing this in a form that doesn't present the truth about passion and society is the whole art of success. So far as there is art in the mass media, it is the art of letting the natural man satisfy his desires within a moral framework; and it is done by a number of easily acquired illusions.

I come again to my chief point: that you cannot give an audience an art that it does not want. There are immense possibilities of art in sound radio, television, and film, but the audience are impatient for the excitements of the emotions. We live in a secular society that has no philosophy of passion, little conception of society as subordinate to God, and not much understanding of the divine in the natural.

The mass audience doesn't want poetry; it wants stories of foiled seducers, of bad men chasing good women into the arms of good men, so that it can gratify its moral sense with the happy ending and its sexual lusts with the story. And since it is ignorant of the significance of passion, it likes dirty insinuations so that it can gloat over what it doesn't understand. The puritan moralist tries to eliminate passion, cut it out by the roots. That is the worst attitude of all. Passion must be an eternal theme of life and art. The high arts have always been concerned with passion. There is a long tradition of passionate tragedy in European art; passion is a form of suffering, intense to the point of longing for death; men, in the past, have seen the choice between sacred and profane love as a heart-breaking choice. They have sought not the abandonment of passionate feeling but the refinement and purification of it; they have seen the passion for God himself as the ultimate passion for which other passions are surrendered. The passionate man loves all creation and the incompatibilities of his passions lead to tragic situations. But such a view of passion is today incomprehensible. All romantic sexual passions, to judge by the films, have an infallible ending in happy marriage, to judge by the film stars in many happy marriages! There cannot be tragedy in a progressive society; it can always find a rational answer. And so the old dramas linger on in a debased form with all their real meaning taken out of them: desire need not be redeemed or punished or sublimated. There are no Dantes.

But no one who has ever suffered passion can accept such a debased assumption. If you listen to the popular love-songs of today, such as 'Eden' or 'I Believe', you will find that they provide a religious sanction for lust. The wailing crooning voices, of eunuchs rather than of men, float upward like cats' on a roof with a semi-religious accompaniment. The effect of this on the unregenerate multitudes puts Bacchus in the shade. You have all seen pictures of crooners being mobbed at railway stations and theatres. A decadent paganism with echoes of Christian religious music provides the spiritual nourishment of the masses. It is an entertainment to sit in the studio while a disc programme is being put out. Many of the technicians involved in putting out such programmes are emotionally superior to the disc jockeys, and pull faces at each other behind the compère and the producer; but often enough the producer has to go home and be quietly sick. However, the producer is often enough in the same sort of position as the worker in the armament factory. Nevertheless, the defence of one's country has some moral justification; I suppose one can say that the armament worker doesn't know if the arms he makes will be used for a just or an unjust cause. Maybe the people who cater for mass taste are also uncertain whether they are doing right or wrong. The people pay for the mass media; without their support they would not be possible, so it is said. Broadcasting, newspapers, and the rest exist to serve the public. Isn't it, therefore, perhaps morally wrong not to give the public what it wants? And isn't it perhaps priggish to dictate what the public ought to have? If the multitude wanted our Lord to reign over Israel as a real king wasn't he letting them down by refusing? He seems to have been a bit of a cad—democratically speaking.

'We must serve the people.' That is the slogan that makes

every evil of mass entertainment possible. We don't serve the Holy Spirit, or Art or Truth; we 'serve the people'. The influence of mass media on the arts reflects the influence of society on the mass media.

Technical invention—that is, the invention of tools which are not actually a part of the human being himself—has two effects: one is to make our tasks much easier; the other it to make our tasks more and more distant and less related to ourselves and our needs. Thus the invention of writing and printing enables the poet to take his poems to people who could never hear them if he were to stand on a mountain top and recite: they tempt him to forget that he writes for the voice and for an audience. Poetry is the supreme instance of an art killed by technical invention. The Greek dramatists, without printing, had huge audiences such as no modern poet, even with books, could hope to command. The only comparable decay would be to imagine music without musical instruments simply read like books. The book of poems is too easy to shove on the shelf and forget. Yet, one might say, as optimists always do, radio will alter all that: now the poet reading his verse can be heard in every home. But, of course, it is too late to revive poetry; it is not an inherent traditional need of the mass of society and therefore radio can do nothing to revive it. People have not rushed to buy gramophone records of spoken poetry, which is a better medium still, since you can put the record on as often as you wish.

Our use of technical inventions reflects our philosophy of life and the sort of people we are. Travel only diminishes our provincial egotism when we have learnt to value what is not ourselves; travel often increases egotism when there has been no spiritual preparation. In the same way, one might think that, when the mass media open up the opportunity to ordinary people to become familiar with the arts, culture would flourish and men's souls would broaden and enrich. That is a charming Victorian idea; the temple doors of the palace of art have been opened to the masses and they have found nothing there; they have made the splendid discovery that art is all an upper-class racket and when they hear the word culture they reach for their football pools. The enjoyment of art, like the enjoyment of travel, requires spiritual preparation and a humble willingness to have one's egotism invaded by forces that are outside oneself, unknown and unfamiliar. The souls of men deprived of religion are clamped down tight over their own egotism; they want neither art, nor God, nor travel, nor the intrusion of coloured races into their sphere of consciousness. All they want to see is their own perfect image writ large over the universe . . . they want to hear exclusively about themselves on television, radio, and in parliament. The spiritual and artistic and political progress of mankind depends upon splitting open this subjective fortress, this unrelaxing central ego in the natural man. But far from any such attempt being made or regarded as necessary, the whole trend of society is to flatter egotism, pander to provincial taste, and make the natural man feel he is indeed the very voice of God on earth: to present the people to the people.

The mass media are a means to power like gunpowder and nuclear fission. The wireless was not invented to provide a means of mass entertainment, just as the explosive now called gunpowder was not invented in order that people should kill each other. But war is a means to power; and mass entertainment is also a means to power, and to vast fame and fortune. Like gunpowder and nuclear fission the mass media provide wonderful, dazzling opportunities for abuse. And one must confess that many of the most eminent figures in the country have succumbed to the temptation, and given this abuse their support and the camouflage of their names, as if a bishop should accept the post of *grande dame* in a brothel. Now what is peculiarly fascinating in our time is that all these abuses, which in the past could be kept within a limited sphere, cannot any longer be kept under. The atomic bomb confronts man with the fact that if he goes on quarrelling with his brother he will annihilate himself; the mass media in the sphere of the arts and culture have brought us face to face with the fact that we are going to be reduced to non-spiritual moronic animals. In the past small sections of society could escape from the pressure of man's basic nature; now nobody can. It is shouted in every home or flung before your eyes wherever you turn. Democracy, compulsory education, and a wider distribution of wealth—have intensified all the moral problems.

I imagine that the frescoes of Giotto were a mass art in their time; when people couldn't read, they taught them the spiritual truths of the Christian religion; they must have been seen by a high percentage of the population of the time. So art intended for popular enjoyment need not be debased. The Greek theatre wasn't, but the Roman theatre was. The need for vulgarity, sensationalism, and spectacle is always present in a bored population that has no creative work to do. The factory bench created the audience for the mass media and the press barons and the publishing houses and the broadcasting authorities set out to gratify it, or they found themselves compelled to gratify these tastes, whichever way you look at it. For unless this need is gratified none of these activities, none of the mass media, can be placed on a sound financial basis. The trap is perfect. The vicious circle has no break in it. The temptation is absolute. Destiny has set the tycoons of entertainment a problem of survival that allows of no compromise and no weakening. It never, almost never, occurs to a tycoon that in the eyes of God it may be salvation to fail and damnation to succeed. So there will be no compromise. In industrial town and factory, the workers on monotonous machines often exhausted, so far as the imagination is concerned, by overtime, provide the bored audience hungering to feel something, hungering to live, hungering for the quickest ways of feeling emotion, hungering for sensation and spectacle: and the tycoons are there to give it to them as if they were charitable benefactors.

Now the Greeks with their sense of destiny would have seen this for what it is—a tragic and irreversible doom laid on mankind at a particular time in history. In a Christian assembly one may point this out without fear of being hooted off the stage as a pessimist. Christianity redeemed the Roman Empire from its materialistic doom partly because it recognized that the spirit is always crucified, that the world always and actively persecutes the spirit; in our day it does this by ignoring its existence. Christianity recognizes the tragedy of existence. But the Christianity of the mass today is a mere lingering sentimentalism; religion is not for them a judgment of themselves, it is a glorification of their way of life.

A civilization which fixes its spiritual sights on the average fallen sinner, not to lift him up, but just to distract him from his real state of being, will get the sort of art and entertainment, the sort of culture it deserves . . . and that the Romans had to an even more extreme degree than we have. Ordinariness is protected by its numbers; so many millions can't be wrong. If audience research says millions enjoyed a programme it must be good. That is our rule of judgment and evaluation.

It looks as if I am starting a hate campaign of my own against the ordinary man. Not at all. I am campaigning against the cult of the ordinary man; for this cult is not a safeguard against tyranny, dictatorship, and vulgarity. It's the quickest way to it. Yet in the long run I think we shall find that the ordinary man grows sick of his own taste writ large over everything. The politicians and business men who have made him into God for the purpose of selling him themselves and their products will find that he will turn against them and accuse them of debauching him. It is not easy to resist the free gratification of daydreams, whether they be Hitlerian dreams of Empire, the Communists' dream of equality imposed by force, or the factory girl's dream of a rich lover. But those who deprive us of our sense of reality by selling us these dreams are in the end recognized, I think, as public enemies; even though the dreams, being latent in nature, spring up again in due course. The world of temptation and the cycles of temptation are part of human destiny and the great religions recognize their place and their reality. The non-religious societies don't. The ordinary man is superior to the culture which is served up to him, which he demands and apparently enjoys. Culture is part of the whole social background of a people. The powers of artistic expression are not aroused in the modern world; the real character of ordinary people is never more than latent. Our cities and our education system and our organization of life do not stimulate the imagination and arouse the passions, except, one is tempted to say, in war.

Culture and truth are inter-related and the beginning of culture is to tell the truth about what is felt; and that is what our culture does not do. We don't present man as he is or man as he should be. To present him cynically as a victim of fate is not true; he has visions of better things and can work better things. To present everything as perfect is worse still; merely to make everything one big joke is blasphemous; to present unrealizable and false dreams as art is treachery to the audience. In my view the educated have betrayed the semi-educated and they are now scared of the proletarian mass whose greed they have created; strikes and the like are a revolt of slaves, luxury slaves, but slaves nevertheless in terms of their monotonous work. The politicians are in a panic; they can think of nothing better than to bribe the mass with bread and circuses—of which commercial television is the most recent example. Putting the whole apparatus of television at the mercy of commercial advertising is a very odd conception of freedom. I am opposed to the B.B.C.'s monopoly myself, but this anarchy is worse. T.V. is now literally bringing the Roman circus into the home. It is simply the cultural domination of the mass. Yes, the Roman circus has come to the hearth. Indeed, if we look back to second-century Rome we see a civilization with a startling similarity to our own. I would say that between the Rome of those days and the Western civilization of today nothing of the kind has existed. For second-century Rome was governed by the needs and tastes of an urban proletariat. It had also an educated bureaucracy that manipulated a welfare state in some ways more indulgent than our own; it had a number of highly cultivated families, who lived a Bloomsbury-like existence more or less indifferent to the decadence and slavery of the rest, provided they could have their exquisite enjoyments; it had religious tolerance, provided no criticism were made of its social system; and it had free entertainments. And what entertainments!

This situation killed any possibility of great art, except the work of the occasional satirist like Juvenal or Martial. The only passion that inspired the sensitive was disgust. We see here the ideal condition of the mass media—the undifferentiated, bored, urban proletariat hungering for excitement and entertainment, and constituting a political estate. So the Colosseum was built and filled with ceaseless entertainment from morning till night at the State's expense for a quarter of a million spectators. The Colosseum was the prototype of the mass media—created as it was to gratify the bored passions of an urban mob running into a million.

The wise emperors vied with the worst in this debauchery of pleasure and squandering of money: and the most ostentatious, the most apparently foolish in the matter was perhaps Trajan, the model emperor whose perfection was held to be worthy of Jupiter. In reality, as Fronto saw it, his wisdom never failed to pay attention to the stars of the theatre, the circus or the arena, for he knew well that the excellence of government lay no less in its care for the amusements of the people than in serious matters, and that although the distribution of corn and money might satisfy the individual, spectacle was necessary for the contentment of the masses.

The brutality of the Roman spectacle is not yet on the radio. But it is on the way. Already it is found in the horror comics with their immense circulation. However, listen to this from *The Observer* of Sunday, 3 March 1957. Maurice Richardson writes on the I.T.V. programme 'Superman':

> I was more shocked by Superman than by anything I have yet seen on television. I honestly believe it might be possible to catch schizophrenia from this fantasm, if your sense of reality was at a low ebb. It is deeply regressive, without a trace of constructive imagination that redeems the crudest science fiction.
>
> Superman, a jowly muscleman thinly disguised as a newspaper reporter with horn-rimmed spectacles and Brooks Bros. suit over his posing slip, defies all the physical laws in a contemporary setting. He flies, just like that. A giant gorilla's stone cosh, brought down on his

head with all the force of a giant gorilla's right arm, shatters into fragments. The pressure of his hand-grip converts a lump of coal into diamond.

This takes you straight back to the phenomenon which Freud called 'the omnipotence of thoughts', that overestimation of the power of wishes and mental processes which amounts to a sort of infant's megalomania. It may serve its purpose in the cradle. It might be permissible as a comic strip on a packet of breakfast food. But to blow it up into a film (live, not cartoon) and put it on for half-an-hour at a time when boys should be doing their homework is the most defiant gesture yet made in the name of the Idiot's Lantern, cretino-cracy rampant. I would sooner serialize *Malleus Maleficorum* than miserable dementia.

The effect of the tradition of Christian morals has been to make it difficult to stage gladiatorial combats or throw people we don't like to the lions—we throw them to the quizzers. So the thirst for perpetual amusement has needed other gratifications. It is being assuaged by a deluge of triviality; endless facts and informa-tion unrelated to the spiritually significant, adults playing children's games and the like. One might be tempted to say that Christianity has served no better purpose than to turn 'Thoughts and afflictions, passions, Hell itself to favours and to prettiness.'

We may echo Pliny the Younger: 'Such favour, such weighty influence, hath one worthless charioteer's tunic—I say nothing of the vulgar herd, more worthless than the tunic—but with certain grave personages. When I observe such men thus in-satiably fond of so silly, so low, so uninteresting, so common an entertainment, I congratulate myself that I am insensible to such pleasures.' We know, too, that under these conditions of mass values the Roman tragedy declined into the modern musical. 'The producer', says M. Carpino in his fine book *Daily Life in Ancient Rome*, 'mercilessly cut the traditional texts of plays and clipped the dialogue, so that after the scissors had done their worst a tragedy consisted of little but lyrics more or less skilfully punctuated by scraps of dialogue. The Roman impressarios thought not of serving a work of art but of exploiting it.'

The similarities between their mass culture and ours are innumerable. It is all based on fear of losing popularity on the part of the ruling classes—or anyway the people with power. Mass entertainment is in fact the ladder to power. And it all leads to hopeless vulgarity and finally to the collapse of the civilization that allows it. The Romans were so attached to horse racing that, when the barbarian was at the gate, they left a Pope to go and challenge him, while they continued with their gambling.

The Roman Empire did many fine things; we do many fine things; we still do them even in the sphere of mass entertainment; but subordination of judgment to popularity dragged down Rome and is dragging us down too. There must be some standard of judgment that is spiritual and transcendent; some discipline of nature such as high art provides; even artists themselves are full of human frailty.

It is within the bounds of possibility that the mass media will ultimately kill the arts in this country. If they don't, it will be because our whole civilization has seen the light about its general philosophy of life. You can't buy out the Spirit any more than you can the barbarian. The Spirit will finish you off and start again if you don't pay a proper and humble tribute to its demands.

The discussion tended toward the view that Mr. Waller had spoilt a good case by exaggeration, but this was not entirely clear. There was some anxiety lest the author should seem to be speaking disparagingly of uneducated people or of democracy; he was in fact referring to the cult of 'the common man' and the cult of 'democracy'. There was agreement that, in any case, in every society the greatest achievements—spiritual, religious, artistic—inevitably proceed from small minority groups.

An important matter was raised about the televising of the Christian liturgy. Horror at what had been done in this respect was expressed by more than one person present. With due deference to the Benedictine hosts of the symposium it was suggested that the televising of High Mass was against the Christian tradition. It was pointed out that the Mass is divided into two parts, the Mass of the catechumens, that is of those who are being instructed, which may well be open to all people, but that the rest of the Mass is a sacred religious act of the Christian body and of no one else. To televise it was to cast pearls before swine. Another person specified the trouble more precisely. Television is a spectacle, but the liturgy is a religious act in which every person present takes part; it is just because most Christians have forgotten what the liturgy is, it is just because they do in fact normally regard it merely as a spectacle which they watch, that they are not shocked by its introduction on a television programme.

17. The Senses

JOHN MARSHALL

Dr. John Marshall is Director of the Academic Unit in Neurology, of the Institute of Neurology of London University and the National Hospital for Nervous Diseases. He was invited to provide the symposium with information about the physical basis of perception. Since each human being is a single whole it seemed wrong to suppose that the physical means by which we become aware of the arts, our senses, could be ignored in a study of the arts. Dr. Marshall provided this exposition of the information for which we asked.

IT is difficult in a symposium in which the Arts are so widely and strongly represented, for a scientist to say anything that is helpful or meaningful. He must walk a tight-rope between two errors. His presentation may be so full of facts couched in a technical jargon that slumber rapidly overtakes his audience. Alternatively, in an endeavour to stimulate and maintain interest, he may propose intriguing hypotheses which, though initially related to known facts, develop during their elaboration an increasingly tenuous connexion with reality. Faced with this dilemma, I have taken a pusillanimous course, and will say in effect that science is science and art is art, and though one day the twain may meet, such a prospect does not, as yet, lighten our horizon. I shall give some account of the mechanism of the simple structures which make up the nervous system, on which our appreciation of the Arts is entirely dependent; I shall endeavour to indicate how the activity of these simple structures is utilized; I shall relate some effects of sensory deprivation upon the human organism; and I shall conclude by emphasizing the yawning chasm which exists between the account which I have given, and the reality of sensory appreciation as seen in the world of Arts.

The nervous system exists for no other purpose than to convey information. It is a signalling system whereby messages can be carried from one place to another. Information from the world without impinges upon receptors such as the eye, the ear, the nose, and the tactile organs in the skin where it is translated into a series of impulses which travel along nerves to the brain. Information from the world within us is likewise picked up by specialized receptors and conveyed centrally. Hence I know that I am thirsty or satiated, hungry or replete, that my heart is beating quickly or that my muscles are tired. The traffic is not only one way, for identical impulses travelling outwards may cause my hand to be raised, my mouth to water, or my pupils to constrict. It is well to remember, however, that of itself the nervous system can effect nothing. The High Command may send the signal for the attack, but effective action depends upon the co-operation of the troops in the field. Likewise, the translation of impulses in the nervous system into effective action requires the presence of muscles which will move the limb, or of glands which will pour forth their secretion. There is, of course, a defect in the military analogy, for the troops are capable of action independently of or even in opposition to commands, whereas the effectors of the nervous system obey without question.

There is another aspect of this activity which must be mentioned, and that is the question of awareness. We have no direct knowledge in ourselves of the actual passage of information along our nerves. We feel the cool breeze blowing on our skin or hear the sound of voices falling on the ear, but of the nervous processes mediating these experiences we have no awareness. More surprising perhaps is the fact that we are not always aware of the activity of the effector organs. Thus, though we may know when we raise our hands, we do not, and cannot, by any amount of introspection know when our pupils constrict. There is also between these two extremes a vast number of semi-automatic activities of which we may become aware by taking thought.

Walking is a good example, for though we may by introspection take great interest in our gait, usually it is an activity which is automatic and to which we pay no attention.

The nervous system is, therefore, a signalling system. Let us consider for a moment how the information is conveyed. The elucidation of this fascinating chapter in physiology is a good example of how science works in this field. Our task is made easier by the fact that though nerve fibres are of different lengths and different diameters, their mode of action is uniform. A nerve fibre consists of a tube or cylinder, the wall of which is composed of a membrane which has remarkable properties. Within the tube is a watery solution and suspension of chemical substances known as axoplasm. The most striking property of the enclosing membrane is its ability to allow some substances to pass through it freely, while remaining impermeable to others. Thus potassium and chloride ions pass readily through the membrane, whereas sodium ions are kept out. This active separation of chemical substances results in an electrical potential being developed on the membrane of the order of one hundred millivolts (a millivolt is one thousandth of a volt), which is quite a high potential for a biological system. To what end is this exclusion of sodium from within the nerve fibre? If the potential at the surface of the membrane is slightly diminished by any means, immediately sodium begins to flow into the fibre and potassium passes out. This flux of ions is the genesis of the nerve impulse, for the movement is accompanied by an electrical disturbance which lowers the potential of the adjacent part of the membrane through which in turn sodium begins to flow, and so the process is propagated along the nerve fibre.

This process underlying the passage of an impulse in a nerve fibre is extremely simple, but the final analysis conveys no hint of the work involved in its elucidation. The description 'a tube or cylinder' tends to enlarge our mental picture of the nerve fibre until it attains the dimensions of a large water main, the inner and outer environments of which can readily be analysed. It is therefore chastening to remember that the largest nerve fibre, the giant axon of the squid, is about 0·5 millimetre in diameter, and that most nerve fibres are very much smaller than this. How then have physiologists obtained their information? Various approaches have been made, and it may be of interest to indicate one or two of these. The electrical potential of the membrane has been measured directly by making a glass electrode of one-thousandth of a millimetre diameter, and introducing it under microscopic control into the nerve fibre. Such a process is easily described but less easily executed. Replacing the potassium by radio-active potassium and then measuring its content by means of a Geiger counter is another method which has been used. A third line of attack has been to extrude the axoplasm from a large fibre which, you will remember, is only 0·5 millimetre in diameter, and to analyse it by microchemical methods. It will be appreciated that all these techniques entail a high degree of technical skill and perseverance, but it is by such means that the knowledge of the nature of the nerve impulse has been obtained.

Now why have I, in defiance of my initial declaration about the danger of too technical an approach to my subject, elaborated to such an extent the mechanism underlying the passage of an impulse in a nerve fibre? My reason is as follows: when we are stirred by the beauty of a picture, when we are enthralled by the pattern of the dance, or when we are roused by the climax of a symphony, a prosaic but essential step in our appreciation is the flow of countless ions of sodium and potassium in accordance with a pattern, which rivals in its order and faultless perfection that of the dance we may be witnessing. Between the movement of ions on the one hand and our total appreciation of the artistic situation on the other, lies a large abyss of which it might be said:

> Between the idea
> And the reality
> Between the motion
> And the act
> Falls the Shadow.[1]

1 T. S. Eliot: *The Hollow Men.*

That the shadow of our ignorance falls heavily between the extremes I have delineated cannot be doubted, but I think it is valuable for us to appreciate at the outset the parameters of our subject.

Let us now look a little farther and see how the passage of impulses conveys sensory information from the periphery to the centre in order that we may enjoy artistic endeavour. All nervous impulses are alike, consisting, as has been described, of movements of ions accompanied by an electrical disturbance which, because of the ease with which it may be recorded, is a convenient outward sign of the disturbance within the nerve. How can identical impulses convey information which may differ widely in its character? There are several methods by which the nervous system deals with this problem. One way is by the implication of a greater or lesser number of fibres. Thus the pressure of a knife edge upon the skin will excite only a limited number of fibres as compared with that exerted by a book or a more expansive object. The number of fibres involved will reflect to some extent the size and shape of the stimulating object. A second way is by the number of impulses which flow in a single fibre. Thus the weight of an object will be reflected in the frequency of the impulses passing along any individual nerve fibre supplying the supporting muscle; the greater the weight the higher will be the rate of discharge of nerve impulses.

But the most important method of obtaining information and making it available to the nervous system is by the development of specialized receptors such as the eye and ear. These organs, as is apparent, respond to one kind of stimulus only. It is of no avail to shine a light in the ear; sound is the efficient stimulus for this organ and only to sound does it respond. Likewise the eye responds to light and the nose to scents. Thus, though the impulses in the auditory, optic, and olfactory nerves are identical, the information which they convey is different because the receptors which excite the nerve fibres respond to different types of stimulus. The appearance of these receptors in higher forms of animal life has, therefore, extended enormously the range of appreciation which is possible.

The development of the specialized sensory receptors did not see an end to the degree of differentiation carried out by the nervous system. The eye does not simply respond to light, but by its agency we can appreciate lights of different colours. How this is achieved is not known for certain, the most acceptable hypothesis being the trichromatic theory. This envisages that the receptor cells, known as cones, are of three types, each of which responds to only a limited part of the light spectrum. Mixing of light from the different parts of the spectrum gives us the phenomenon we call colour, hence the proportional excitation of the three types of receptor is the basis of our colour appreciation. This has a wide range, for it has been estimated that as many as 165 hues can be distinguished. The artist presumably has a greater awareness of the vast potentiality of his colour appreciation than does the ordinary person.

This question of potentiality in a sensory modality is worth examining a little farther. There can be little doubt that the great majority of us glean only a fraction of the information that our sense organs are capable of gathering. Proof of this is seen in the remarkable achievements of those who, for some reason, are deprived of one form of sense experience, and so develop the potentialities of other senses beyond all expectation. The tactile and auditory abilities of the blind are too well known to require elaboration here. The most outstanding example of this compensatory development is surely Helen Keller, who, though blind and deaf, has achieved so much by means of her sense of smell and touch. Describing a drive with her, Frederick Tilney, the American neurologist, relates:

> Her first observation was that we were then making our way through open fields. This proved to be the case, for the road ran through a golf course. Later, she said we were passing trees. The road at this point made its way through a small grove. She then called attention to the fact that we had just passed a house with an open fire, and looking back I saw a small cottage with smoke pouring out of its chimney. . . . Shortly after this Miss Keller called attention to the fact that we had just entered Garden City and were passing the plant of Doubleday

and Doran, her publishers, which actually was the case. Her realization of this fact, she told me, was due to her olfactory recognition of
the ink from the presses of this publishing establishment, with which
she was familiar.[1]

In describing the importance of the sense of smell in her life,
Helen Keller herself wrote: 'I wonder how many people are
aware of the complex odours in a house that has been lived in for
a long time. They give me a comfortable sense of hospitality.
They suggest cheery winter fires and peace and sweet family
intimacies. There are lingering scents of perfume and garments in
closets and drawers, and appetizing odours of cooking which some
people find extremely unpleasant, but which seem to me kindly.'

The comparative neglect of much of our sensory capacity must
impoverish our appreciation of the arts. For not only is knowledge
of the particular discipline required for a full appreciation of an
artistic creation, but also the ability to absorb completely the
sensory data which the medium presents to us. Experience may
indicate what features are important, and for what we should look
or listen, just as in medicine the doctor seeks certain signs because he knows their significance. But does not training also
develop the discriminatory powers of the sensory mechanism,
quite apart from our awareness of the need to direct it to the
relevant points? I should think it does, and the colour discrimination of the artist or the tone perception of the musician is greater
than that of the untutored person by reason of his training.

The importance of sensory experience in our lives has been
emphasized by observation of the effect of sensory deprivation.
These observations have come from two sources. One is of
patients whose sensory pathways have been interrupted by disease
so that the patient receives little or no sensory information. Such
a patient tends to lie immobile with open eyes but taking no heed
of what is happening around. Spontaneous movement is absent,
and it is only the most vigorous stimulation that will provoke a
reaction. The patient is also mute. During recovery, when it is

1 Tilney, F.: Archives of Neurology and Psychiatry (1929), 21, 239.

possible to establish communication with him, it becomes apparent that he had been unaware of his orientation in space and time during the period of his stupor. It is important to realize that there is no defect of the effector mechanisms in these patients, but the loss of the stimulating effect of sensory information renders the patient inert, although he is perfectly capable of movement or action.

The other striking illustration of the need we have of a constant stream of sensation is the change produced in those unfortunate persons who have been kept for a long period in solitary confinement. The loss of sensory information produces a state in which the prisoner (it is usually a political prisoner who is subjected to such treatment) loses contact with reality. He loses count of place and time, and often slips into a dreamlike state in which he is unsure of what is fact and what is fiction. Hallucinations may also occur. It is while in this state that he is so susceptible to indoctrination, or brain-washing as it is often called. Prisoners under such conditions have emphasized the need for undertaking deliberate mental activity such as counting numbers or surveying the words in their vocabulary; by these means they are able to some extent to compensate the loss of natural sensation, and to minimize the worst effects of their treatment. These phenomena have also been studied experimentally in volunteers who have been confined in a sound-proof room, wearing goggles which permit the entry of light but do not allow any pattern to be distinguished, and with their hands enclosed so as to prevent any tactile stimulation. The subjects of these experiments report that loss of the power of concentration and of awareness of reality rapidly develop under these conditions.

I have, I hope, said enough to illustrate how vital is sensation for the proper functioning of man, and so far I have kept very close to the experimental and factual line. The difficult step comes when we try to penetrate farther and understand what happens to this sensory information when it reaches the brain. How is all this information integrated to form the living reality which we know in our everyday experience?

We have seen that a stimulus which is physical or chemical in nature is applied to a sensory receptor, and that this excites in nerve fibres trains of impulses which are nothing more than the movement of ions with an electrical accompaniment. These impulses travel centrally, and in turn excite further impulses in the complicated nerve network which constitutes the human brain. As a result of this activity we experience a sensation which seems to come not from the brain where the disturbance is occurring but from the skin, or even, in the case of sounds and sights, from some place entirely outside our body. This experience we call a percept. We must remember that a percept is an intensely personal and private matter having no existence outside ourselves. Thus, a wave of a certain frequency only becomes colour when it is perceived by someone. By various means we agree that the experience produced in ourselves by a certain physical stimulus we shall call red or blue, but the percept itself remains a personal matter. But the unique problem which has exercised great minds for a long time is how the impulses which traverse the nerve net of the brain produce a percept in the mind. We can analyse the nature of the stimulus, we can determine the nature of the nervous impulse and follow its progress from periphery to centre, we can even obtain some very approximate notion of the pattern of activity in the nerve net of the brain, but beyond this to the percept we cannot go. It is obvious that it is exactly here that the realm of artistic appreciation starts, and so we begin to see the gap that lies before us. For, so far, we have talked of simple percepts such as colour, touch, or sounds, but how much greater will be the gap when we come to think of an artistic experience with its nuances of light and shade, the emotions it arouses, the memories it evokes, and the symbolism it conveys. We say that a piece of music conjures up a picture of this or that; how can we hope to understand the links between an auditory and a visual percept, when we do not begin to understand the link between each percept and the stimuli which give rise to it?

These difficulties have driven many to adopt a wholly mechanistic view of our being, likening us to the great electronic calculating machines which modern science and technology have produced. No doubt there is much in the construction of such machines that is analogous to the structure of the human brain, and much about man that can be learned from the study of these electronic contrivances. But we cannot do better than quote the words of Professor Sir Geoffrey Jefferson in this regard when he declared: 'Not until a machine can write a sonnet or compose a concerto because of thoughts and emotions felt, and not by a chance fall of symbols could we agree that machine equals brain. . . . No mechanism could feel pleasure at its successes, grief when its valves fuse, be warmed by flattery, be made miserable by its mistakes, be charmed by sex, be angry or depressed when it cannot get what it wants.'[1]

And so I have reached the chasm yet cannot bridge it; being human, however, I can appreciate and enjoy the actions of those who disport themselves in the less exacting but more pleasurable regions beyond it.

[1] Jefferson, G.: *British Medical Journal* (1949), *1*, 1105.

18. The Mind

RITA PAGE BARTON

A principal purpose of the symposium was to examine the practice of the arts; it was not to be a series of abstract hypotheses about the arts, unrelated to the artists and their works. Hence the section of witness by artists themselves, who were asked to come and talk of their work, in spite of their preference for communicating in their own chosen medium, not that of reflective discourse.

This empirical bent led to an attempt to avoid mere theorizing in this paper on art and the mind. For this reason an invitation was sent to someone actually concerned, in the course of her daily work, with the relationship between mental life and artistic work. Artistic work is here understood in the wide sense, used generally in the symposium, as any craft which involves the making of any sort of symbol.

Mrs. Rita Page Barton is a psychotherapist who uses painting, modelling and art activities as a supplement to an analysis in her task of healing sick minds. She gives a description of her approach to this work.

Lovers and madmen have such seething brains,
Such shaping fantasies, that apprehend
More than cool reason ever comprehends.
The lunatic, the lover, and the poet,
Are of imagination all compact:
One sees more devils than vast hell can hold,
That is the madman; the lover, all as frantic,
Sees Helen's beauty in a brow of Egypt:
The poet's eye, in a fine frenzy rolling,
Doth glance from heaven to earth, from earth to heaven;
And, as imagination bodies forth

The forms of things unknown, the poet's pen
Turns them to shapes, and gives to airy nothing
A local habitation and a name.

SHAKESPEARE: *A Midsummer Night's Dream*, V, i, 4-17

THE subject of Art and the Mind is too vast for me. I cannot put
on paper the thoughts of a lifetime, even though in my youth I
was specially privileged in learning the history of art from a
teacher[1] so enlightened and cultured that during the spell-binding
period of her lectures one was there in the atelier grinding the
colours with van der Weyden, Titian, or van Eyck; one experi-
mented *with* Leonardo da Vinci; one strove with Michelangelo,
and was on one's knees with Fra Angelico.

The whole world over, Art has had to serve religious, mythological and historical ends, and so has been a visible and tangible
means of exteriorizing the workings of the mind, and indeed the
life of the spirit. Interest in the past is so closely dependent on the
problems of the present that, as the present changes, both its
specific curiosities and its way of looking at works of art also
change. This, rather than the discovery of new materials,
valuable though they may be, is the reason why the history of the
past has continually to be rewritten.

Heraclitus would have it that we cannot dip twice in the same
stream. What is there that we can repeat, seeing that neither
within nor without are we and our universe the same for two
consecutive seconds? It becomes increasingly obvious that our
reactions to the works of art of the past differ greatly from the
reactions of the people who first enjoyed those works of art.

The true creative artist depicts, as well as he can, what he sees.
Yet first in interpreting and digesting what he sees, and secondly
in selecting and deciding what to portray, the artist will surely be
swayed by the general climate of thought, or *Weltanschauung,* in
which he lives. This is inescapable however individualistic or
iconoclastic the artist may be. Even as a rebel against the prevailing opinion he will still be affected in that very rebellion. This

---

1 Mère Léocadie, Dames de Marie, Brussels.

general mental outlook therefore will inevitably reappear to some degree and in some manner in his painting. Those too who study art or who look at pictures will also absorb or notice something of the spirit of the age in which the paintings were produced.

The Six Arts of the ancient Chinese were Ritual, Music, Archery, Charioteering, Calligraphy, and Calculation. Some time later mention is made of the Four Arts of the scholar, which turn out to be Music, Chess, Calligraphy, and Painting. Thus, instead of artists eager to communicate form and idea, a rather dilettante approach to art is produced, it would seem, in old China. In Egypt a formal stylized art was used mainly in conjunction with a formal religious doctrine. In Greece man's untrammelled far-questing mind, combined with an appreciation of the works of nature, saw the flowering of bold and confident art-forms and unrivalled sculpture and architecture.

In Europe during the Middle Ages people thought about and artists painted aspects of Christianity. The spirit of inquiry which spread abroad with the Renaissance was marked by an effort to bring meaning into life based on fresh and unprejudiced experience. It is interesting to note the change in the expression of the eyes in paintings of this time. It would seem that an inner process of becoming that had been developing for centuries, a struggle perhaps to reconcile the opposites of ego and non-ego, was resulting in a greater individuation. The eyes look more self-conscious. Individuation springs from the idea that each person possesses an immortal soul.

The Victorian Age with its interest in morality was marked by the painting of pictures which aimed at edification. The fashion for 'problem pictures' pointing more or less obliquely at a moral solution was a revealing development and the popularity of these pictures at the time derived from the general preoccupation with ideas about morality. I will not now dwell on the significance of the complete oblivion of this type of picture. The Age of Reason and Elegance saw artistic interest directed to landscape, to portraits, to animals, and to satires on society.

What can be deduced about a period which has produced Surrealism, Abstracts, and a feverish search after originality, apparently for its own sake alone? Surely it indicates a confused general outlook, or at least a lack of certainty, of settled acceptance and of confidence? One may also say: 'these new art forms are indications or growing pains of further individuation'.

This use of Art as a clue—or, as it may often become, as a key—can be of great value when applied diagnostically on the individual level. Also, in addition to diagnosis, direct therapeutic use can often be made of the paintings produced by patients. So although I have a lively and continuing interest in Art in all its forms, which causes me to dash off to see what is being shown whenever I can, I am confining myself here to the smaller compass of 'Art and the Sick Mind' because nearly all my time is devoted to psychotherapy. The therapeutic value of the arts in eliciting the patient's own healing powers is constantly shown and never fails to be awe-inspiring. When we ripen for an experience it is often some work of art, visual, verbal, or musical, that reveals the full sense of it and helps us to its utmost enjoyment.

Dr. Marshall's paper leaves us on the exciting and important threshold of perception, and immediately I am moved to recall that 'beauty is in the eye of the beholder'. Although this has been so repeated as to have become a cliché, and may often be said without any appropriate significance, it is nevertheless a wise and profound observation which hints at the Law of Reciprocities existing within the Self, the Total Man. It indicates the interplay of his light and dark sides, self and shadow, which must end eventually in the assimilation of the shadow. It recalls the pull of Yea and Nay, of Earth and Heaven, *yin* and *yang*, interdependence which is always operating in that marriage of opposites which occurs on any level whenever an act of integration takes place. Some degree of this activity is manifest every time we achieve a moment of harmony, however fleeting it may be.

We know that the disciplining of the senses has an effect on the mind, though this should not lead to frustration but rather to a loving participation in all life. It will be my endeavour in this paper to show how what seems merely an exercise in sensory perception, aimed at an enhanced aesthetic appreciation of visual phenomena, really leads to just that loving acceptance of all life.

A creative participation in the life of the senses through the arts does in effect enable a patient to get beside his problem instead of beside himself. Not infrequently art will facilitate the first step in detachment from his problem for a patient who is unable to achieve this through a more rational method or through contemplation of his dream material. Among the labyrinthine ways of patients' mentalities, checked and cornered by personal concepts and inhibitions, some form of art activity may help this release. Exteriorization of the unconscious contents of the mind helps the work of therapy; it favours a harmonious and reciprocal attitude to life. Then the doors of the mind may be opened enough to discriminate between what is real and what unreal, what is desirable and what is not, and to distinguish the pairs of opposites. I want to speak of those struggles of the sick mind which further typify the growing-pains of individuation. Perhaps the best thing is to give some examples.

E. G., aged twenty-five, had been in the Wrens and then a student-teacher in a kindergarten. It was imperative that she should pass her exams at the first attempt in order to earn her living. She could not concentrate, her hands were always wringing wet, and she suffered from claustrophobia. She was the elder of two children, her sister being ten years younger. Both parents were living. Mother was delicate and wrapped up in the shining perfection of her house and home, which father ruled kindly. 'No; no family worries', she said; she just could not concentrate and could I give her some exercises for it, please, as the examination was in six months' time?

The first picture was done for the third interview in two weeks. At the end of the month she brought the news that she would be unable to pay and so would have to stop coming to me. I replied that I would wait till she had passed the exams and had the job and then she should pay. Next week she brought the only other picture in this story, and the title is hers: 'Mirror, mirror upon the wall, who is the fairest of us all?' Hers also was the explanation: she is going to consult the mirror and her mother and sister are following behind. Unconsciously she had been identifying herself with mother in relation with father and was becoming mother's rival. Her unconscious guilt had been stealing away more than half her psychic energy, with consequent deprivation in her conscious life.

She improved from this time, and a part of our weekly interviews was used for a review of the week's lectures, always with a strongly synthetic trend. Picturing her home and the private drama on paper had enabled her to take this necessary step in detachment. At the end of the year she paid me, for she was embarked on a successful career.

The study of primitive art shows us parallels with the formulations of modern psychology; primitive art speaks to the primitive creativeness within ourselves and is an expression of the primordial images in our psyche.

I have noticed that the paintings and modellings of patients suffering from anxiety states are of a marked primitive nature, and I find an interesting corollary to this in the fact that primitive peoples, living in the collective in an undifferentiated condition, suffer almost constant anxiety that this or that power should be appeased. The ego of these patients needs strengthening, for they also are marked by a state of some undifferentiation.

H. B. was an office worker aged thirty who had striven to better herself. In this she had succeeded, but was still only found attractive by men of her former class whom she now considered 'beneath her'. Marriage was not to be thought of and she suffered from frequent bouts of anxiety. She said 'I want to make something of my life but I'm terribly lonely.' Dream material was copious and one interview was hardly enough to discuss it; it represented a completely different life, which she related to me in the manner of an onlooker. I told her to type out these reams of dream material and to send them as stories to various papers. Soon she returned, having done so, and three months later she showed me her first literary cheque, which was a quite encouraging one. The only painting done was in beautifying the walls and furniture of her little flat; and this kept pace more or less with putting her inner house in order. Periodic anxiety was fast disappearing and eventually the proximate cause of it also went. She has acquired more friends through her writing, which she no longer has to dream up. There is a good flow of material in full consciousness and I wish I had half her facility.

In this case too I waited for payment, which came entirely from her literary earnings. Her restrained pride was a joy to see.

In the kind of patient for whom God's love is thought of as conditional on a permanent state of virtue, the releasing effect of painting, or possibly of dancing, is most marked. The condition of such a patient is like that of the primitive in the dark forest endeavouring always to propitiate hobgoblins and demons, without hope of ever really doing right or even occasionally scoring a 'good mark'. The blessedly irrational nature of the plastic arts allows a certain homeopathic sort of operation whereby love and humility get a chance to come through, unimpeded if I could dare to say so by good works.

K. T., a Roman Catholic aged twenty-seven, had been a member of an aircrew. Six good years of his life had been passed in that close aircrew fellowship, with frequent sorties of considerable danger, poor rations, wrong clothing and equipment. These difficulties were, nevertheless, offset by the interdependence and trust existing in the group. The empty vastness of the desert had almost created a group soul for these men.

He was demobilized and living at home with his widowed mother in her ultra-tidy house, and doing an office job with conscientious application and little liking. He was allowed no hobbies; a bicycle 'would make the place dirty', and so would a cat or dog or carpentry. He was suffering from washing compulsions, scruples, a sense of impending doom, and a sorely irritating skin eruption, and proclaimed himself 'disillusioned with women; they always go off and marry someone else'.

During our talks his sense of loneliness and frustration became increasingly evident. Having left the 'father-mother' Air Force in

15

whose service he had enjoyed freedom, he had returned to a
veritable slavery with his natural mother. His overt aggression
against her mounted as his skin eruption subsided. After I'd seen a
canal and a ship or two in his paintings, I suggested that as cycles
were taboo he might like messing about in boats. Like many an
Englishman before him he took up the idea with enthusiasm and
spent his summer holiday learning to sail.

Then I suggested that as he kept the long narrow garden in
order he might have earned some rights there and could build a
'glory-hole' out of sight at the end. He said he would put it to
'Mum', who categorically refused, as I expected. 'Never mind,' I
said, 'what else would you like?' 'Goldfish', he replied. 'That's a
good idea' was my answer, and he fixed up a small aquarium in
my consulting room which gave lots of fun to the other patients.
In assembling this aquarium with its gadgets, all the perfectionist
idiosyncrasies of the scrupulant were more than adequately
manifested, but we got through it and hand-washing somehow got
mislaid. I never knew where it got to. Or did I?

Now he began to have open rows with his mother, who was
Irish and pious, though her temper was such that several ding-
dong battles took place. After these the patient always looked
better in health but full of self-reproach. I encouraged him to
build a shed and a boat, and most fortunately he had a confessor
who told him to follow my instructions to the letter. Timber
delivered to the house while he was at work was sent away again,
and had to be brought in with the help of his chums from the
church on Saturday afternoons. Construction began on the spot,
after which they all went to confession and the men's club.

One day we were sitting in silence on either side of the
fire in my consulting room when he suddenly jumped up and
walked hurriedly away. I sat still and made no comment. 'I wanted
to hit you then', he said, sitting down again. 'You raised your
hand in a gesture like my mother. And then I felt such love I
didn't know what to do; it is so much harder to handle than
hate.' So the aggression was detached from his mother.

The unconscious of analyst and analysand are at work on these problems no less than the conscious mind, so that my unconscious gesture had its place in the task of bringing the hidden treasure of his great love to light. None of his creative efforts were wanted at home, and it is hard indeed when no one wants your treasure. He had to learn that it is no use giving what someone else cannot take. For a time I bore the mother-image. He invented more and more perfect gadgets, and one day even walked under a ladder without calamity, though he was a bit shaken to realize that he had not noticed it!

About this time someone gave me a pot of early chrysanthemums and he thought it would be a fine idea to grow the flowers for the house. After his mother's acceptance of this gift, the first of his efforts she could sustain, doom became less impending. He dreamed of, and painted, a golden crocodile, the kingly emblem of Egypt. The last of his phobias left him; the boat was made and launched.

Sometimes when a patient is 'bogged down' (and often then he is 'slumped down' too), I chatter and paint away myself, and soon, by dint of distraction, I find that he or she is setting to work with gusto at something that could not be achieved before because of trying too hard. The give and take of conversation have induced him or her to breathe properly and then to start. After keen observation it seems to me, in retrospect, that the creative moment occurs after expiration and before inspiration. In an unseen fashion a higher principle appears to take over the situation and unites the two opposites; the unifying principle begins to be born on a very humble, down-to-earth level. Straining towards a goal has in the heart of the act the seeds of its own destruction or reversal.

M. N. was such a one. In her case a little while spent in piano playing produced a firmer person. In the consulting-room atmosphere she achieved recollection and firmness. The music she plays is light but the end is achieved, for the discipline of the musical phrase affords her a framework in which she feels secure.

Contemplation of another's work may also favour a harmonious approach to life if it triggers off something in the mind of the beholder; but the effect of creating something of one's own is far deeper. It is not necessary that anything at all should be verbalized, in criticism, say; the music, painting, or model is its own interpreter, and really, in its work of helping along the inferior function and reconciling the conscious and unconscious, needs no language. By 'inferior function' is meant that function which is least well developed. Environmental conditions rarely allow a man to develop equally well all sides of his nature, and not unnaturally he tends to concentrate on the things at which he thinks himself to be most gifted, or on those things which he prefers, and so by dint of specially feeding the one he starves the other, which is said to be 'inferior'. The inferior function remains in arrear in the process of differentiation, since it is almost impossible for anyone to bring all his psychological functions to simultaneous development. Through the unconscious condition of the inferior function, its unused energy is transferred to the unconscious, whereupon the unconscious becomes unnaturally activated, resulting in the production of phantasy at an equally primitive level. Retrieving such phantasies enables a new sense of balance to be achieved.

Although a man can only keep alive through the exercise of his leading functions, be they introverted or extroverted, it must also be remembered that during the process of absorbing unconscious contents of the mind, revealed perhaps by painting, it is only through a very gradual process of training that he can safely cultivate characteristics that are opposed to his predominant ones.

Since so much of psychotherapy hinges upon the healing power which is concealed, as it were, in the inferior function, it might be useful to give a short definition of the four psychological functions as delineated by Professor Jung.

THINKING is an apperceptive activity and can be divided into Active and Passive, though still activity. Active thinking is an act of the will or directed thinking, the faculty for which is termed *intellect*. Passive thinking is an occurrence and might be termed *intuitive* thinking.

FEELING is primarily a process which takes place between the Ego and a given content, a process that imparts to the content a definite value in the sense of acceptance or rejection. It is an entirely subjective process and can also convey mood.

SENSATION or sensing is that psychological function which transmits a physical stimulus to perception. It is therefore identical with perception. Sensation is related not only to the outer stimuli but also to the inner, i.e. to changes in the internal organs. It is sense-perception or perception transmitted through the sense organs (kinaesthetic vaso-motor sensation, etc.) A distinction must be made between the above and *Abstract Sensation*, which represents a differentiated kind of perception that might be termed 'aesthetic'. Abstract sensation is mainly suited to the artist, and like every abstraction is linked with the will, the element of direction. The will that is directed towards the abstraction of sensation is both the expression and the activity of the aesthetic sensational attitude.

INTUITION is that function which transmits perceptions in an unconscious way. It is often coloured by thinking, feeling, or sensation but is none of these. It is an instinctive apprehension and transmits the perception of mythological images, the precursors of *ideas*.

It is a great advantage for the therapist to know the Art languages, for in the work of 'one-ing' the soul to God, in the work of reconciling the opposites, qualities both good and bad are brought into the open. Negative and positive reactions may be looked for, and though anticipated need not be commented upon. Experience indicates that the good is likely to be much better when revealed, and the bad far worse.

Mr. K. said to me after some months of reductive analysis in which disclosures of a really revolting nature were made:'Why do you never condemn? I *know* it's bad.' The turning-point was here; for by the light within him he could now discriminate, and if the light be clear enough the wholesome is always preferred. Premature comment or explanation is unwise.

I do not think it helpful to give things names before they are properly born. Even a really evil-smelling inferiority complex, when it is brought forth at the appointed time, may bring with it certain compensatory factors such as a sense of positive guilt: a wholesome awareness of one's creatureliness *vis-à-vis* the Creator, for example.

Mr. J., an actor keeping the very worst of company, had been born a Catholic in Ireland, but because I had a fairly prominent bronze Buddha in my consulting room he supposed me to be a Buddhist. One day he said to me, 'Oh, you would not understand, of course, but in our religion we have the Sacrament of Penance.' He had not followed his religion for many years. However, by dint of making me understand it, during which time I needed everything explained, he talked himself back into the Faith and the practice of his religion. This helped him to change his company, his address, and his habits about which he had been referred to me. These habits were rooted in a considerable un-conscious inferiority complex. His drawings helped in dealing with this and so he was enabled to write plays as well as acting in them. He is now reading History.

Representations of images and feelings detach themselves in the shadowland of the unconscious and are shown as entities in painting or dream. Things repressed or forgotten come back again. This is a gain, though often a painful one, for the inferior and the rejected clings, nay belongs, to me as my shadow. It needs a lot of humility to let the shadow sit and look at you, even when it is only on canvas or paper. When it is not so safely anchored as that, it seems that the only remedy is in humble prostration, for when in that lowly position my shadow ceases to haunt me. If you are flat on the ground where then is the shadow?

In one of my painting groups where the sharing of a common consciousness seems to result in a share-out of libido, I often find that members paint a monster. Then, if I am not quick enough to stop them, they paint it over and cover it up by painting a vase of flowers on top. These 'rescued' monsters from whom we hide behind flowers or pieties or what you will, are most interesting and improve upon acquaintance, often indeed having the quality of the 'gargoyle-guardian'. They have value and significance, and tolerance of the monster on paper may well be the first step towards an inner attitude of reckoning with the dark side. Sometimes a face, not always that of a monster, possibly of the analyst, but very often resembling an ancestor, not of conscious significance to the painter, is perhaps the first real clue to a drama involving 'the sins of the fathers' or the unlived lives of the parents. Troubles often spring from parents' 'unlived lives', when a parent unconsciously harbours a sense of failure and so makes demands, perhaps also unconsciously, on his child to achieve what he did not. The child thereby confers on the parent the vicarious satisfaction of success through his child, who, however, is thus debarred from following his own bent and developing his own talents, and so experiences frustration and heaven knows what before he wanders into the consulting-room of some skilled therapist.

Often these monsters, if given a courteous reception, are transformed into the sort of helpful animals familiar to us in fairy-tales. The first aim of analytical work is to know ourselves, and we would do well to bear in mind Nietzsche's Zarathustra and 'the ugliest man whom we must love'. Jung says that the ugliest man is always oneself. Love therefore enables the evil to be transmuted and put in its place. Evil is good out of place.

Another patient who painted no monster but a pallid and solitary daffodil, or gently toned water-colours of misty landscape, left her real problem lurking at home in the shape of a sado-masochistic attitude to life involving a joyless and rigorous morality in the world, offset in the land of dreams by scenes of butchery. In this case dream relation was of more significance than the innocuous paintings in enabling this patient to assimilate the shadow.

It is very necessary that these things should be dealt with by someone with tact and discrimination (i.e. one who can tell what signifies what in these drawings) and skilled knowledge in also knowing how the artist should be treated, for such matters can only be exteriorized with safety if dealt with skilfully by someone with experience and understanding: this means in effect an experienced psychotherapist with insight and skill in both interpretation and handling the person who has painted the 'dynamite'.

S. J. was a factory worker, an ex-seaman with 'a chip on his shoulder'. He was disgusted with the world and people when he came to me with his hand in plaster. In the lecture which he had heard me give before he came to ask me 'to put some meaning into his life', I had suggested that the inner world of the Microcosm, if better known, might throw some light on the (for him, rejected) Macrocosm. In the group he offered little comment but tried to make friends on the way home. Soon I sent him to modelling classes. His stumbling after truth was an unfolding of the pattern of relationships, and he used to bring me his attempts to construct groups and conversation-pieces in the clay. One day he told me he was engaged on something very exciting. Instead of building up the clay in the usual way, he started with a huge lump and took bits away from it in order to disclose whatever should be within. What came forth was a Galatea, a real human figure which was so good that it was put on exhibition for a visit of the Duke of Edinburgh.

In the patient the attitude of readiness to contemplate his painting or other art-form, and in the therapist an aptitude for reductive analysis and synthesis alike, enables the patient to allow a free flow to his phantasies, in art as well as speech, and helps later in the healing assimilation of all these unconscious contents.

I have hardly mentioned the Dance. When Aristotle says (*Poetics*, ch. 1, 1447 a 28): 'By the rhythms of his attitudes the dancer represents the characters of men, their actions and passions together', he only states half the case, for a dance can be a catharsis for the dancer too. Movements somehow influence the mind for good or ill; as you move, so you are. I caused a very sullen and aggressive man, who also suffered from bouts of hysterical running through the streets at night, to go and learn judo. The self-recollection, non-aggression, rhythm and courtesy of judo, combined with a certain 'flanking movement' during the

analytical sessions, a little akin to the teachings of Zen, brought
about a really co-operative attitude to life. The man's inward
grace was matched by an outward *modestia* indicative of his
retrieved equilibrium. He had found his true centre.

I hope these few inadequate words of mine have given some
idea of the light which may be shed on the aberrations and distortions, in amazing complexity, which beset us poor mortals and
harass our feeble minds. The arts are often a beginning of diagnosis and of treatment whether by painting, modelling, music,
mime, or writing. Yet who can say, finally, how health and
balance are regained except by ascribing to the never-failing Grace
of Almighty God the wonderful transformations observed.

*The discussion led to this conclusion: Patients and artists are both
making symbols. The artist is a professional craftsman, but he only
achieves his end when he has created, by his special technique, a symbol
which has some validity, and some therapeutic quality in a general way
for mankind, and in a special way for the men and women of his own time.
The patient, lacking all expertise, is unable to create a symbol of value
for other people; but he can create the elementary outlines of a valid
symbol, with a therapeutic quality, for himself.*

*The artist is a person of heightened sensibility who accommodates this
sensibility in a work of art. This is not 'pathological' and it achieves its
own integration. But, as is well known, the greater the sensibility, the
more finely is the artist balanced and the greater the tension, and the
greater is both his ability to achieve the masterpiece, the archetypal
symbol, and the greater his own vulnerability.*

IV

PHILOSOPHIZING ABOUT THE ARTS

The symposium was not an attempt to formulate a system of aesthetics, and disagreements between papers in this section have not been ironed out. It was impossible to summarize discussions in the form of end-notes, which have been dispensed with entirely.

19. The Mediaeval Tradition

E. I. WATKIN

Mr. E. I. Watkin was invited to contribute to this volume a paper describing theories of beauty to be found in the works of philosophers from St. Augustine until the modern age. His paper was not read or discussed, but its reference to the papers contributed by the artists, and by Dom Illtyd Trethowan and Dom Sebastian Moore will be obvious.

WITH the exception of Augustine and Boethius there are no treatises devoted specifically to aesthetics by Christians in the first millenium, or later by the Schoolmen. The aesthetic teaching is incorporated into a more comprehensive philosophy and needs extraction.

The work has been accomplished by Professor Edgar de Bruyne of Ghent in a work of three volumes: *Etudes d'Esthétique mediévale*. The first volume covers the period from Boethius to John Scotus Eriugena, the second the period from Eriugena to the end of the twelfth century, the third deals with the thirteenth century. Later Professor de Bruyne summed up the results of his detailed studies in a résumé entitled *L'Esthétique du Moyen Age*. Recently a German-American of the University of Chicago, Professor Otto von Simson, in his essay *The Gothic Cathedral* has expounded the aesthetic philosophy of the twelfth century as it determined and was expressed by the birth and development of Gothic architecture, in particular Abbot Suger's St. Denis (the earliest Gothic church) and Chartres cathedral.[1]

So far as I know these are the only source books available for the traditional aesthetic of the Catholic schools, and of the three one

[1] I propose to refer to de Bruyne's *L'Esthétique* by the letter B, to Simson's *The Gothic Cathedral* by the letter S.

only is in English. Whatever I shall have to say is derived from
de Bruyne or Simson (apart of course from personal appreciation
or comment), and their findings are substantially identical.

Mediaeval aesthetic descends from pre-Christian classical
sources, philosophers, manuals of rhetoric, and the like. The
philosophy from which it derives is Platonism, not indeed as
formulated by Plato himself with his erroneous view of art as the
copy of a copy of reality, but as it took shape in Neoplatonism.
Confirmation was found in biblical texts. Professor de Bruyne
maintains that the classical formulas were deepened, in fact transformed, by Christianity. I venture to doubt it. The transformation, had I believe, been achieved already by Neoplatonism. St.
Augustine's aesthetic treatise was written in the earliest days of
his conversion. Boethius in his philosophy was Neoplatonist
rather than distinctively Christian. Eriugena was Neoplatonist,
possibly even at the expense of Christian orthodoxy. It was the
Neoplatonists of Chartres who, as von Simson shows, determined
the architecture of Chartres cathedral. All we can say is that, in
this sphere, Christian faith confirmed Neoplatonism and by its
doctrine of the Word Incarnate reinforced it, deepened and
extended its application.

That mediaeval aesthetic is essentially Neoplatonist may account
for what appears to me the fact that St. Thomas contributed little
that is original to this department of philosophy, which in turn
may perhaps account for the failure of so many Thomists to make
themselves sufficiently acquainted with scholastic aesthetics. This
traditional aesthetic, and on this we cannot insist too much, was
objective. Beauty is not in the beholder's eye or emotional
reaction but is a quality of objective reality grounded in its very
nature. St. Thomas, it is true, speaks of visual beauty as *id quod
visum placet*—that the sight of which delights. But this dictum
cannot offset the fundamental objectivity of his aesthetic as he
derived it substantially from the accepted philosophic tradition.
He wishes to express the distinctive reaction produced by visual
beauty. The difficulty that many, I fear most, people find pleasure
—so far at any rate as artefacts are concerned—in ugly objects

does not seem to have occurred to him. Indeed, so far as I know, it did not occur to any mediaeval writer.

Moreover, taken in the abstract, it is strictly true that beauty is that which gives aesthetic pleasure. However evil in the concrete the object of choice may be it can be chosen, willed only *sub specie boni*, for the sake of some good in it however perverted and defective, or projected into it. Evil as such cannot be willed. So is it with beauty. If an ugly object is regarded, indeed experienced, as beautiful it is in virtue of some beauty in it or projected into it. Nevertheless, from the fact that in the abstract beauty alone is the object of aesthetic experience and delight, we cannot conclude that in the concrete every object so experienced is beautiful, any more than we can conclude from the fact that good alone is the object of the will that every choice in the concrete is morally good. St. Thomas we may well believe in this definition of beauty is thinking abstractly rather than concretely. And the concrete comes to its rights elsewhere.

One of the fundamental aspects of the traditional aesthetic, is, as Professor de Bruyne terms it, musical. Beauty consists in a harmony, a music which is essentially a mathematical proportion. 'Between arithmetic which studies proportions in themselves, in their scientific value, and the audible music which translates them for sense into movements of sound there is a definite relation. Beauty is mathematics incarnate in objects of sense perception.'[1] For this music is not confined to audible music. It extends to every form of beauty. Architecture, for example, is indeed frozen music.[2] For everywhere the harmony of mathematical proportions is the source and nature of beauty. 'Augustine uses architecture, as he does music, to show that number, as apparent in the simpler proportions that are based on the ''perfect'' ratios, is the source of all aesthetic perfection. And he uses the architect, as he does the musician, to prove that all artistic creation observes the law of numbers.'[3] 'At the root of all beauty, whatever its

[1] B, p. 62.
[2] This metaphor is challenged by the musician.   Cf. page 144. ED.
[3] S, p. 23.

nature, shines forth the immaterial world of numbers governed
by immutable relations. This world . . . does not depend on man
for its existence. It lives in God but is reflected in matter where it
gives birth to the music of the universe. Regarded in time the
world is like a fine piece of oratory or a great poem, regarded in
space it is spread out like an immense tableau embracing innumerable shades of colour. . . . It may be compared to a vast
symphony.'[1] Of such a musical vision Gothic architecture was
born. 'That the laws of music embody a cosmic principle, that
they "embrace everything" and extend to all the arts' was an axiom
frequently expressed during the High Middle Ages.[2] For music
understood in the widest sense embraces, we may say, all things,
God and creatures both incorporeal and corporeal, heavenly and
human, and all forms of knowledge theoretical and practical.
For Thomas of York, 'to understand music is to understand the
order of the universe'. 'When you contemplate', writes William
of Auvergne, 'the beauty and sublimity of the world, you are
aware of the universe as a most beautiful song . . . and creatures
in their wondrous variety composing in mutual harmony a
concert marvellously sweet.'[3] Physical, mental and moral health
also are music, the observance of a proportion: surely a classical,
humanist, and Hellenic view. In aesthetics at least the traditional
contrast between the classical and the mediaeval is unjustified. We
should think rather of the latter as the former integrated with a
deeper vision, a vision however already seen by the Neoplatonists.
The mediaeval did not destroy, it fulfilled the classical.

When Suger built at St. Denis the first Gothic church, he
explained his intentions in a tract in which he 'unfolds before us
a mystical vision of harmony that divine reason has established
throughout the cosmos'.[4] Suger's 'language is emphatically
musical. Like his contemporaries, the Platonists of the School
of Chartres, he conceives the universe as a symphonic composition.'

1 B, p. 65.
2 S, p. 42.
3 B. p. 129.
4 S, pp. xviii–xix.

Eriugena before him had seen it as a vast symphony. Suger's architectural design 'reflected the vision of cosmic harmony and was so to be understood'.[1] His tract on the Consecration 'opens with the intellectual vision of divine harmony that reconciles the discord among conflicting things and infuses in those who behold that concord the desire to establish it also within the moral order. The construction of the church is the subsequent realization of that vision both in the work of art and in those who have undertaken it from a desire to "be glorified by participation in the Eternal Reason".'[2] 'At the beginning of the Treatise the ultimate peace in God is divined through the experience of a cosmic symphony. . . .' Suger, according to the booklet, took care to 'equalize "by means of geometrical and arithmetical rules" the new parts of his church with the old one. . . . His desire to achieve concord and homogeneity among all parts of the church is mentioned repeatedly in the work.'[3]

This mathematical-musical aesthetic—extending as it does from Pythagoras through Plato's final identification of ideas with numbers to Sir James Jean's view of God as a cosmic mathematician, and receiving biblical confirmation from the text of Wisdom, that God created all things by measure, number, and weight—presided over the supreme masterpiece of Gothic architecture, Chartres cathedral. The English Bishop of Chartres, John of Salisbury, sees music as embracing the universe, 'reconciling the dissident and dissonant multitude of beings by the law of proportion. . .'. It is the Boethian notion of a triple music, cosmic, human, and instrumental. 'Since, moreover, musical writers of the Gothic age explicitly compare music and architecture because of the cosmic applicability of the laws of harmony, we may assume that the Platonising views John of Salisbury expresses about music applied equally to architecture.'[4] 'Mediaeval metaphysics conceived beauty as the *splendor veritatis*, as the radiant

1 S, pp. 124, 126.
2 S, p. 131.
3 S, p. 132.
4 S, pp. 191-2.

manifestation of objectively valid laws. The elevation of Chartres Cathedral is the supreme vindication of this philosophy of beauty. The perfection of this great architectural system is the perfection of its proportions, proportions that the master developed not according to his personal intuition but by exact geometrical calculations.'[1] 'In Chartres, proportion is experienced as the harmonious articulation of a comprehensive whole; it determines the ground plan as well as the elevation; and it "chains", by the single ratio of the golden section, the individual parts not only to one another but also to the whole that encompasses them all . . . proportion is perceived as . . . "symphonic" in Chartres.'[2]

No aesthetic surely could be more objective, more intellectual, scientific even, than this aesthetic of mathematical harmony. Suger and his fellows, in particular the architects of Chartres, contemplating the cosmic harmony and seeking to give it an architectural expression, saw its perfection in the heavenly society of angels and saints. Accordingly, as von Simson has shown,[3] the structural harmony of the Gothic church was intended to represent, as it reflected, that celestial order. 'Notre Dame of Chartres, like every mediaeval church, is a symbol of heaven.' The tie of analogy that connects the cathedral of Chartres 'with its celestial prototype is the clarity of order that number and light [see below] establish in both.'[4] This theological application, however, does but confirm an aesthetic philosophical in origin and justification.

'An order of number and light'. For the aesthetic of proportion is in another aspect of mediaeval aesthetic reinforced by the aesthetic of light. Throughout Scripture light is the symbol of God and his favour to man. St. Augustine had celebrated it in the rapturous terms of a well-known passage in his *Confessions* and the philosophy of the Middle Ages is truly a philosophy of

[1] S, p. 211.
[2] S, p. 214.
[3] S, pp. xvii–xix, 135, 154.
[4] S, p. 227. S. denies Sedlmeyr's opinion that 'an illusionistic image of the heavenly city' was intended. In view of the stained glass window I am disposed to think that *in addition* to the structural analogy it was.

enlightenment.[1] 'If all things are proportionate', writes De Bruyne, 'they are also luminous. Proportion confers on them harmony and order, light nobility. . . . Light is universally regarded as a source of beauty. For it constitutes the very substance of colour, as also it renders it visible. . . . Of all bodies, said St. Bonaventure, physical light is the best, the most delightful, the most beautiful. . . . According to Robert Grosseteste, one of the fathers of modern science, "light constitutes the perfection and beauty of corporeal objects, as light is the beauty and adornment of every visible creature".'[2] Light for Grosseteste and his school is an energy imprisoned more or less in inert matter. The more it overcomes the latter and frees itself from this captivity the more luminous the object in which it shines.

Grosseteste attempts a synthesis between the aesthetic of light and the aesthetic of harmony. For 'he derives both colour and proportion from the fundamental energy of light, differentiating itself according to the various degrees of resistance opposed to it by matter, a differentiation effected in accordance with simple mathematical laws represented by lines, surfaces and volumes determined by the primary proportions and manifesting itself according to the same proportions in mixtures of luminosity and opacity by the fundamental colours and their innumerable shades'.[3] In more metaphysical terms Albert the Great and his disciple, Ulric of Strasbourg teach that proportion is the metaphysical matter of beauty, light its form.

Possibly the attempted synthesis of the aesthetics of light and musical proportion is incomplete. May we not regard patterned energy generally as the nature of created being, light and its differentiations as a particular example of it? In any case we can surely agree with the traditional aesthetic that light and harmony

[1] It must be admitted that the thinkers of the eighteenth-century Enlightenment, whatever their blindness in divinity and metaphysics, in their suggestions for the improvement of human society—for example by a more rational and humane penal code—were truer to the logic of the traditional philosophy of light than its orthodox exponents.

[2] B, pp. 71, 73, 75.

[3] B, p. 77.

are fundamental constituents of beauty, physical light and proportion of material beauty, spiritual light and harmony of immaterial.
Gothic architecture, it is certain, was the birth and expression of
both aspects of mediaeval aesthetic. The Gothic church must
manifest the beauty of light as well as the music of harmonious
proportion, and indeed light was itself a harmonizing agent. 'Light',
writes von Simson of Gothic architecture, 'which is ordinarily
concealed by matter, appears as the active principle; and matter is
aesthetically real only in so far as it partakes of, and is defined by,
the luminous quality of light. . . . In this decisive aspect . . . Gothic
may be described as transparent, diaphanous architecture.'[1] This was
the practice and architectural principle a century before Grosseteste formulated his scientific theory. 'In the aesthetics of the
twelfth and thirteenth centuries . . . light is conceived as the
form that all things have in common, . . . that imparts unity to
all . . . like unison in music.'[2] 'Suger', as we have seen, the father
of Gothic, 'was the first. . .to conceive his windows not as wall
openings but as translucent surfaces to be adorned with sacred
paintings. This dual "invention" distinguished Suger's style from
Romanesque and is indeed the basic novelty of Gothic architecture.'[3] We cannot, I think, over-emphasize the fact that this
objective aesthetic musical proportion and light produced an
undeniable concrete result, Gothic architecture. By its fruits
surely we may know an aesthetic doctrine for true or false. Nor
was Gothic its sole product. Baroque, the inspiration of a classical
idiom of the Gothic spirit, the continuation and, in so far as the
increasing tension between the sacred and the secular permitted,
the fulfilment of Gothic, expresses the same aesthetic. Baroque
architecture and the sculpture and painting integral with it are,
as connoisseurs of Baroque such as Spengler, Barthel, Sacheverel
Sitwell recognize, arrested music (petrified, frozen are terms
too chilly, too dead)—arrested music, an arrested dance.
Corresponding to the greater complexity of contemporary

[1] S, p. 4.
[2] S, p. 54.
[3] S, p. 122.

polyphony and ballet the rhythms of Baroque are more elaborate, more subtle, than the rhythms of Gothic, the motion thus arrested more evident. Professor von Simson describes the effects of lighting in the Gothic choir of St. Reini (at Rheims) and the south transept of Soissons cathedral: 'Their style is at once *fiery* and *delicate, dramatic* and *graceful*. . . . The light penetrating through the gallery windows tends to render shafts and colonnettes even slenderer than they actually are, and seems to suffuse the forms of the edifice with a luminosity that dissolves their contours.'[1] In just such terms we might describe a Baroque church, the subtle effects of lighting devised by a Bernini or an Asam. Moreover, the Baroque ideal, to be taken up later by Wagner, of a fusion of all the arts collaborating to one effect was in truth mediaeval. 'The Middle Ages cherished the ideal, as they felt the longing for its attainment, of the perfect work of art which with perfection of form would express by appropriate images and an enchanting music the totality of human wisdom . . . scientific and philosophic, profane and sacred. . . . The perfect work of art combines dancing, poetry and music as had been the case in classical drama. The art of harmony indeed comprises harmonious gestures and choreography, the harmony of voices and instruments, the harmony of poetic "speech". For Roger Bacon "Perfect aesthetic satisfaction is produced by a synthesis of the pleasures of sight and hearing (also of touch) composing conjointly a harmony of harmonies."' And Professor de Bruyne points out that such an aesthetic synthesis is in fact realized by the celebration of High Mass.[2] Have we not then to do with a permanent aesthetic law founded in the nature of things? The Middle Ages, it is true, entertained, as Dante in his *Purgatorio* and *Paradiso* is a sufficient witness, an excessively realistic view of art. But this was due in part to the childlike naïvety which marked the mediaeval mind, in part to the fact that painting must perform the task now performed by photography. In consequence the mediaevals did not consistently draw the aesthetic conclusion

[1] S, pp. 215–16.
[2] B, pp. 225–7.

from the truth of which they were nevertheless well aware, that owing to the intrinsic limitations of corporeal being, the ideal forms, the ideal harmony are imperfectly realized in nature, one object moreover interfering with the perfect development of another, and that it is for the artist to disengage and produce a more perfect pattern. In fact, however, owing to his devotion to musical proportion, the artist did this, and art to the end remained, what it should be, idealist. Nothing indeed could be less realist, less photographic than Grosseteste's view of art. 'The nature of things may be contemplated in the full, clear and noble light of their ideal structure, in which case the artist's exemplar is modelled on the exemplar in God, or one may be content with perceiving things in the shadow of matter, in which case to the blurred and flickering image which is the creative there will correspond a passive image in the memory.' And for St. Bonaventure also the artist's 'model which lives spiritually in the creative imagination is far superior to the image which is but the shadow of the material object in the sensible memory'.[1] At this point however I am sensible of an unsolved tension in mediaeval aesthetics between realism and idealism, but which a consistent application of its principles can solve.

As we have seen, harmony for the mediaeval thinker is unification, the multiplicity, the variety of things unified by the proportion between them which integrates them into a whole, into one integral pattern which as such reflects the ultimate Unity which is the source of all created variety. 'Quantitive proportion is reduced to order as such, that is to say to unity in multiplicity.'[2] For Eriugena 'Beauty in its profound structure cannot be understood in corporeal terms. It is realized most fully by the world of indivisible ideas harmonized in the simplicity of the One God. Beauty [as we have seen] is harmony. Harmony however is the reduction of the many to the one, of inequality to equality, of the diverse to the homogeneous by coadaptation and conformity.'[3]

[1] B, p. 175.
[2] B, p. 80.
[3] B, p. 80.

Meyerson, it is worth recalling in this connexion,[1] has displayed
the ideal of science in precisely the same terms as this aesthetic
ideal, as the progressive discovery of unity in the manifold of
sensible phenomena, an ultimate identity in the multiplicity.
Grosseteste speaks the same language. 'A being is perfectly
beautiful when it is in perfect harmony with itself. . . . For
this reason God being supremely simple is supremely beautiful.
. . . What produces identity produces beauty. . . . Whether we
are concerned with light or harmony, matter or spirit, beauty is
identity.'[2]

These mediaeval thinkers however are perhaps insufficiently
aware—Meyerson certainly does not recognize it—that this ideal
identity whether of perfect beauty or scientific knowledge must
somehow comprehend and identify a multiplicity, cannot be a
bare identity. It must integrate and therefore comprise the
multiplicity it unifies. Catholic intuition sees the many though in
one and as one.

Beauty, as the mediaeval thinker understood it and the
mediaeval artist strove to express it—nor was the aesthetic and
art of Baroque otherwise inspired—is thus the reflection in this
corporeal world of an ideal, an exemplary order of perfect
proportions and intellectual luminosity. It is therefore *splendor
formae*, the 'resplendence of form', of the idea. Nor did the later
Aristotelian emphasis upon the form immanent in the object and
making it what it is—would it not be better to call it the
formative principle?—rather than upon the form as it exists in
the Divine Mind, alter this conception of beauty and therefore of
the artist's work. As St. Albert defined it: 'Beauty is the resplendence of a substantial form in a matter in every part perfectly
proportioned and determined by it. . . . A man is beautiful . . .
to the extent to which his appearance expresses the domination
by the human Ideal of a corporeal matter in every respect
perfectly adapted to it. And a man's spirit is beautiful in so far as

[1] *Du Cheminement de la Pensée.*
[2] B, p. 82.

in its faculties and actions it realizes the perfection of the Form'
(the ideal in God's mind) 'which is the law of its being.'[1]

It is easy but disastrous to exaggerate the difference between
Platonism and Aristotelianism. For both alike, as must be the case
with any spiritual philosophy, the spiritual, the intellectual is
more real than the corporeal, as an object is more real than its
shadow.

Such a metaphysic leads inevitably to symbolism. For the
genuine, the natural, as opposed to the purely conventional,
symbol is precisely the fuller and higher spiritual reality as it
exists in the lower reality of a corporeal object which is its
reflection, is indeed itself on a lower plane of being, possessing a
lesser degree of reality. This in fact is the justification and meaning
of the symbolic metaphorical use of language, the reason that we
can for example speak of digesting information and our dinner,
of a spiritual and a physical ascent of Mount Carmel.

This 'metaphysical aesthetic', writes Professor de Bruyne,
'leads inevitably to symbolism. If beauty is . . . the resplendence
of the Form, the Law, the Essential Nature, the Idea, Unity in the
matter which it illuminates and which it causes to shine out
visibly, the sensible appearance must be the symbol of a simple,
immaterial metaphysical principle.'[2] For Eriugena 'Objects are
beautiful in so far as, direct symbols [by direct I take him to mean
what I call natural as opposed to conventional], they display in
their perishable, changing and imperfect fashion the perfection of
the One, of Mind, of Love. Everything beautiful is a theophany' a
manifestation of God. 'There is no visible object which does not
signify something incorporeal and intelligible.'[3] Though Eriugena
was later condemned for at least an appearance of pantheism, this
metaphysical and symbolic aesthetic, as also his view of the
universe as a symphony, persists throughout later Christian
philosophers. 'For mediaeval man', writes von Simson, the
physical world 'has no reality' as compared with the spiritual

1 B, pp. 84, 85.
2 B, p. 86.
3 B, pp. 87–88.

'except as a symbol' of the latter. He 'conceived the symbolic instinct', I should say rather, symbolic vision, 'as the only reliable guide' to an understanding of the world. 'Maximus the Confessor ̄. . .. defines what he calls "symbolic vision" as the ability to apprehend within the objects of sense perception the invisible reality of the intelligible that lies beyond them.'[1]

For this symbolic aesthetic every object of beauty, indeed every sensible experience, is at once a revelation and a veil of the Divine. It is a revelation inasmuch as it reflects and communicates its Creator, a veil inasmuch as the Divine Light, too brilliant for our mortal vision, is refracted and screened by these imperfect created reflections. Von Simson quotes from Hugh of St. Victor a passage in which he speaks of the veils with which the Divine Light is tempered to our 'blear eyes' and thereby rendered accessible.[2] And it is Hugh who in the infinite variety of material beauties and in every sensible perception and experience finds a ladder of ascent to God.[3] For Hugh 'lovely forms, delicious flavours, sweet melodies, fragrant perfumes, pleasures of touch are related directly to the Eternal Beauty, infinite Sweetness, Spiritual Savour'.[4]

This immanence of the spiritual in matter, of the Divine in creatures, of the Intelligible Order in the sensible whereby the latter is symbolic of the former, was confirmed when for the Neoplatonic Intelligence or Spirit the first necessary creation of the One, Christianity substituted the Divine Word coeternal and consubstantial with the Father, and this divine incarnation in bodily creatures was for the Christian thinker crowned and completed by the personal Incarnation of the Word made flesh.

As von Simson points out, this symbolic aesthetic, idealist-realist, immanental and transcendental, the veiling revelation of the Light Inaccessible, found expression in the Gothic invention of the stained glass window which refracts into colours the light of

[1] S, p. xix.
[2] S, p. 120 note.
[3] B, p. 105.
[4] B, p. 140.

an invisible sun and uses it to display its images of holy persons
and scenes. Its later equivalent will be the Baroque dome with
its painting of the heavenly society upwards to the supreme light.

For this traditional aesthetic, though so insistent upon the
rational, intelligible, even scientific factors of beauty, order,
proportion, mathematics, was far from unaware of its other
aspect, the experience it produces of what cannot be understood,
of the ultimate mystery. As we are conscious of a sunlight too
brilliant to permit direct vision—in fact light itself is invisible
and we see only illuminated objects—so the spirit at the height of
aesthetic experience is conscious of a light whose dazzling
brilliance admits no clear vision, 'dark with excessive bright'.
According to Hugh of St. Victor 'all forms of contemplation may
involve rapture, *mentis excessum*'.[1] 'The aesthetic of Thomas
Gallus', the Victorine commentator on the Pseudo-Dionysius,
'culminates in an ecstasy in which all is united, the good and the
beautiful, love and vision, the pleasure of sight and the joy of
possession, perception of light and the warm sensation of life, the
sovereign delight of combustion in God the aboriginal Fire and
an outpouring of self freely willed. If this ineffable ecstasy is the
highest state to which the contemplation of Beauty may rise, and
if, on the other hand, it begins on a lower level by the perception
of corporeal forms, are we not justified in concluding that
already in the aesthetic pleasure derived from sensible objects an
ecstatic condition may supervene, in which the apex of the spirit
"its inmost and highest" thrills with love and concentration,
while the entire sensibility is flooded with delights both vital
(scents, tastes, caresses) and contemplative (the sight of images,
the hearing of music)?'[2]

For William of Auvergne—a powerful exponent of the musical
aesthetic[3]—'beauty arises from the meeting of a given object
regarded in its well adapted structure with the soul in its

[1] B, p. 102.
[2] B, p. 125.
[3] B, pp. 129, 134.

orientation towards the ideal'.[1] 'Our spontaneous delight in beauty is due to the fact that in a form in itself right,' as it should be, 'we are aware of a reflection of God, the Absolute Ideal. . . .' In our soul, 'which harmonizes with the beautiful form, we are vaguely conscious of an irrepressible aspiration towards God. . . .'[2]

Aesthetic intuition therefore 'should combine a definite "aesthetic" appreciation' (delight in the perception of a definite pattern) 'with an indefinite, confused, indescribable emotion. For within its limits a form canalizes the Infinite. . . . The same suggestion of the Infinite, the Sublime, is given by Grosseteste, himself influenced by St. Augustine. 'God is the perfection beyond all perfection . . . the beauty of all that is beautiful. We become aware of this when in a flash we know what the word beauty means.' Even in the feeling evoked by the precisely delimited pattern of a piece of music, a poem, a picture, we experience, the mediaeval man believed, not only a foretaste but to some extent the actual possession of a Happiness which exceeds our grasp. In the pleasure of hearing music we taste, so Cassiodorus tells us, something of the immutable joy, of the repose which is activity, the activity which never tires. What, asks Alcuin, is easier than to love fair forms however fugitive? But if it is natural to love them despite their limitation, what is easier than to love the eternal Beauty which upholds them? In the beauty that passes, that leaves us or is left by us, why do we not love the Beauty which abides the same everlastingly? The Eternal in the transitory (Alexander of Hales), the Infinite in the finite (Isidore), the Ineffable in what may be defined (Eriugena): of this the Middle Ages more than any other epoch was aware not only as a conclusion of speculative thought but as an aesthetic experience.[3]

'William of Auvergne', writes de Bruyne, 'goes still further. The activity of creatures is a fragmentary expression of the

[1] B, p. 111.
[2] B, p. 113.
[3] B, pp. 156–7.

Divine Action immanent in them. The desire for what is beautiful, the joy of vision, the aspiration towards beauty are manifestations of the primal Energy. . . . God floods us like a stream of good, a torrent of delight gushing out violently to fill countless streams and rivulets. Not only do we enjoy the Divine Beauty in beautiful created forms, our capacity for such enjoyment is itself a manifestation of the Divine Act present and operative in ourselves.'[1]

Nevertheless the artist or simply the aesthete may insufficiently disengage the Transcendent from its immanence, may be content with the aesthetic-mystic experience of the Transcendent as immanent. Such at any rate was the fear entertained by mediaeval teachers.

It was the purpose and task of Christianity—though the later Platonism had prepared its path—to raise man from the Immanent and Natural to the Transcendent and Supernatural. Inevitably, therefore, it must stress detachment from the creatures in which God's Immanence is circumscribed rather than appreciation of them for that Divine Immanence. Greater emphasis will, at least for practical conduct, be placed on the unlikeness of creatures to their Creator than upon their reflection of his Beauty, on their comparative unreality as shadows rather than on the reality which even shadows of Infinite Reality must possess. Hence inevitably there has been a puritan suspicion of natural and particularly of artistic beauty, even at times an hostility to it. Witness St. Augustine's fear of the attraction he felt for physical light, or his scruple about the delight he felt in ecclesiastical chant. After all, might it not be simple pleasure of the ear, not an ascent of the spirit to God. Hence also the *volte face* in valuation, though not in ontology, made by Hugh of St. Victor when, despite his lyrical appreciation of all forms of sensible beauty as reflections of God, he makes the disconcerting statement that from the standpoint of religion we should prefer to contemplate ugly rather than beautiful objects. For whereas a thing of beauty tempts us to repose in it, forgetting its limitations, an ugly

[1] B, p. 113.

object by the repulsion it excites thrusts us above itself.[1] This, it is true, is an altogether exceptional dictum. But the puritanism it expresses has been persistent in Catholic thought and feeling, thwarting in many ways its comprehensive and balanced humanism. Though the aesthetic value and significance of the dance as harmonious and patterned motion follows from a Catholic aesthetic of harmony and proportion—and to watch a great dancer may be and often is an occasion of the aesthetical-mystical experience of which, as we have seen, Catholic philosophers have spoken so eloquently—the Curé d'Ars was by no means the only Catholic teacher to see in dancing only a form of sexual licence. And the theatre has fared little better. Yves de Paris, the seventeenth-century Capuchin studied by Bremond, repeats Hugh of St. Victor's comprehensive aesthetic but, unlike his predecessor, he does not turn back upon it in his practical advice. We may well learn from him.

This kinship in aesthetic philosophy over six centuries between Hugh of St. Victor and Yves de Paris supports my conviction that, in the field of aesthetics at least, the contrast too generally supposed between the classical and the mediaeval, the Renaissance and Baroque, does not in fact exist. The continuity between classical and mediaeval aesthetic is, as I have already pointed out, evident. As von Simson points out[2] the aesthetic of the Renaissance architect Philibert Delorme continues, if it does not exaggerate, a mediaeval naïvety. For he regards the biblical measurements of Noah's ark, the Tabernacle, and Solomon's Temple, as proportions divinely revealed for the architect's guidance. Since Baroque art, as we have seen, expresses the same aesthetic principles as mediaeval, it is a reasonable conclusion that its aesthetic philosophy was substantially the same. And in fact the aesthetic which can be disengaged from the writings of the puritan Platonists John Smith and Peter Sterry agrees with the aesthetic of the Platonists of Chartres. Professor de Bruyne's investigations should be carried forward by a study

[1] B, p. 159.
[2] S, pp. 227 f.

of the later Schoolmen, such philosophers as Cajetan and Suarez, of Renaissance and Baroque writers on art or literature. The result, I am convinced, would be to establish a continuous aesthetic tradition from the classical philosophers to the disintegration of the European cultural tradition.

The philosophy of beauty determines the philosophy of art. I have therefore been led inevitably when considering the traditional understanding of beauty to speak of its view of art. I only need add, I think, that, although the Middle Ages were not unaware of the distinction between the crafts and what we term the fine arts, emphasis was laid on the technical aspect of art, on its craftsmanship, and the arts were thus integrated solidly and healthily with the crafts happily uncontaminated by mechanism. They had no place—nor had Baroque—for an art intelligible only to an élite of initiates. Their art was an art of high aesthetic worth yet with wide popular appeal, such art as is exemplified by the Gothic cathedral, the Baroque village church, the drama of Shakespeare. It was, however, it could not have been otherwise, the product of a satisfactory aesthetic—objective, intellectual, even to a large extent scientific—but at the same time exceeding intelligibility and comprehensible pattern in its contact with man's central spirit, its awareness of Divine transcendence. It was the aesthetic of the traditional Catholic schools, to which we should be well advised to return.

20. The Retreat from Meaning

JOHN COULSON

Before coming to Downside, where he now teaches, Mr. John Coulson was for ten years in charge of centres for education and the arts at Salisbury and Bristol. His paper, which discusses the effect of the philosophical tradition initiated by Descartes on aesthetic theory, is integrated with a number of other papers, but complements particularly closely that of Mr. Cameron on language.

OUR world forces us to think clearly and logically, or it does not permit us to survive. Members of a scientific and industrial civilization, children of the managerial revolution, however much we may envy the flamboyant gesture, the pure 'play' of the expressionists, the neo-Buddhist's immersion in non-being, we must do so in our spare time as Sunday painters or Sunday mystics: bluntly, we dare not risk such meaningless joys, because our survival depends upon our being able to think 'meaningfully' —an ugly but expressive word—and that implies being able to think conceptually. Conditioned as we are, it seems odd, therefore, that when we come to talk about the arts, we should appear to take up two quite contradictory attitudes, but I want to suggest that each must be understood as a reaction from the other and that we are really oscillating between thesis and antithesis: at one moment artists are inferior or even pseudo-thinkers, and at the next they are semi-divine, the high priests of the pre-conceptual. The thesis is that the arts merely adorn or even obscure what could be more essentially expressed in some other way, the antithesis is that the arts are an autonomous, extra-logical activity, a non-conceptual revelation which cannot be related to other aspects of experience even approximately. Either the arts mean very little, or they have meaning only in a special, Pickwickian sense.

The first point of view, the thesis, is much harder to answer than it seems, and although it is as old as Plato (the poet, if you remember, was no more than an imitator of imitations), it is with Descartes that the charge receives its more characteristic definition.

Descartes' celebrated method of doubt led him to become particularly suspicious of any information which purported to come to us by means of the senses. He supposes in his first meditation 'that some malignant demon . . . has employed all his artifice to deceive me; I will suppose that the sky, the air, the earth, colours, figures, sounds and all external things, are nothing better than the illusions of dreams, by means of which this being has laid snares for my credulity'. He was driven by this method to conceive one criterion only of certain knowledge, viz. 'that all things which we very clearly and distinctly conceive are true'. This assumption is forcibly expressed by Bacon, Sprat, Hobbes, and many other writers who, with Descartes, formed the minds of the seventeenth and eighteenth centuries.

Bacon's main purpose was, by his criticism of what he thought to be the abuses of language, to produce a language fit for the new science, because it would be a more accurate means of describing reality. He inveighed in *The Advancement of Learning* against knowledge which is 'steeped and infused in the humours of the affections', and he evolved a new aesthetic criterion which can be particularly clearly seen in his attitude to analogies, imagery, and illustrative figures. In more representative Elizabethan writers, such as Hooker or Donne, there is what one might call a feeling for both sides of the analogy, so that the metaphor sometimes has too vigorous a life of its own to be strictly accurate or useful as scientific description. A typical example is Donne's 'Every sin casteth another shovel of brimstone upon him in Hell.' For Bacon the image is necessary only to make clear to the layman something which is already abundantly clear to the

author, because such a use of language is merely a game, and if it
is taken seriously, if we concentrate too much upon the form of
our statement, its images, rhythms, and other deceitful adorn-
ments, then we shall be producing a 'contract of error'. To avoid
such a 'contract', Bacon decides to adopt his now celebrated
aphoristic style, putting forward what he has to say in a short
almost abrupt way, for, by this means, he is 'representing a
knowledge broken, which invites men to inquire further'.
Aphoristic writing is not likely to be betrayed into the flowing
period, or the seductive image, and it is a prose purged of
irrelevant associations so that words can be made to stand clearly
and without equivocation for the realities they point to. The
suggestive powers of words arouse his deepest suspicions, for 'as
the tartar's bow [they] do shoot back upon the understanding of
the wisest'.

These strictures upon everyday language begin to take on an
ironically contemporary ring when, in 1604, the year in which
Shakespeare wrote *Othello* and two years before *Lear*, Bacon
complains in *Novum Organum* of words which 'stand in the way'
and 'resist change'. Poetry 'cometh of the lust of the earth', since,
because it is not 'tied to the laws of matter, it may at pleasure join
that which nature hath severed and sever that which nature hath
joined, and so make unlawful matches and divorces of things'. This
deep suspicion of poetry, of words detached from things, of the
emotions, and of all that obscures the really real world underlying appearance, the world of clear and distinct ideas, is a force
which grows in power and influence during the century. It does
not merely stem from Descartes, it is a great river fed by many
tributaries—Seneca, Bacon, Montaigne—but of these Descartes
is perhaps the greatest, and it is no wonder that Rousseau
accused him of having cut poetry's throat.

For a time, writers were, so to speak, bi-lingual; accustomed
as they were to doing much of their thinking by images and to
developing their thoughts by extended analogies, they had to
translate this native and immediate awareness into the requirements of the new plain prose. They were exhorted to do this by

Thomas Sprat, the historian of the Royal Society, who was famous for his castigation of poetry and ornate writing: 'This vicious abundance of phrase, this trick of metaphors, this volubility of thought' must be eliminated in favour of 'a mathematical [sic] plainness'. We must prefer the language of artisans and merchants to that of wits and scholars and must banish eloquence 'as a thing fatal to peace and good manners'. It is, once again, interesting to note when this was being said. It was in 1667, barely thirty years after the first collected edition of Donne's poetry had appeared and at the time when Dryden was establishing his reputation as a dramatist.

An interesting and amusing example of the two languages is given by Joseph Glanvill—known to us as the author of *The Vanity of Dogmatising*, from which Arnold took the story of the Scholar Gypsy. This book was first published in 1661 and was then recast by its author in the scientific style, being republished under a different title in 1676. The changes made by Glanvill are highly significant. It is clear that he goes to immense pains to cut out all adjectives which make a direct appeal to feeling. ('The frigid air' becomes simply 'air', and 'pretty images' become 'images'.) Any descriptions which betray imagination or enthusiasm are ruthlessly pruned ('loosely wandering up and down in the water' in the revised edition has been substituted for 'playing up and down within their liquid prison', while 'A truth . . . that to go about industriously to prove it, were to light a candle to seek the sun' of the first edition becomes in the second 'that I need not stay to prove it'). Another interesting change is towards the standardizing of words in the interest of restricting oneself to a vocabulary which is limited, accurate, and able to express what can be measured and classified, ('midnight compositions' become 'dreams', and 'praeter-lapsed ages' become 'past ages').

This suspicion of the emotions and of language which arouses deep feeling together with a preference for what can be clearly and dispassionately conceived are at the root of all Augustan thinking about the Fine Arts: the distaste for enthusiasm, the desire to rewrite Shakespeare, the judgment of Donne as uncouth, and of Chaucer as needing to be 'improved', the use of the term 'Gothick' as a synonym for 'farouche'. And faced by such a challenge—that art provides merely the trimmings and that prose, because it is best able to express thought, is a superior instrument to poetry—the artist is frequently driven to a series of improvisations. He tries to do what science so far has not achieved, but it does not last: the Pre-Raphaelites are put out of business by the colour photographer. You cannot put science in its place like that, because the field of scientific research is perpetually widening, and many subjects may now be profitably studied which the nineteenth century had confidently reserved to the non-scientist.

Are we then to take Peacock's line and hold that poetry belongs to the early pre-scientific stage of man and that if the artist will not be useful he must, as Plato insisted, be banished? And if we turn from what might be called the historical case against the Arts to what the modern Empiricists have to say, then the case seems bleaker still.

Bertrand Russell and Rudolf Carnap, beginning on orthodox Cartesian lines, decided to go beneath what they considered to be the deceptions of everyday language ('the idols of the market place', as Bacon had called them) to the indivisible logical particles or atoms which, they believed, could be identified, isolated, and then employed in the construction of a higher and more accurate language. This language could not be formulated in words but only in symbols. Some philosophers, particularly in America, still undertake this work, and if you are interested you can always read Carnap's *The Logical Syntax of Language*, or the shorter account given by Captain Lemuel Gulliver in that chapter in his travels dealing with the Academy of Projectors.

A much more important line was worked out by Wittgenstein in the *Tractatus Logico-Philosophicus*. He came to believe that the old way of regarding logic as a technique or method which was applied to certain constants or terms in a proposition was quite mistaken. A thought was not a series of coaches coupled together by logic, something made out of detachable pieces, but a functional unity from which the logical form could not be separated any more than the visual field can be separated from what we see. Wittgenstein was led to assert that 'logic is not a theory but a reflection of the world', that it precedes experience, being before the What but not before the How. Logic was not something which could be put on one side, as a discarded tool, but it was part of our way of seeing reality, a built-in component of our perceptive apparatus. The logical form set a limit to what language could do, and the limits set by language were, Wittgenstein thought, limits set to experience: 'the limits of my language mean the limits of my world'.

This position carries the following implications: that what cannot be expressed in terms of the propositions of logic, has no meaning, because meaning and logic are aspects of the same fact, that although there may be an aspect of experience (Wittgenstein called it 'the mystical', but he also meant ethical and aesthetic values) which cannot be expressed in this way, we must be silent about it, because we can say nothing to which any meaning can be strictly attached, and if we try we shall probably talk nonsense. Such a view rejects, a priori, Coleridge's classical counter-stroke to the Cartesian attack upon poetry. For him, the imagination was an insight parallel to and superior to that of the intellect, melting, diffusing, dissipating the ordinary insights in order to recreate a reality which corresponded more closely to the fundamental aspects and values of our experience. But to claim to diffuse and to dissipate our everyday perception would be to claim to be outside it—which, a priori, we cannot be; and, in any case, we do not create what is intelligible, it is created for us. The imaginative power as described by Coleridge would be to Wittgenstein a prime example of the 'meaningless'.

Wittgenstein closes his Tractatus with a warning which is so ineffably Teutonic that I think it is best given in its original German: Wovon man nicht sprechen kann, darüber muss man schweigen, a remark which has been wittily paraphrased as 'What we can't say we can't say, and we can't whistle it either.' I think the paraphrase gives us a clue to the limitation of this position. It used to be assumed that whistling was not without significance, that is if it took the rather more sophisticated form of a Beethoven quartet or a Mozart symphony, and that the composer expressed himself in music rather than, say, in the conceptual forms of a logician, because it was only in his chosen medium that what he had to say could be said. What was not questioned was that quite a number of things could be whistled that could not be spoken, but that in judging a work of art—in whatever medium—some attempt had to be made to discover what might be a rough and ready conceptual equivalent to the artist's intention; we had, in other words, to discuss his intentions.

This view is now challenged, and when one realizes some of the weird excesses to which its unquestioned acceptance led, one is not sorry. Essays on 'Whither is Browning tending?', books on the religion of Shakespeare's heroines, and some of the pro-gramme notes of the late Rosa Newmarch on the Beethoven symphonies, were among the most amusing. Nowadays both artist and critics seem agreed to avoid all discussion of content and intention in case it should be thought that a work of art can be evaluated in terms of its 'meaning'. A new work on aesthetics entitled *Aesthetics and Language* published in 1954, edited by William Elton and containing contributions by leading British empiricists, confirms my point; and a great deal of the poetry, music, and writing of the past twenty-five years can be explained in terms of such a reaction: surrealism, the poetry of E. E. Cummings, or even some of Dylan Thomas, the glorification of the 'primitive' in children's art.

A certain type of artist tends to concentrate on the purely formal qualities of his work to the exclusion of all else. If he is told that his latest canvas has its point of departure on Battersea Bridge on a rainy night, he will either resist the suggestion with vehemence, or feel that his painting is to that extent defective and lacking in the true aesthetic value. But, as Wyndham Lewis has pointed out in his retractation of these views, if the artist is always to be driven in upon himself for his inspiration, the range of his experience will become narrower and narrower. If he refuses to deal with what other people can understand, then all sorts of bastard art-forms will emerge that have precisely this purpose: the novel does the job that poetry fails to do, the cinema takes over from the painter, the manifesto writer from the philosopher of aesthetics—the outsider from the insider. The job still gets done under different names; and, of course, the retreat from the intelligible varies in depth with the economic requirements of each art-form. Ink and paper are cheap, so anyone can write out a stream of consciousness in any incoherent shape he fancies. Paint and canvas, at least for the Sunday painter, are well within the power of limited means to provide, so if you must produce paintings which look as though they are studies of yellow fish in blue frying-pans, there is no one to stop you, even if you insist that your pictures are not studies of fish and frying-pans, although visitors to your studios always trip over the pan and complain of the smell of decaying fish.

The modern movements in music and architecture have been less extreme, because these arts cannot exist in a subjectivist vacuum but must make some concessions to their backers in the shape of tunes, efficient drains, and walls that keep out the damp. Art must have some contact with intelligibility, and this is something that every schoolboy knows but ceases to be sure of when he becomes an undergraduate. The values which a work of art possesses are not autonomous and cannot be evaluated merely in terms of its own form, or of the form or structure of the responses it creates. When I compare two novels on a similar theme, and say that one has a better shape, a greater economy of form than the other, I mean that in so far as I have grasped the similarity in intention of the respective writers, I believe that one writer has expressed his intention more effectively, that he has mastered the complexity of his material more convincingly than the other writer. I cannot really avoid a discussion of meaning.

But where I agree with the empiricists is that I cannot discuss the meaning of a work of art easily or in the same way as I discuss the meaning of a proposition. Is this merely because of the views which stem from Descartes, Bacon, and Hobbes that the Fine Arts are merely embellishments to Truth suitable for the younger and weaker intellects but merely distractions which the best minds soon learn to throw over? Can the real meaning of a Hamlet soliloquy be written on a postcard? The trouble is that the meaning of *Hamlet* seems a different one to different people, even to the same people at each successive performance; and what is worse is that we feel not only that it is right that this should be so, but that part of the play's quality is to be ascribed to that very fact.

It is a truism of criticism to say that the meaning of a work can never be exhausted and therefore comprised in any number of conceptual statements. These will always remain approximations. In the past, artists and critics had believed that an exhaustive analysis and explanation of a particular art-form was not only possible but could supply the means of a successful revival of that form. The nineteenth-century Gothic revival is the most recent example, and one has only to compare the best of the Gothic Revival churches with Salisbury or Wells to see that something is missing, and that what it is will never submit to the limitations of a conceptual formulation. Revivers of culture are so very like those Lord Mayors who, faced with the social trials of their office, ruefully discover that it takes three generations to make a gentleman; and it is the possession of this awareness which stops the modern artist of integrity from building other than very simple and unambitious buildings, whilst it is the lack of it which allows his less high-principled colleague to produce what he likes to call 'buildings of refinement in the Georgian manner'. The values that each in his way admires and strives to isolate in order to emulate are too firmly embodied in the context of their culture to be separated in this way; we can only achieve a steriliz-ing eclecticism, never a living embodiment. And yet the Georgians were apparently able to produce a successful revival of Greek and Roman forms in building, dress, and literature—but this is to anticipate.

Apart from confirming by illustration the existence of these conflicting ways of talking about the arts, I hope I may have been able to establish the following points: that although there may be more to the arts than can be expressed in conceptual terms, directly the arts cease to be intelligible they evaporate; that it is not so easy to evade this difficulty by insisting that the arts mean more than they say, because it is difficult to see *how* we can mean more than we say. Here it would be appropriate to protest against those philosophers who invent a special language for describing the arts and a special theory of knowledge to go with it, who talk of the pre-conceptual, and, in the teeth of Descartes, Bacon, and Wittgenstein, try to justify the function of the arts in terms of counter-assertions about the nature of reality.

So far I have been concerned with the attitude of outsiders— critics, scientists and philosophers—to the arts, and when one turns to the attitudes of the practitioners themselves one notices a very significant addition to our vocabulary. Artists stress the emotions, and this is, of course, a serious complication for philosophers to whom the emotions are those perpetual poor relations whom they would like to cut but never can; and yet we cannot conceive a work of art from which emotion is absent. To play down the emotional aspect of our experience always leads to explosive reactions of which the Romantics, D. H. Lawrence, and Freud have been some of the more interesting; but to speak of emotion is to raise hundreds of problems. I propose to restrict my analysis, therefore, to one art—poetry—and to quote Wordsworth's account in the Preface to the second edition of the *Lyrical Ballads* (1800) in which he says: 'Poetry is the spontaneous overflow of powerful feelings: it takes its origin from emotion recollected in tranquillity: the emotion is contemplated, till, by a species of reaction, the tranquillity gradually disappears and an emotion, kindred to that which was before the subject of contemplation, is gradually produced, and does itself actually exist in the mind.'

Wordsworth is not writing as an interested party in a metaphysical dispute, but with incontestable authority: poetry is, after all, what a poet does. In Book XII of *The Prelude*, he tells us

that these moments in which powerful emotion is aroused are
related to certain key expressions or 'spots of time', so that it
might be reasonable to suggest that the emotion is to be regarded
adjectivally, or, in the language of the psychologists, as a strong
affective tone to an important experience. Perhaps also there is
some relationship between the value of the experience and the
strength of the emotions, as though the emotions were acting
as indicators, pointing to particular thoughts and sensations,
perhaps even guaranteeing or authenticating such sensations by
means of the strength of emotions aroused:

> And I have felt
> A presence that disturbs me with the joy
> Of elevated thoughts; a sense sublime
> Of something far more deeply interfused,
> Whose dwelling is the light of setting suns,
> And the round ocean and the living air,
> And the blue sky, and in the mind of man.

Wordsworth also implies that the artist is conscious of a
distinction between his experience and his expression of it, in
that the original experience is not the same as the experience
which the artist has as he writes, it is something re-created. The
quality of consciousness which the artist possesses during the
second stage is crucial; if it is defective in any way, then what he
produces will reflect these defects. Perhaps there is a clue here as
to what constitutes the relative degrees of success and failure in
a work of art to realize what, in an obscure and imperfect way,
we come to grasp as the author's intention. 'Emotion recollected
in tranquillity' is somehow less private than the original experience because it is accompanied by the search for a form or
structure which alone can ensure a successful re-enactment:
what T. S. Eliot calls 'a raid upon the inarticulate' is about to
begin. The struggle that the poet has is not merely with words
but with an order of words, because he is attempting to relive an
experience so important that even to remember it causes him
excitement, and the order in which he expresses himself will be

as important and probably more important than the individual meanings of each individual word.

But as the emotion is only the signal and the starting point, so the right order of his words—the form of his work—is only intermediary to his intention, which is, as it were, to push the words beyond themselves so that we respond not to them individually but to the whole which they convey, as we respond to a house and not to the bricks or stones that compose it:

> Only by the form, the pattern,
> Can words or music reach
> The stillness, as a Chinese jar still
> Moves perpetually in its stillness.[1]

And this account holds good whether the poem is about the highly debatable subject matter of the *Four Quartets* or 'that sweet disorder in her dress' which fixes for ever a moment in carnal love.

That is why we cannot account for a work of art in terms of the emotion it arouses or of its skill in the employment of technique. These are undoubtedly characteristics of success, but the life which a masterpiece achieves is gained only on the farther side of such excitement and skill when it has, as it were, passed over into the silence before the storm of applause. We instinctively value tragedy above pathos and catharsis above tears, as though the emotions aroused can only be acceptable if they are the signals of an essentially cognitive awareness which has to be gained intuitively rather than by logical inference, and is immediate and certain in its effects rather than discursive and probable. Such awareness has been variously described as the moment of truth, of consciousness, of vision—'the still centre in the turning world'—but however it may be characterized we know that we are not so much concerned to ask 'What does it mean?' as 'Is it true?'

What Descartes and his followers could not see is that there are more significant aspects to an experience than that which is

---

[1] T. S. Eliot: *Burnt Norton*.

the clearest and most distinct. If we judge a work of art solely in terms of its meaning, of course we shall find it frequently defective and always unnecessarily foggy; conversely, if we fail to base our medical science upon clear and distinct ideas, patients will die like flies in a welter of necromancy, astrology, and pretences to divine inspiration. An artist is, of course, saying something and, therefore, making a statement in reference to thoughts and facts, but this is incidental to his purpose, which is to recreate the relationship and growth of a complex of thoughts and facts, showing not merely their logical relationship but all the other relationships which are sometimes hidden away under the title 'emotional'. In this sense there is an emotional as well as a logical precision, and there is a biological as well as a methodological development of ideas. It was Cook Wilson who pointed out that why philosophers seemed never to be very much concerned to alter their ideas after the arguments advanced in their recommendation had been confuted, was that they never develop their main ideas by the same means as they choose to defend them.

But what of the claim put forward by Wittgenstein that all we can and do in fact see in reality are those constants between which logical relations are possible, because logic precedes experience? How can we claim to go outside the perceptual field? First of all, I want to suggest that we do not need to deny that logic precedes experience in order to find a fundamental place for the emotions, which neither precede nor displace logic; what they do is to accompany it, as anyone who reads the controversies of logicians will know. The mistake is to ignore emotion by pretending that it does not exist or rightly belong when we are thinking. The Schoolmen were not mistaken when they spoke of more than one kind of thinking, of *intellectus* as well as *ratio*, which suggests that the mistake which is made is to become possessed of too naïve a notion of what thinking really is. If we reflect on the way in which we really do our thinking we find that unless we are cranks or believers in the validity of mediaeval disputations, we investigate our concepts, check that they are properly related in a logical way both to one another and to their situation, but that we then go on to investigate the emotional structure in which these concepts are embodied in order to assess the quality of awareness from which they spring. Two different speeches could be written (and frequently are written by politicians turned journalist) urging a course of action. They use the same concepts and the same logic, but since each bears a distinct emotional charge, each will have quite a different effect upon the minds and intentions of an audience. One speech may produce conviction, another merely notions which are soon forgotten, and to explain this distinction in terms of a 'surrender to the emotions' is to know very little about the purely adjectival status of the emotions. Hopkins puts this distinction rather well when he contrasts 'an equation in theology, the dull algebra of the Schoolmen' with 'knowledge that leaves their minds swinging; poised but on the quiver . . . the ecstasy of interest'.[1]

The analysis of our experience made by Descartes and Wittgenstein is not false; it is merely incomplete. There is more to the perceptual field than what we see clearly and distinctly in front of our eyes, because there is a kind of experience that comes, as it were, obliquely and, indeed, will not come if we seek it. We can see it out of the corner of our eyes, it was there but we did not notice it until we remembered the event some weeks later. It is what Hardy calls the 'self unseeing':

> Childlike, I danced in a dream:
> Blessings emblazoned that day;
> Everything glowed with a gleam;
> Yet we were looking away!

Eliot refers to it in the *Dry Salvages* as 'the unattended moment':

> the moment in and out of time,
> The distraction fit, lost in a shaft of sunlight,
> The wild thyme unseen, or the winter lightning,
> Or the waterfall, or music heard so deeply
> That it is not heard at all, but you are the music
> While the music lasts.

[1] Gerard Manley Hopkins: *Letters*, Vol. I, pp. 187–9.

or it may be the sudden flash of irony with which Edward
Thomas ends a poem:

> Some day I shall think this a happy day.

All the great philosophers, including Wittgenstein himself, have
acknowledged this special kind of awareness. In the *Tractatus* he
refers to the 'mystical' and to the peculiar status of aesthetic and
moral judgments; and it is only his most fanatical devotees who
have wished to deny what they experienced so long ago and so
very feebly. In his later work, the *Philosophical Investigations*,
Wittgenstein goes a little farther by making the distinction
between the dead language of the puzzle-solving type of analyst
which is, as he puts it, like 'an engine idling', and language in its
natural condition: alive and purposeful. Speaking of those aspects
of our experience which are hard to define, he refers to the
difficulty of pinning down an aspect, because directly it is pinned
down it seems to vanish or to change into something else: 'It is as
if we had altered the adjustment of a microscope.' This is an
excellent description of our response, say, to a Shakespearean
tragedy: we are continually having to change focus; at all times
the perceptual field is much less simple that we had supposed.
What Wittgenstein still believed was the impossibility of tran-
scending the world out of which language had been constructed,
the world of everyday sensory experience. But in poetry, or at
least some poetry, this is precisely what the artist achieves: his
words go beyond themselves in the process:

> Words strain,
> Crack and sometimes break, under the burden,
> Under the tension, slip, slide, perish,
> Decay with imprecision, will not stay in place,
> Will not stay still.[1]

All the greatest artists have made this attempt, usually at the
end of their lives, and we think of the late Beethoven quartets,
the later Turner, the Shakespearean 'romances', and the later

---

[1] T. S. Eliot: *Burnt Norton.*

Rembrandt. Words, sounds, and colours do indeed belong to the world of sensory perception, to the directly perceived sensory field; but they can be and have been made to convey this other awareness by means of approximations, analogies, 'hovering between images', and all the other devices so vehemently denounced by Bacon, Hobbes, and Sprat. There is a rational discourse which can be undertaken very effectively in these terms, and anyone familiar with having to teach the great Shakespearean tragedies will know that they can only be effectively commented upon in such terms. How fundamental are the images of loss and insubstantiality in *Antony and Cleopatra* and of blood and grace in *The Winter's Tale*.

The mistaken views about the nature of art and of poetry in particular proposed during the seventeenth and eighteenth centuries by Bacon, Sprat, Hobbes and their followers can be attributed to their thinking that the sole question to ask of a work of art was 'What does it mean?' This is an important question, but not one which can be asked of a poem or picture as a whole, and to describe our total response a word with a wider connotation is needed, such as 'significance'. This distinction between meaning and significance is one which is used increasingly by modern philosophers in other fields. Meaning is certainly part of the whole which is the work of art and a specially privileged part, because without meaning a work of art would be without significance, but as meaning is implicit in the initial experience of the artist, so it is to be found implicit in our experience of the whole: its position of privilege applies not merely to the artist's awareness but to the critic's method of evaluating his response.

The mistake which has vitiated more aesthetic theory than any other has been to regard the artist as a thinker and the work of art as a series of thoughts, because the artist does more than think: he makes, and what he makes is public property because it is made with public materials—the King's English (as distinct from philosopher's English), the building trade's bricks, the members of the musicians' union. An artist can only create what he is allowed to create, and only if these public media are conducive to successful expression can what he makes be said to 'live'. Thus the Gothic revival was defeated by the Victorian building tradition—or the lack of it—and the Georgian neo-classical revival succeeded because the public conditions existed for which the forms of Greek and Roman art were organically appropriate.

Since the artist is a discoverer, we are often able to draw his attention to an aspect of his work he did not know was there, because what he makes is so much wider than what, in a strictly conceptual sense, he intended to create. Discovery includes intention and making includes meaning, in the same way as the mind is included in the person and the emotions are part of an experience. Conversely, meaning cannot be regarded as an impurity in an otherwise pure work of art, nor can it be regarded as one of a number of equally valuable components in our total response, because although we are more concerned with finding out what a work of art signifies than what it means, with how a meaning has been embodied than with what the meaning is when it is divorced from its embodiment, nevertheless, nothing can exist which is not intelligible without being nonsense, even though its content of intelligibility may be minimal. The negative test is crucial: a work of art ceases to be such when it is meaningless, and as nonsense can never make poetry, so the meaningless sounds of the Aeolian harp jingling in the wind can never become music.

21. The Desolation of Aesthetics

FR. VINCENT TURNER, S.J.

Fr. Vincent Turner, S.J., of Campion Hall, Oxford, has written and lectured for a number of years on art. His paper ranges over the field of aesthetic theories which have dominated thought about the arts in Europe for the last hundred and fifty years. Along with Mr. Coulson's paper it provides a sketch of the background, enough in itself for many books, of any philosophical consideration of the arts today. Fr. Vincent is not however a merely detached observer, any more than is Mr. Coulson. His paper is not only a work of introduction, it is also a work of demolition—and although he has shortened it this double task makes it long.

WHEN in the first instance I was honoured by an invitation to contribute to this symposium it was suggested that I do a paper on the failure of scholastic aesthetics. To this I demurred. By aesthetics was meant a philosophy of art, and it seems to me that scholasticism of the vintage years has no general aesthetic theory, no theory of art, either to be successful with or to fail with. It also seems to me that this is something very much to the credit and good sense of the scholastics. But what of neo-scholasticism? It is impossible not to be impressed with the ingenuity with which is elicited out of St. Thomas what he would have said in answer to questions of a type that never crossed his mind; in a way, what he was already saying without knowing it; and the germs and seeds of aesthetics, philosophy of art as well as philosophy of beauty, have also been extracted from him and cultivated in many a hot-house and many a cold-frame. Beyond doubt, in neo-scholastic learned journals and in books, there has been plenty of high aesthetic theory.

There was about these theories a curious and at first sight elusive feature. The more closely one scrutinized their ghostly outlines the more nearly they merged with the similarly ghostly outlines of a general body of metaphysics of art that happened to be contemporary with them, large parts of which, moreover, have passed into the vocabulary and tools and presuppositions of a considerable number of writers who, without being in the least professional philosophers, none the less write aesthetics in the grand style (I am thinking here of, for example, the writings of Sir Herbert Read); or at any rate large parts of this general body of aesthetics chimed with current ways of talking about the arts. The process still goes on; with regard to the neo-scholastics M. Maritain's Mellon lectures of 1952, published as *Creative Intuition in Art and Poetry*, are a conspicuous and distinguished example of what I have in mind.

If neo-scholastic aesthetics, then, merges into a general body of aesthetics, it seems worthwhile to make some attempt to suggest, however briefly, what are the outlines of this general body of aesthetics that I have spoken of. It might turn out possible to hazard some guesses about why it is that its ghostly outlines seem to reappear in so many writers, and indeed in the manifestos and declarations of artists, who do not read professional philosophy. Is it that this aesthetics enjoys a pervasive and directive intellectual influence, and gets into the air, so that on account of it men think about the arts what otherwise they would never have thought? Or is it that in some queer way this aesthetics is reflecting and bringing into an intellectual self-consciousness what people are feeling and vaguely thinking anyhow? Or is there a two-way traffic more complicated still?

I shall try, then, to suggest what are these ghostly outlines. Far be it from me to attempt to disentangle them. I am only too acutely aware that this is holy ground, picketed with signs that warn trespassers to keep out, a field where criticism is construed as failure in comprehension.

For if a man embarks on any conscientious re-reading as a preliminary to any such paper as this, there is strongly borne in on him a feature about aesthetics, philosophy of art, that is most remarkable but not often remarked. Epic, lyric, tragedy, comedy, music, painting, relief, sculpture, architecture: these are activities whose history is several thousand years old. But aesthetics as we have come to use the word, that is to say systematic philosophy of art, is a quite modern subject. Reflection on literature and music and sculpture and painting is at least as old as Plato, as is reflection on beauty. Perhaps there have been few centuries in which men have not thought about these things, or some of them, and indeed had theories about them. To come nearer to our own time, the eighteenth century is full of these puzzlings and abounds in theories. But all of them are different in kind from what we now call aesthetics. For one thing the question is rather 'What is beauty?' or 'What do the arts do to the soul?' than 'What is art?' For another thing, although they are usually philosophical and naturally, therefore, carry the imprint of their author's philosophy in other respects, as for instance his theory of knowledge, they are none the less comparatively fragmentary and unsystematic. There is no mapping of the universe of human activities; no allocation of appropriate places to the human spirit's self-expression in religion, art, morals, craft, and so forth; no attempt made to localize the genesis of these activities in the spirit of man. In fact aesthetics as we now know it is German in origin and post-Kantian in date.[1] It grows up with metaphysical Idealism.[2] But it is a slow developer. Even in Hegel

[1] Kant's *Critique of Judgement* was published in 1790.

[2] Monistic idealism would perhaps be a less misleading description. But all labels are deceptive. There is a sense in which not only Bishop Berkeley but also David Hume might be called a 'subjective idealist', and the theory that we see not things but representations 'of' things, our impressions or ideas, and that things are families of sense data, is a jumping-off ground not only for philosophical idealism—'reality is experience', in the dictum of F. H. Bradley and Bernard Bosanquet—but also for the systematic British empiricism current in the present century. It is quite impossible to give a brief account of Idealism. On its epistemological side perhaps as good a clue as any is furnished by Croce's own restatement in *Problemi di Estetica* (1910) of Kant's 'Copernican revolution in philosophy': 'If knowing is not making or re-making what

18

it is astonishingly modest—I had almost said astonishingly empirical; perhaps with an eye on the historical process and on organic growth I ought to say adolescent—in fact amateurish and impressionistic. Indeed, and this is very odd, it reaches its maturity and manhood not before Croce, I fancy; that is to say, not until the present century, for the *Estetica* was published in 1901 and the *Breviario* in 1913. For the first time in Croce, and nowhere before, do you have the feeling of what is now currently called aesthetics, although you appreciate that the growth has been continuous. I mean such things as the feeling of system and the feeling that common enjoyments have been outgrown and left behind with childhood's random toys, the feeling that we know what are and must be the genuine self-expressions of spirit, their inter-relations and their place on the cosmic map; above all, perhaps, their exclusiveness.

You will observe that I have already in large measure identified what earlier I called the general body of aesthetic theory with the aesthetics of Croce, with, that is to say, a fully grown, very confident, very tightly knit idealist metaphysical aesthetics. The evidence for this can only be had in the reading, and that *in extenso*, of the literature; my own perfunctory historical sketch is only a statement of a conclusion. But with regard to the reading of Croce we are lucky; we can do it almost without tears. In 1938 the late Professor Robin Collingwood of Oxford published a most readable volume entitled *The Principles of Art*—elegantly written, amusing, high-spirited, gay, learned, urbane, wilful, perverse, opinionated, dogmatic—to replace his earlier *Outlines of a Philosophy of Art* (of 1924) and to do 'penance for youthful follies'. But the volume remains vintage Croce and is therefore

---

the mind itself has produced, are we not returning to dualism, to the thing confronting the thinker, with all the absurdities dualism involves?' For a sympathetic account of all this see A. C. Ewing, *Idealism: A Critical Survey* (1935); and, since Croce does in a most remarkable way resume his idealist predecessors, Wildon Carr, *The Philosophy of Benedetto Croce* (1917). For an account of absolute or teleological idealism the reader may be referred to the chapter 'The Philosophy of Spirit' in Isaiah Berlin: *Karl Marx* (1939).

indispensable reading for my topic. I shall try to honour my promise, but for the flesh and blood of these dry bones I shall refer the curious to this volume and to Croce's article on aesthetics in the 14th (1929) edition of the *Encyclopaedia Britannica*.

But first of all a preliminary comment to underline one character of all this mode of philosophy of art and to give substance to one or two earlier and opprobious remarks of my own. In the preface to his book Collingwood explained that his earlier work on aesthetics needed replacement and not revision, not only because he had in the interval changed his mind about some matters but also because in the interval there had been a change in the situation both of art and of aesthetic theory in England. 'There has been at any rate the beginning of what may prove an important revival in the arts themselves.' He is referring to the period between 1924 and 1937, but as usual he does not condescend to tell us what these new beginnings are. 'We have', he says, 'a new poetry, and we have a new way of painting. We have some very interesting experiments in a new way of writing prose. These things are gradually establishing themselves; but they are much hampered by rags and tatters of moribund theory which still encumber and intimidate the minds of people who ought to be welcoming the new developments.' Yet in so far as concerned the visual arts 1924–1937 were years of the hey-day of the Fry-Bell theory of significant form, of the irrelevance of morals and of subject-matter, of the pure aesthetic emotion; and the first Post-Impressionist exhibition had been held as long ago as 1910. Collingwood comments that between 1924 and 1937 there had been a new and lively 'if somewhat chaotic' growth of aesthetic theory and criticism and that most of it had been written by artists, and this, he continues, is the reason for the appearance of *The Principles of Art*.

> For I do not think of aesthetic theory as an attempt to investigate and expound eternal verities concerning the nature of an eternal subject called Art, but as an attempt to reach, by thinking, the solution of certain problems arising out of the situation in which artists find themselves here and now. Everything written in this book has been

written in the belief that it has a practical bearing, direct or indirect, upon the condition of art in England in 1937.

This sounds most attractive. It is again pure Croce, who could also commit himself to the paradox that philosophy is as nearly history as makes no difference.

Scepticism [wrote Croce in his *Autobiography*, which I quote in Collingwood's translation (1927)] is inevitable and invincible, given the concept of a static reality outside the historical process. But the concept of truth as history tempers the conceit of today and opens up hopes for tomorrow; for the despairing sense of struggling in vain to pursue a quarry that always flies and hides, it substitutes the consciousness of always possessing a wealth that always increases; for the melancholy picture of a blind humanity groping in the darkness it substitutes the heroic picture of mankind rising from light to light.

Is it, I wonder, fanciful to detect here a tone of voice that echoes throughout the work of Sir Herbert Read?

However this may be, Collingwood's programme is at first sight an attractive one. It suggests that our aesthetic thinking is going to have some observable and corrigible connexion with its material; and we remember, too, that Collingwood was brought up in a household familiar with painting. But the hope is belied. In the pages of *The Principles of Art* we do indeed learn that, apart from some music, almost the only works that deserve the title of art proper are those of Jane Austen, Cézanne, and Mr. T. S. Eliot; but then there is never a mention in his pages of any particular works of painting or sculpture. The only contemporary British artist mentioned is, I think, Sir Frank Brangwyn; no foreign painters or sculptors are noticed, not even, for all the talk about new trends, Picasso; no French painter is mentioned later than Cézanne (the subject of a foolish and sometimes silly page—'Of course Cézanne was right. Painting can never be a visual art. A man paints with his hands, not with his eyes.') and the Impressionists, whose aims Collingwood would seem to find incomprehensible. It is very odd in a book about art, this serene disregard and almost bland contempt for descending to the consideration of its particular works.

But there is a reason for it, an important reason but one that it is very difficult to state both lucidly and briefly. The difficulty lies in the fact that this aesthetics is solid system and the part is difficult to get hold of in isolation from the whole, and the whole is objective (or subjective?) metaphysical idealism.[1] Roughly, very roughly, the ghostly outline that I want to bring into focus runs like this. Aesthetics, or philosophy of art, is not reflection stimulated by particular works of art, for the real work of art is a total imaginative experience and not any physical thing in a particular medium. Aesthetics, as Croce put it, is the whole of philosophy, of the understanding of spirit, but with special reference to the manifestation of the human spirit in artistic activity. The activity of spirit is the one and only subject-matter of philosophy, but spirit expresses itself in various modes or grades; there are two grades of theoretical, or contemplative, activity and two of practical activity. The first and purest mode of the spirit, prior to all the others and presupposing none but presupposed by all, is aesthetic contemplation. This is pure and unique experience of the unique individual, pre-logical and pre-conceptual, undifferentiated awareness and response to an individual concrete situation, an activity of soul that, being preconceptual, is a spontaneous expression of emotions or sentiment or feeling (the word is not to be pressed); the experience is called by Croce (and by Maritain) intuition, by Collingwood imagination. The second mode of spirit is again contemplative, but the complex of spontaneous feeling is analysed, manipulated, classified, into concepts and judgments; it is no longer individual and concrete but abstract and classified into general ideas. It is concerned, as the first mode cannot be, with truth and falsity, not, as the first mode alone is, with beauty and ugliness. And at this point

---

[1] With regard to Croce's aesthetics the best and most sympathetic recent study in English is Mr. Bernard Mayo's essay 'Art, Language and Philosophy in Croce' in *The Philosophical Quarterly* for July 1955; useful, too, especially in its early pages, is Mr. E. F. Carritt's paper 'Croce and his Aesthetic' in the October 1953 issue of *Mind*.

it is relevant to interject that the material world, and nature, belong to this second mode of spirit—a concept, an abstraction, and already at one remove from the reality that is the pure and lyrical activity of the spirit.

Presupposing these two modes are the two practical grades of spirit, economic (or magical) and ethical. Practical activity is guided by thought, but it may be inspired by desires and directed towards ends and be concerned with the useful and the useless and with technique; or it may be inspired by will and governed by principles of conduct and concerned with good and evil.

By application of this doctrine of the four modes of self-expression of spirit both Croce and Collingwood issue some interesting negative definitions of art. It is not physical fact, for this is to allocate it to the category of the concept and of reason; it is not a means to pleasure or entertainment or the production of any intended effects by a technique, for this is to allocate it to the category of the economic and the magical, of desire and utility; it is not moral, for this is to allocate it to the category of ethical activity, of will and of principles of good and evil; it is not knowledge, being preconceptual, but (since it does not presuppose knowledge) better than knowledge.

This, very roughly, is the anatomy of spirit. Those of you who have read *The Principles of Art* will remember the entertaining polemics throughout most of its first book, that entitled 'Art and Not Art'. Craft is not art, for craft involves a distinction between means and end, between planning and execution, between raw material and artefact; art has nothing to do with technique or any special skill; there can be no religious art; art has nothing to do with beauty as we ordinarily use the word,[1] for there is no quality in things in virtue of which when we contemplate them we enjoy what we recognize as an aesthetic experience: the aesthetic experience is an autonomous activity which arises from within

---

[1] Collingwood does, however, want to find a common characteristic corresponding to the common word. 'The word "beauty", wherever and however it is used, connotes that in things by virtue of which we love them, admire them, or desire them.' This is not very informative.

—not any specific reaction to a stimulus proceeding from a specific type of external object. Representative art is not art proper—not, however, that art and representation are incompatible, for the representation can be emotional: the feeling evoked by the artefact resembles the feeling evoked by the motif; representation is always a means to an end, the re-evocation of certain emotions, and according as these are evoked for their practical value or for their own sake it is called magic or amusement. Neither is strictly art proper, although magic can become art; amusement art is hedonistic and therefore not at all utilitarian, but the work of art, so called, that provides the amusement is strictly utilitarian, being strictly a means to an end and unlike a work of art proper having no value in itself. An example of such amusement art is

> not only the representation of nudity which reappeared in European painting and sculpture at the Renaissance, when art as magic [Collingwood here means mediaeval religious art] was replaced by art as amusement . . . the novel, or story based on a sexual motive, which dates from the same period, is essentially an appeal to the sexual emotions of the audience, not in order to stimulate these emotions for actual commerce between the sexes, but in order to provide them with make-believe objects and thus divert them from their practical goal in the interests of amusement.

All such art, all such Renaissance and mediaeval art, is art as technique and therefore not art proper; art proper is not an arousing of emotion but an expressing of emotion, not of course a description of emotion (for all description generalizes) nor yet a betraying of emotion, but an expression to oneself of an emotion in the act of which we apprehend and individualize it. Since art is not a craft the work of art is not an artefact, and not therefore anything visible or audible or tangible; art is the expression of emotion: when an artist paints a picture he is in possession of an experience (this is what expression means) quite other than that of seeing the colours he puts on the canvas, an imaginary experience of total activity more or less like that which we construct for ourselves when we look at the picture.

Such, again very schematically, is the series of points made in the first book of *The Principles of Art*.

One thing is painfully clear, namely that the bulk of what we call art is not art at all. Another thing painfully clear, but it is really the same thing, is that this theory of art takes no account of any particular works of art; it is not in any ordinary sense an empirical theory. A third thing that is clear and gives no less pain, but again it is the same thing, is the apparent inability to comprehend, not indeed particular works, for these are never mentioned, but large tracts of artistic activity: the unqualified pronouncement about the Renaissance nude is only the most glaring example. The reason for all this is, I think, both simple and far-reaching. It is that the theory of art is but one facet of a theory of spirit, and that this theory is an extreme form of, after all, absolute idealism. Both Croce and Collingwood were humanists and immanentists; Croce rejected Hegel's World-Spirit. But as Feuerbach pointed out many years before him, if this which is responsible for the behaviour of the universe is not itself some sort of entity, however mysterious and queer, then it is nothing but a pompous name for all there is; in which case to say that everything is as it is because it is the manifestation of spirit is to say nothing at all. A few years ago Professor Isaiah Berlin recorded his opinion that this was the crucial dilemma on which, for all his richness of mind and culture, Signor Croce's entire system broke to pieces[1]; and I agree with him.

But since his philosophy is all of a piece and aesthetics sets the tone for it, as he often said, his aesthetic breaks on it too. 'Spirit', some of his defenders have urged, is just his name for the totality of human activity, and the tenor of Croce suggests that this is indeed what he wants to mean by the word. But if it is, there is only one way of understanding the spirit of man, and that is to examine the activities of man and the works of man, and this in close detail; but a close matter-of-fact investigation of this sort is an enterprise that, for all the countless references to the con-

[1] In *Mind* for October 1952, p. 577.

crete, neither Croce nor his disciple Collingwood ever consented
to undertake. Instead there is rather a polished contempt for
descending into the arena of vulgar particularities. But it remains
odd, except on one hypothesis, that, humanist as he was, Croce
should reflect upon the activities of spirit as if spirit were not at
all just the sum of human activities but as if it were after all some
central directing hypostatized Spirit that manifested itself in
modes and grades; which modes a man could contemplate *a priori*
and in themselves, and must so contemplate them if they are to
be understood in their purity. It is very much as if the emotional
drive behind the philosophy is still some sort of faith in the
progressive self-realization of Spirit. That there should be this
faith is a hypothesis that makes some sort of sense of this oddity,
and one that is to some extent confirmed by the Crocean attitude
towards history that we have seen, an attitude also shared by
Collingwood.

By sense I mean that to some extent we can understand on this
hypothesis why this philosophy proceeds as it does, why, that is to
say, there is all this talk about pure art, or art proper, the essence
of art, as a primary self-expression of spirit through emotion. I do
not mean that the talk itself is sensible. For after all, to be blunt
about it, what is art that there should be a pure essence of it, of
whatever kind? There is no such thing as art. Art is nothing but
a general word, of quite modern coinage, to designate the
activities of epic poets and lyric poets, of writers of tragedy and
comedy, some historians and philosophers and novelists, of
painters on walls and boards and canvas, of sculptors in stone and
bronze and metal and cement, of architects of cathedrals and
churches and houses and castles, of musicians—but I will not
continue the list. These are *some* of the activities designated by the
word 'art', and there is not the slightest reason to suppose that
to the one name there corresponds some one essence, nuclear and
self-identical in all these activities, that can be grasped by
apprehending a primal pre-logical mode of consciousness
intermediate between the psycho-physical and the intellectual, or
in any other way whatever.

The prejudice that a common word denotes a common essence dies hard.[1] Surely we do not use the one word without any reason at all. Of course not; for one thing, all art is gratuitous, but this has nothing to do with essences. And if a man says that surely there is some one nuclear essence shared by all forms of artistic activity that we can discover if only we look long and hard enough at all these activities, the candid answer is a brief one, namely that the longer and harder we look the more diverse do these activities come to appear to be and that a purity of essence in which they are all seen as one and the self-same act is a dream and a delusion that turns into a nightmare. What is the essence shared alike by *Pride and Prejudice*, Beethoven's last quartet op. 135, the *Iliad*, Aristophanes' *Frogs*, Catullus's *Miser Catulle, desinas ineptire*, Westminster Abbey, *King Lear*, *The Laocoon*, Botticelli's *Birth of Venus*, Michelangelo's last (Rondanini) *Pietà*, Géricault's *Raft of the Medusa* or by, to take a single pair of paintings, Blake's *God creating Adam* and Monet's *Le Bassin aux Nymphéas*?—but one must stop sometime. Assuredly not a few aestheticians have answered—and it is a near-Crocean answer, but whether Croce is responsible for it or whether there is a climate of opinion and sentiment that is responsible both for it and for him is another question that calls for further investigation—that there is indeed something common to all these works, namely expressiveness of emotion. But this is an empty answer, as empty as the answer that they are all productive of pleasure or delight. For there is no such thing as delight-by-itself that these things 'produce': the delight is in every case of a quite particular kind, nor is it anything 'produced', nor is it separable from the media in which these works of art are done. Similarly with emotion, or lyrical consciousness or intuition or imagination or whatever word one uses; similarly, too, with their expressiveness: this also is quite particular and inseparable from the media in which the works are done.

1 Cf. Clive Bell: 'For either all works of visual art have some common quality, or when we speak of "works of art" we gibber.' From the chapter 'The Aesthetic Hypothesis' in his book *Art* (1914).

'Painting', said Turner, who knew a great deal about it, 'is a rum business.' Consider for a moment paintings and indeed English work of our own time, to restrict the area still more. What is the pure essence common to David Jones's *Aphrodite in Aulis* and to an abstract of Ben Nicholson's, to Gwen John's nuns and Stanley Spencer's *The Resurrection, Cookham*, Paul Nash's *Landscape of the Vernal Equinox* and Wyndham Lewis's *The Surrender of Barcelona*? Many writers would no doubt still say— this is not Crocean theory but it has affinities and belongs to the same climate of thought and feeling—that they have this in common: that they generate a specific and self-identical aesthetic emotion, and this through a uniquely satisfying apprehension of purely formal qualities or of significant form. But this formula, too, is empty and for the same reasons as before. There is no self-identical aesthetic emotion generated by these works: the emotion is quite particular in every case, nor is it an emotion. Perhaps it is a mode of consciousness? But to say this is only to use a high-sounding phrase for what these pictures do to us; it is not to give any account of it. Nor yet are the formal relations (Ben Nicholson apart) purely formal nor can they be: a visual curve is not pure curve but the curve of something, and it makes a difference, a difference to the appreciation and significant form of the curve, what it is a curve of.[1]

It is impossible, then, to find this elusive essence even when we restrict our inquiries to twentieth-century English works in the one medium. But it will already, I think, begin to be apparent that the Crocean denial that 'art' can mean works of art, paintings or buildings or statues, for example, and his affirmation that, on the contrary, 'art' is what goes on in people's heads, the head of the artist, that is, and those of his public, are quite essential to his

---

[1] This is, of course, altogether too brief and hurried. The doctrine under criticism here becomes, at its purest, the doctrine to the effect that all art proper is abstract art. The most intelligent and effective appraisals of this doctrine up to date will be found in Mr. Robin Ironside's essay 'Painting' in *The New Outline of Modern Knowledge* (ed. Alan Pryce-Jones, 1956) and, more philosophically and with respect to Sir Herbert Read's enunciation of it, in Sir John Rothenstein's essay on Ben Nicholson (*Modern English Painters*, vol. II, 1956).

theory of art's having a pure essence. (I think it is essential to any
such theory; it is honest and courageous of Croce to recognize it,
and silly of him to stick to it.) There are, of course, many difficulties about any such view besides its non-empirical character.
For one thing a painter, for example, expresses his emotion or
intuition, brings it to consciousness and thereby transforms it;
we should agree, I take it, that the phrase 'expression of' is very
misleading, and that expressing *is* the feeling but transformed
from something simply sensuous into something imaginative, in
much the same way as appetite is transformed into desire. On
this point Croce and Collingwood are correct and Collingwood
is illuminating. A painter, then, expresses his emotion and in the
very process consciously apprehends it, for himself and for us;
but he does not express it in his head through a merely external
and instrumental act of painting; the act of painting is the expression, and painting is nothing if it is not doing something with
brushes in one's hands to a piece of canvas or hardboard or whatever it is; and what goes on in his head as expressed to him and to
us, communicated, is nothing if it is not the painting, the physical
thing that he makes. Croce quotes with approval the Paterian
dictum that all art constantly aspires towards the condition of
music, and there is some sense in saying that Beethoven's op. 135
is not the physical score. At a stretch, a strained stretch, his
account might be made to fit poetry. Did not Shelley say that 'the
most glorious poetry that has ever been communicated to the
world is probably a feeble shadow of the original conceptions of
the poet'? But yet Gerard Manley Hopkins's expression of his
'intuition' is inseparable from its verbal embodiment and the
poem is what we declaim from the printed page. In painting, the
view that art is what goes on inside the head begins to look pretty
silly; for sculpture it is still more palpably silly: Mr. Henry
Moore has some blessedly down-to-earth things to say about how
a sculptor learns, and not only in 'technique', from actually
working on his material; nor is Michelangelo's expression of his
'intuition' in the Rondanini *Pietà* separable from its being
sculpture, it could not be translated into paint. And as for

architecture—but I said a little while ago that the thesis that
'art' is not the artefact is essential to any account of art as pure
essence, as some one act, and with this thesis goes also, of course,
the thesis that the common distinction between the 'arts' in
terms of medium (painting, sculpture, words, etc.) is a vulgar
superficiality and an irrelevance, as also, and necessarily, is
technique. But architecture, though not more recalcitrant to this
mode of theorizing, is more blatantly so. 'Does the Idealist
aesthetician', a critic has asked, 'seriously maintain that one act
of imagination is responsible for, say, Cologne cathedral?'

The idealist will not be deterred by this question, or by any of
mine. 'Reality is Experience.' It is a curious thing about this
manner of aesthetics that no objections to it ever count; that
nothing counts as evidence against it but, on the contrary, everything is evidence that the theory is right and the only right one;
for everything is either interpreted as being really a confirmation
or else is dismissed as irrelevant (not art but pseudo-art) or as the
vulgarity of the immature mind. Naturally a philosopher becomes
worried about a situation of this sort in which a theory about our
activities is systematically irrefutable; for if a theory about art is
not empirical then it is probably a myth and (in Collingwood's
sense) a would-be magical myth, a *mythus* propounded to inculcate
a point of view or a certain attitude to things.

I think indeed that this is just what the Crocean theory is and
that it is in this respect exactly like the other grand aesthetic
theories of our time, or rather (for there is no other theory
coherent enough to be called grand) the bits and pieces that
might make up such a theory. I am thinking again of Sir Herbert
Read, whose writings are no less non-empirical in the sense
described above than are Croce's or Collingwood's. But of this
more presently.

My concern in this paper is not to expound or criticize
Croceanism beyond the minimum necessary for the elucidation
of characteristics of it that are to my purpose. My purpose, if I
may remind you, is to draw the ghostly outlines of a central
metaphysics of art and to suggest why I think it central and in

what sense; why, that is, and in what sense of 'formative' I think
that it is formative of and sets the tone for an array of contemporary art theory that at first sight might seem to be remote from
it. Many will find this suggestion a surprising one. How can anything quite so peculiar as a Crocean idealist metaphysic be
directive of the theories that go about the market-place? But
perhaps it is odd and peculiar only because it happens to be the
only completely elaborated aesthetic theory there is and the only
one worked out by a couple of highly intelligent men who knew
exactly what they were doing. *The Principles of Art* is not about
art and not, except incidentally (but it is full of incidental
excellences), about anything at all; but it is the only coherent
treatise about aesthetics written in English.

But perhaps it is not as a theory that it is formative. Perhaps we
get nearer the root of the matter if we entertain the possibility
that it only happens to give systematic if peculiar expression to a
set of opinions and attitudes about the arts that have been current
in Western Europe for some few decades. Perhaps, that is to say,
its character is not to examine the arts but to give intellectual
respectability to what many people think and feel anyway. To say
this is not, of course, to be opprobrious to the gentlemen whose
ideas I have been describing; it is only to say something that is in
line with their own (and Hegel's) cherished thesis that philosophy
is history. Are there any such opinions and attitudes? I think
there are, and that it is worthwhile to make a brief and by no
means exhaustive list.

The reference to Cologne cathedral suggests the first and
perhaps the most important of these. I can imagine an aesthetician
of the type we are considering replying that Cologne cathedral,
or any large and largely organized structure, is not of course a
work of art but is and can only be an agglomeration of moments
of art proper. In much the same way you will find it assumed that
epic poetry is not poetry proper but a succession of moments of
'pure poetry' held together by the paste and glue of epic narrative.
(Henri Bremond's theory about *poésie pure* ran something like

this, and it has been a common enough theory, not least when not explicitly stated.) The idea is that pure poetry, or poetry proper, or the essence of poetry, is the lyric, and that the other so-called 'kinds' are either the necessary vehicles of the lyrical moments, and psychologically necessary, too, since we cannot always live at this high lyric altitude but need our moments of relaxation and respite; or else are impure poetry or, like declamatory poetry, pseudo-poetry.

You have the same attitude in regard to painting and sculpture. In painting there has been and is a preference for the sketch over the finished work of which it is the sketch, and which is some-times opprobiously called the 'machine'. Constable's sketches are regarded as expressive of more of pure art than his finished pictures; the finished pictures with their elaboration and organiza-tion adulterate the primal imaginative experience expressed to us in the sketches.

You may recollect that at the Omega Workshops initiated and directed by Roger Fry in London shortly before the First World War, there was a systematic avoidance of the polished and finished look in their artefacts and a studious preference for the appearance of a wilful and sophisticated clumsiness.

With regard to painting and sculpture this attitude does not arise out of the void; it is not simply some mysterious alteration in the human spirit, although of course there are such things. It is closely connected with the decline of patronage, although not completely explained by it. When painters and sculptors are commissioned to do work that is going to be lived with in a church or some other public building or in the patron's house, nobody is likely to have much preference for the first aesthetic shock. It is one thing to live with a picture, and another to see it in a studio or on the walls of an art gallery. Here it is the first impact, the immediate lyrical moment, that tells. It is not very surprising that the uncommissioned easel picture should occasion a new set of responses and of preferences. But there is nothing in this of any consequence for the development of the human spirit.

It is part of the attitude I have been describing that narrative

pictures, conversation pieces, wall paintings commissioned by a
church and indeed anything commissioned, even the portrait, or
any largely organized work, are, like the epic and the cathedral,
impure art redeemed by their passages of pure art or creative
intuition (this is M. Maritain's word) or whatever you call it;
much as Lucretius's *De Rerum Natura* was thought to be redeemed
by its occasional felicities. Commissioned art, as Croce charmingly puts it in the *Breviario*, is art 'bidden to play the harlot
(since her original sin cannot be rooted out), but all in the service
of Holy Church and of morality—*meretrix ecclesiae*'.[1] But, again to
live with, commissioned wall paintings can yield a conclusion
quite different and a satisfaction quite different from the Crocean
in kind. For really to see paintings with one's eyes and to be
visually familiar with them, which is a rare thing, suggests conclusions quite different from ideological reflection about them or
about art and the situation of the artist, which is a common thing.

But secondly, to confine myself for the moment to painting
only, the obsolescence of patronage, which most practising
painters deeply resent for very many reasons, was accompanied,
as was but natural, by the obsolescence of the apprentice system
and its substitution by the art school. Conjointly these two factors
have had a host of consequences. When paintings were commissioned and painters learned how to paint in the studio of a master,
there was no occasion for a man to suffer either headaches or
neuroses about what to paint or how to paint it; nor was he made
aware, through photography, of a multiplicity of forms and styles
and ways of looking at the world culled from every corner of the
globe and from most centuries of recorded time—a multiplicity
bewildering for any but the strongest digestions and the most
assured imaginations. With his subject set him, unexposed to the
distracting competitiveness of other forms, with the discipline
of the studio all about him, the painter was the freer to realize
what was in him and to express the vision that was his own. There
is nothing peculiar about this; when all possibilities are open and
there are no dykes to hold the flood, a man hardly knows how to

[1] I quote Mr. E. F. Carritt's translation, from *Philosophies of Beauty* (1931).

decide where to go and the river spreads aimlessly over the water-meadows.

This, however, is no part of my story. I have referred to the obsolescence of patronage and of art-apprenticeship, whose effects, I have suggested, are aggravated by photography (but not by photography only, as we shall see) only to illustrate or give some substance to a second feature of the modern climate in the arts that I am trying to characterize. It is, in a word, an obsession with the freedom of creativity, the freedom of the personal vision, with subjectivity (all these phrases are echoed in M. Maritain's aesthetics but they are common form everywhere); an obsession that takes some odd forms. To judge from not a few declarations, particularly of art theorists, the artist's whole struggle is a struggle to assert himself against reactionary forces and opinions that obstruct his free creativity. There are now no longer, however, any such forces or opinions or conventions.

It is much as if, freedom being felt as a choice between alternatives presented by one's society or culture and as a self-assertion and self-expression in a resistant discipline, now that all possibilities are open and there are no resistances, it is psychologically necessary to invent them. At the root of the matter there is a deep *malaise*: what is a painter to do with the absolute freedom that is now his?

I have wandered far from patronage and studios and jumped many decades in the wandering: I am aware that up to shortly before the First World War, painters, and sculptors, did have to fight against established conventions and against indifference; and the fight is bitter when a man has to earn his living and support a family. The point I have been trying to illustrate at some little length in this digression is that when the uncommissioned easel picture succeeded to the commissioned fresco and portrait and the rest, and there was no longer any studio tradition but in their stead a new middle class and conventions from which the life had ebbed, a painter's freedom to express himself as he personally saw the world took a place in his attention that it could not have taken before. Before, the question did not arise; it solved itself *ambulando.* It was an important question and it sank itself deep in consciousness, so deep that there has had to be a pretence in the last few decades that it is a vital interest for the defence of which there must be unrelenting war. It is not a new freedom; what is new is only that the question of it arose.

The situation is faithfully reflected in all aestheticians and in Croce; it is made retrospective and a simple version of it is rationalized into a story about the essence of pure art. Art is not craft and has nothing to do with technique; there can be no religious art; magical art and hedonistic art are not art proper; art is the primary self-expression of spirit, a pre-logical spontaneous expression of pure imagination; art is pure subjectivity, and this is pure freedom, or rather (I quote from M. Maritain's *Creative Intuition in Art and Poetry*) 'in proportion as the creativity of the spirit strives for greater and greater liberation in order for the Self to be revealed in the work, Nature discloses greater obstacles, or, rather, demands from poetic intuition a ceaselessly growing power, in order for things to be grasped and expressed in the work, without hampering or thwarting the simultaneous expression of subjectivity and the freedom of creative spirit'. It takes a philosopher to elevate contingent historical facts into a mode of the necessary self-expression of the human spirit and the pure essence of art, and a neo-scholastic to make out that they follow from the first principles of a metaphysic of man.[1]

Of course, if what is meant by all this talk is that a painter, let us say, can do good work only if he is free to paint as he genuinely thinks or feels and that his work will be bad—not 'art' at all, if you like, although this way of putting it begins to beg many questions—if he pretends to what he does not feel or if he produces simply the branded goods that the public happens to esteem, then no one would disagree with anything so elementary. But, we may legitimately ask, why not say just this in half a dozen simple sentences? Why sky-rocket into a world of essences and pure subjectivity? Why be so solemn?

[1] See also, with regard to M. Maritain, the present writer's essay in *The Month* for November 1954.

But, thirdly, aesthetics is nothing if not exceedingly solemn, and there are reasons for this too. One is obvious enough. 'Art', as T. E. Hulme once said, has come to be 'spilt religion'. A generation that has lost belief in a Redemption and even in God the Creator has not lost the hope of salvation from the Old Adam. (At the moment the especial hope is put in the visual arts. If painters and sculptors are the prophets of the Lord, then the critics and scholars are the theologians, and this is in part why the London art world is the Hobbesian jungle of calumny and malice and bitterness that it is—*homo homini lupus*; the *odium aestheticum* of the twentieth century has much the same quality as the *odium theologicum* of the seventeenth.) Who shall deliver us from the body of this death—of practical affairs and practical and moral thinking, of the conceptual round? The obvious claimant is 'art'. Not 'art' as technique, of course, or as didactic or as pleasurable, as representational or enhancing the act of living; these things belong still to the body of this death; but 'art' as the preconceptual and unpresupposed self-expression of spirit, the greatest Liberator of them all.

I have already pointed out that, historically, aesthetics as a carefully thought out and rounded business is a part of philosophical idealism. Idealism itself has always been an alternative to Christian religion, a philosophy that claims to be 'a philosophy of life' (the only one that has ever made so grandiose a claim), the occupant of a pulpit and a pulpit alternative to the Christian pulpit. There is no need here, I think, to develop this point. For my present purpose it is enough to remind you of the unction of the idealist tone of voice ('It's just like being in church', as Lord Hailsham once said, I believe, after a lecture by Professor Joachim of Oxford) and to invite you to recollect the tone of voice of those writers on 'art' who 'take aesthetics seriously', of, for example, Sir Herbert Read. If I am right, this is no accident. I have suggested already what I have come to believe, that writings on aesthetics of this century are bits and pieces of a central body of doctrine and that this doctrine, to be found at its most self-conscious and at its most reflective and most professional in Croce and Collingwood, is integral to an idealist metaphysic. Naturally, too, it has affected most disciplines that grew up in nineteenth-century Germany.

It is small wonder, if I am right, that aesthetics should be solemn, or that it should suggest as strongly as it does a higher gnosticism; and small wonder that 'art' in this generation should be what the mystery religions were in the Greco-Roman world. The satisfactions are the same.

Nor is it surprising, fourthly, that most contemporary writing on aesthetics, and indeed much popular contemporary art criticism and history, should underwrite what has been called the revolutionary principle, but what might be better called applied evolution myth.[1] Of Sir Herbert Read himself it has been said that he has been present at the birth of every new movement and the demise of none. The attitude is that whatever is new is valuable and that its value is in proportion to its novelty, and this because it is a fresh self-expression of the spirit and, being so, is more expressive also, somehow, of the real nature of the human spirit and of its place in the world. But the most interesting characteristic of this attitude is that 'is', in the sentence in which I have very crudely tried to convey it, means not 'is' but 'must be'; the most interesting thing about it is its *a priori* character.

Again there are many historical reasons for this attitude. The most obvious and perhaps the most powerful, where the arts are concerned, is that in the nineteenth century and up to the First World War, and especially in France, every departure from accustomed ways of doing things was greeted with howls of execration; new work was neither exhibited except by the personal initiative of the artists nor sold; and the artists really did starve. Courbet, the Impressionist group, Cézanne, van Gogh, Gauguin, the Fauves—the list is an impressive one. And there is always the inertia of established manners; and after all, Sir Alfred Munnings is a contemporary. Scholars and critics and philosophers

[1] For this use of the word see Professor Stephen Toulmin's essay 'Contemporary Scientific Mythology' in *Metaphysical Beliefs: Three Essays* by Toulmin, Hepburn and MacIntyre (1957).

of art now are very conscious of this and have no wish that it should ever happen again; they keep open house. What could be more admirable?

But if a man keep open house we do not expect him to believe implicitly that all his visitors must be God's anointed ones, must be so, somehow, by definition. Whence comes the *a priori* character of the belief? Again there are historical reasons at work, some of them deep down in the political and social and philosophical and religious history of the nineteenth century, and they make a story far too complex to be unravelled with any brevity. I have mentioned already some of these, and there will shortly be occasion to mention more.

At this point I would add the axiom, which came into being in the nineteenth century, that innovation is a thing good in itself, and also that nothing is of moment that does not lead to something else. It may simply be an expression of the endemic restlessness of Western European man, with his periods of tumescence and brief relaxation, energy and repose; I do not know. It is now, as I have indicated, axiomatic. In our own age, as Sir John Rothenstein has recorded, 'it is an unconscious assumption that the great artist is a man who innovates, who is original. Originality has become a part of the meaning that we assign to the word "greatness". It has not always been so.'[1] The idea is one that you will find controlling historical study, for instance, as in the neglect, up till recently, of Sienese painting, which neither initiated anything new nor led to anything; beautiful but a backwater.[2] The idea you will find in the complaint of the literary critic that so-and-so's recent production continues what he has done so well before and marks no progression, is no contribution to his *œuvre*. When ideas are taken for granted, they become axioms and the spectacles through which we see; a contingency becomes a necessary element in the constitution of human nature and of the activities of spirit that deserve the name of spirit.

[1] Introduction, *Modern English Painters*, vol. I (1952).
[2] Cf. John Pope-Hennessy: *Sienese Quattrocento Painting* (1947), p. 23.

Or a mode of the self-expression of spirit. For all this history is resumed and intellectually justified by the idealist metaphysician. I have already quoted Croce's *Autobiography* to the effect that 'truth as history' affords us 'the consciousness of a wealth that always increases'. Why should it? It is clear why it does so for Croce; idealist optimism is grounded in idealist—indeed Hegelian—metaphysics of Spirit, and the first and primary grade of spirit is art. I see no reason whatever to believe in the idealist fairy story and every reason not to. But I do see that for a man who believes in it optimism about innovation in the arts is justified, and I see, too, why for such a man the belief that what is new *must* be valuable is justified. I see whence comes the *a priori* character of the belief. And I am suggesting that idealist aesthetics of the Crocean type are central to all aesthetics of our time for this reason also, that it is they that justify innovation, originality, the revolutionary vision, as spiritual progress. Outside such a metaphysic there is no reason whatever for the *a priorism* I have been describing; and it may well be that it is a dim recognition that there is not and—for few British aestheticians now are metaphysical idealists and would probably not be very clear about what metaphysical idealism is—a vague worry about what else does justify it that is responsible for the belligerency, and worse, of some parts of the art world. People unsure of themselves are apt to turn nasty, particularly if they think they are not being taken seriously.

Fifthly, in the climate of opinion about the arts in modern times, there is the belief that subject-matter is irrelevant. There are, yet again, historical reasons why people came to think so, and I have, by implication, already hinted at some of them, particularly in remarks about the lyrical moments of the organized work of art and about the freedom of subjectivity. There are others still closer to hand. 'There would seem to prevail today among artists'—I quote again from Sir John Rothenstein's carefully pondered analysis[1]:

---

[1] Introduction, *op. cit.*

little of the sense of the majesty of the world and the excitement of the human adventure. What has taken the place of the mediaeval artist's exalted conception of a God-centred universe in which every man and woman, and every created thing, had its value and its function? Or the Renaissance artist's intoxicating confidence that man, by the intense cultivation of his understanding, his inventiveness, his daring and all his faculties, might himself become godlike? Nothing, except an intense preoccupation with his separate and individual self.

At bottom, what has happened is a religious change; our society is no longer either Christian or theist or pagan. But there are other changes that have run concurrently. Once it was thought that an unremitting scrutiny of natural appearances might enhance both delight and understanding; and it was recognized that, in any case, appearances are for a painter all the clue to reality that there is, seeing that the world of the outer and the inner eye is all the world he has. In modern times, however, it has come to be thought that appearances are deceptive and systematically deceptive; the majesty of the oak and the radiance of human beauty, and indeed their colours and their shapes, are constructions of the human mind. 'Out there' there are atoms and the void, or perhaps (a phrase, I think, of Bertrand Russell's) the wild and whirling world of sense-data. What the eye sees is not what our forebears confidently thought they saw. Nature and all the surfaces of nature are our 'ideas', our theoretical constructions; and one degree removed from the reality, for the reality is pure activity of spirit.

I have reverted yet again, you will remark, to Crocean terminology. Not that I am suggesting for a moment, of course, that it takes a metaphysical idealist to talk about the appearance of the world like this. Scientists can talk like this and so can British empiricists; they have done so for some few centuries and in a very close systematic way for several decades.[1] It is, I think, this sort of talk from these sorts of sources that has contributed to the

---

[1] For some idea of this see, for example, Bertrand Russell, *Our Knowledge of the External World* (1914) and Professor H. H. Price, *Perception* (1932).

making of the climate that I am describing. Too little of the whole man was indeed expressed by Impressionism for this painting to give lasting satisfaction, and too little of the hard structure of the world; but how far are we now from the Impressionist's delighted confidence in the surface of things, and how far for that matter from Cézanne's patient and tenacious scrutiny of the enduring rock and bone beneath them. And for the same reason. But whether in eighteenth- or twentieth-century style, whether it be David Hume or Bertrand Russell or Professor A. J. Ayer, British empiricism has fathered no aesthetics. Aesthetics is the child of philosophical idealism, and to these doubts and misgivings about the appearances of the world about us idealist aesthetics has given a home and a location in the panoramic map of Spirit and of Spirit's self-expressions.

I do not want to caricature. There is nothing in Crocean aesthetics from which one could strictly infer the axiom so dear to Sir Herbert Read and to countless other writers—the 'absolute presupposition' of much of their thinking—that the more representational a work of visual art is the less is it a work of art proper. Morals would appear to enter into the absoluteness of this presupposition: a moral puritanism about appearances and their representation, a repugnance for the natural world. It is, however, a tenet of Crocean aesthetics that representation and subject-matter are quite irrelevant: representational art is not art proper, for all representation is a means to an end, namely the arousing of emotions; art proper has nothing to do with ends, being itself a pure expression of emotion. And of course it must be the case that representational art is not art proper. For the scrutiny of nature is the study of a concept, of a mode of spirit second to that mode which is art. As Croce puts it more picturesquely, 'a man, faced with natural beauty, is exactly the mythical Narcissus at the pool'. Its representation, therefore, is and cannot but be a depiction of a man-made abstraction, a petrification, therefore, of an inferior activity of spirit that can be tapped more immediately at a higher source.

Again for the same set of reasons you cannot, sixthly, say that one form of art is of a higher quality or more engaging of more of a man's self or leaves less out, than another; nor are there degrees of beauty. A cathedral is no finer of itself than a dower house, nor is a tragedy greater than a sonnet, or a Crucifixion than an abstract, or a nude than a still-life of apples. These negations, I need not remind you, have done yeoman service in their day and in the nineteenth century were even necessary to clear away a mass of lumber. Yet, as it happened, the great revolutionary movements of that century achieved their aims through representation and through a passionate love of nature, and a conviction, therefore, that some subjects and emotions were worth far more than others. It would be too tiresome to trace in contemporary writing the reiterations of these negations; it is enough for my purpose to underline that these too are a necessary corollary of the idealist model of spiritual activity. But to say that some subjects and some emotions are more worthwhile or more engaging of more of human nature than others is to grade them and to make a moral judgment; and moral judgments are a quite other mode of the expression of spirit, which the spirit's self-expression in art does not presuppose.

To be true to its essence, art proper, pure art, must discard not only concepts and nature then, but also moral feelings and not a little of human nature. How lucky for us that Titian, for one, was unaware of it. But here, too, I must not make a caricature. Collingwood himself is insistent that a genuine artist cannot be indifferent about his subject-matter; he must take it seriously.

> I said that the emotion expressed by a work of art cannot be merely an 'aesthetic' emotion, but that this so-called aesthetic emotion is itself a translation into imaginative form of an emotion which must pre-exist to the activity of expressing it. It is an obvious corollary of this, that an artist who is not furnished, independently of being an artist, with deep and powerful emotions will never produce anything except shallow and frivolous works of art.[1]

Still, there is nothing a man cannot take seriously, if taking it seriously means having deep and powerful emotions about it.

[1] *The Principles of Art*, p. 279.

There are, I know, those who have gravely, and on principle, welcomed the lyrical self-expressions in drawing and painting not only of children but of psychotics in mental homes. The impulse is the familiar one: to prize the 'act of what Croce has called lyrical intuition' precisely for being pre-logical and preconceptual and pre-moral, and for expressing, therefore, and revealing 'imagination', 'the wider margin of what Freud calls the pre-conscious mind'.[1] Nor is there anything inconsistent with Croceanism in this undifferentiated and especial esteem; quite the reverse.

If you cannot, then, grade the subject-matter of art or the emotions that beget it, it is little wonder that to the pagan and mediaeval and Renaissance imagination there has succeeded for most painters 'nothing except an intense preoccupation with his separate and individual self'. Little wonder either that not only are we far from the Impressionists and Cézanne, but far also from Gauguin and Van Gogh; the emotions expressed in the visual arts have progressively narrowed in their range. Of course, if every-thing is, as a matter of dogma, of equal interest and on the same level of significance, then nothing is of special interest or of greater or less significance. The only thing that matters is that an artist should feel strongly about his ego, his 'vision', the expres-sion of which is the entire function of art proper. The dogma is called a humanism; the description is, no doubt, a peculiar use of English.

But the last feature of the climate of aesthetics to which I should like to draw your attention is the use of language. Of course, it hardly need be added, questions about language are never questions merely about language. What I have in mind is not so much the woolliness of aesthetics that appals and bores so many. It is arguable that all writing about the arts, and particularly the non-literary arts, must of its nature put language to strained uses, so strained that it will take a mind of unusual power and discipline, and one fastidious in the use of words, to keep the

[1] These phrases are quoted from the last few pages of Sir Herbert Read, *Art Now* (1933).

writing out of the bog of indeterminacy to which we have grown so accustomed; and in the general run of critics no less than of aestheticians these qualities are excessively rare. It is arguable, because most of the arts are in a different medium from that of words, and because, no matter what the medium, concepts are one thing and experience is another. It may indeed be the case—I think it is—that one of our endemic diseases is to believe that all experience is translatable, more or less, into talk; and certainly among the hundreds who talk endlessly and who write about the arts there are not more than dozens who look and feel and respond. But there is nothing to complain of in strained language, so long as the lines of communication with workaday language, language whose meanings can be cashed, are kept clear; so long, that is, as there are open communications with the home base.

The lines of communication, however, are usually not kept clear, and this for a most excellent reason. The woolliness of aesthetics is not, I have suggested, a central peculiarity. Behind the woolliness and responsible for it is something very peculiar indeed, namely that aesthetics, the central body of aesthetics whose ghostly outlines and whose climate I have been endeavouring to capture, is not a descriptive study at all. It is not, that is to say, a study that attempts to describe, at however high a level of altitude and generality, particular works of art; it is not an attempt at a theory that will do justice to what particular artists are doing in their works and to what they do to us.[1] It is not an empirical study. In the conduct of an empirical study in which a man is trying to discern and account for common characteristics in a multitude of instances, there are, of course, features that go to confirm his hypothesis and features that count against it; the theory is offered, therefore, as a probable story that does better justice to more aspects of the matter than another; he is ready at any moment to reconsider it. But aesthetics in the grand style is not like this at all. It is not empirical. One of the first characteristics one notes about it is that, according to it, a great number of

[1] From some of these strictures, though not from all, I must, of course, exempt Roger Fry; Fry's precepts always stuck close to examples.

things that one would have called works of art are not really
works of art at all, and that a great deal that one would have
thought relevant is systematically left out; another characteristic
that one comes to notice is that nothing counts as evidence
against the theory, but that, contrariwise, everything counts as
evidence for it; what appears to count against it is either liqui-
dated (it is not art at all) or construed in terms of the theory.
Thirdly, this process of liquidation and reconstruction is not
accidental to the theory and done from time to time, but essential
to it and systematically done. The theory is, in other words,
irrefutable and systematically irrefutable. It is, that is to say, not
a theory at all but a dogma of a special kind of metaphysics.[1]
Its key propositions are not descriptive of works of art but *a
priori* propositions regulative of what are works of art.

I cannot forbear directing your attention, however, to a
second oddity about the use of language in aesthetics, although it
is implicit in all that I have just been saying. The language, then,
is non-empirical and non-descriptive; it is *a priori*; it is also, and
inevitably, prescriptive. That is to say, instead of describing how
things are, it lays down what experience of art must be like if it is
to be experience of art proper, what art must be if it is to be art
proper. It is, in other words, a set of concealed imperatives.

It is a very short step from these hypothetical imperatives to
categorical or moral imperatives. Or rather, it is no step at all;
these imperatives are already moral. For art proper is a pure
expression of spirit that is degraded or adulterated or corrupted
or prostituted or frustrated by art that is not the genuine article
and the real thing, by interests alien to its essence; by, for
example, representational art. These words—'real', 'essential',
'genuine', 'pure', 'proper'—are persuasive words, and none of us
wants to be a degraded specimen of human-kind; the words, then,
are crypto-imperatival. 'Thou shall not worship false gods nor any
art that is representational nor any art that tells a story'—and so

[1] For more on this matter see Beryl Lake, 'A Study of the Irrefutability of Two
Aesthetic Theories' published in *Aesthetics and Language* (ed. William Elton, 1954).
Miss Lake discusses Croce and Clive Bell.

on and so on. It is no accident that in a man who takes the visual arts as seriously as does Sir Herbert Read, to refer yet again to him (and I refer to him as often as I do *honoris causa*), aesthetics is pervaded by moralism and indeed reads sometimes like a passage of ascetical and mystical theology, or like, at any rate, a piece from a book of devotional literature.

It is again part of the climate of modern times: art is the liberator of the Old Adam. It might appear odd that an aesthetics one of whose essential tenets is the amoralism of art should itself be impregnated with morals and, indeed, puritanism in morals. But the oddity is of a type discussed earlier in these pages. This non-descriptive and prescriptive use of language that merges into the issuing of concealed moral imperatives is itself integral to an aesthetics of idealism and the idealist story of the pure expression of spirit. It is thoroughly thought out only in such an aesthetics. Outside this philosophy of art it is more like a set of axioms or unconscious presuppositions; it reflects not a mind, perhaps, but a mood.

May I conclude by drawing these themes together as best I can and as briefly as I can?

I have attempted to delineate the ghostly outlines, as I have called them, of a body of doctrine that is common to most of the aesthetics done in our time. By aesthetics I mean not literary or art criticism but a comprehensive and panoramic theory of art as art, although it is obvious that the two live together and do not merely coexist; in particular aesthetics affects a good deal, and in my own view most, of current popular criticism. Not, however, as doctrine; by this body of doctrine I mean not so much explicitly held tenets as, rather, a body of shared assumptions: not theories that you make the better to understand and to clarify and illuminate the facts, but spectacles through which you look at the facts, barely conscious schemes of interpretation to categorize no matter what facts. I am conscious that my documentation is incomplete and that for exact accuracy my argument calls for more qualification that there has been space to give. But I believe that my picture is a recognizable one. M. Maritain's aesthetic, for instance, is nothing if not fashionable; but I have most frequently had in mind the aesthetical writings of Sir Herbert Read. To Sir Herbert I have referred often, but infrequently in detail; it is the over-all picture that I have tried to describe and appraise. Sir Herbert both catches and by conceptual elaboration of what he catches sets the tone of much English thinking about the arts, and I believe that my delineation may be verified by reference to his serious and many works.[1]

I have attempted also to show that to this body of doctrine, or rather to this set of shared assumptions, there corresponds in fact a body of explicit aesthetic doctrine, a systematic corpus of theses held to be justified by a comprehensive and explicit philosophy. I have tried to show, further, that this corpus itself was not something just thought up by philosophers; that contrariwise it reflected a state of affairs that had historically come into being.

But by so reflecting it confirmed this state of affairs in being, for it built it into a comprehensive doctrine, or dogma, of what art proper is. In this sense it intellectually justified the process of history, and the ephemeralities of flux became essential moments in the life of the Spirit.

I have argued, further, that aesthetics, as a philosophy of art elaborated by men who knew what thinking is and what they were doing, is in fact a child of metaphysical (and indeed absolute) idealism and of nothing else; that this and only this is the explicit and comprehensive philosophy that legitimates it. The assumptions of current aesthetics are self-conscious and mutually consistent doctrines in idealist aesthetics; outside such an aesthetics they are merely taken-for-granted assumptions. I have referred to Croce and to Collingwood not because they are academics and so am I, but because they are not conduits of a mood but minds, learned and powerful, who knew what they were about. Their philosophy of art is part of a philosophy of history, of a philosophy

---

[1] I do not, of course, wish to be construed as suggesting that there are no inconsistencies to be found in these works, or that everything said by their distinguished author belongs easily to this picture or is, indeed, compatible with it.

of nature and of a philosophy of mind. And their work recapitulates and resumes in a most striking fashion the main themes of continental (and British) idealism since Kant, and therefore a pervasive cultural *milieu*.

Of course philosophy is not history, and in spite of its essential relativism (I am thinking here of Collingwood's doctrine of 'absolute presuppositions')[1] idealist aesthetics comes to wreckage on the thesis that it is. The essence of it is a belief that art is and only is lyrical expressiveness; a phase of how Europeans felt about literature and the arts is erected into an essential mode of spirit; but there it is fixed, arrested, immobilized, an absolute in a platonic world of Forms. Yet there is in fact nothing absolute about it, and tomorrow people may feel quite differently. In consistency, any new way of feeling that emerges in history is equally a mode of the activity of pure spirit in art; and 'pure' here means the dominant way in which contemporaries feel. This is not, however, how Croce and Collingwood talk or what they mean by 'pure', and *The Principles of Art* is concerned to show, once for all, what is and what is not art proper. At bottom, I need hardly add, the wreckage is that of the original Hegelian delusion, towards which Croce and Collingwood stand in an ambiguous relation. 'What really evolves', wrote Croce, 'is . . . the universal spirit', and it evolves spontaneously; 'true progress is our own progress, the progress of the world in and through us, which is always going on and so is without end'.[2] It is vintage teleological Hegelianism. Everything is explained and justified by the self-development of Spirit, but Spirit is the spirit immanent in human-kind; so that nothing is either explained or justified: everything is as it is and comes to be as it does because this is what it is and this is how it happens. But, as I said earlier, it is the Hegelianism that provides the optimism.

Not that this is the only rock on which this kind of idealism breaks. 'Objective' or 'subjective' idealism (but the label does

[1] See *An Essay on Metaphysics* (1940).
[2] From the essay 'In Praise of Individuality' published in *My Philosophy* (trans. E. F. Carritt, 1949).

not matter) is about as false a philosophy as even a philosopher
could devise. But I have argued also that it and only it is the hearth
and home for the kind of aesthetics current in England now. This
is a very surprising thing to argue, but I mean it quite seriously.
Sir Herbert Read would perhaps be appalled to learn of the
company that he is keeping; it is company that he has disowned.[1]
But this is the company. In the aesthetics of the moment there are
no minds of considerable power and none trained or learned in
philosophy, and they do not know what they are doing. They are
to all appearances unaware that if the moods that their assumptions
reflect are to be more than expressions of the passing show and
are to be significant and vital expressions of spirit, if they are to
have any validity (for they do not make much of a showing for
any such validity in their own right), it is from philosophical
idealism that they must borrow their validity and their significance above the flux. They are unaware that the positions they
take are bits and pieces, severed arms and legs, of a coherent
corpus of idealist dogma, and that only as integral parts of this
body of philosophy do they take on either life or even hypothetical sense.

I have argued, then, that the self-conscious and articulate
intellectual drive behind the unconscious and tacit assumptions

---

[1] 'Croce, of course, has made the attempt' (i.e. to give 'this sphere of the human
spirit—art—a just place within a unified view of the universe'), Sir Herbert has
written, 'but . . . it is the last flicker of a defunct idealism, and I do not propose
to stop to examine it. It is daily earning discredit and will not for long embarrass us
with its terminological confusions.' Very oddly, Sir Herbert characterizes it as 'a
species of solipsism that attempts to identify aesthetics with linguistics'. (*Art Now*,
1933, pp. 52–4.)

On the other hand Sir Herbert has also declared that 'we have now reached a stage
of relativism in philosophy where it is possible to affirm that reality is in fact
subjectivity, which means that the individual has no choice but to construct his own
reality, however arbitrary and even "absurd" it may seem. This is the position
reached by the Existentialists, and to it corresponds a position in the world of art
that requires a similar decision. . . . But Existentialism is but the latest phase of a
development of thought that reaches back to Kant and Schelling, and it is difficult
(from a point of view inside the stream) to see any other direction which philosophy
can take (it already carries along with it the contradiction of Christianity and
atheism).' ('The Modern Epoch in Art', 1949, republished in *The Philosophy of
Modern Art*, 1952. See also *ibid.* the essay 'Human Art and Inhuman Nature'.)

of current aesthetics is metaphysical idealism. That this is so and that it is unrecognized may well be an element in the malaise of our aesthetics; if a child is unsure of himself it is all the worse if he does not know who his parents are. But there is no reason why we should be idealists 'subjective' or 'objective' or 'absolute' or of whatever kind, and every reason why we should not be. Does it follow that current aesthetics is unsound from top to bottom? It does.

All aesthetics historically is the offspring of metaphysical idealism. Does it follow that it is all unsound? It does. And for this primary reason. Aesthetics now asks what is art, and this is a question that makes putative sense within and only within such an idealism. If we forget philosophical idealism, the question is clearly a silly one. There is no one common activity or essence called art; art is an umbrella word under which shelters a mass of activities in a mass of different media. It is small wonder that aesthetics is non-descriptive, non-empirical, prescriptive, and systematically irrefutable, and no wonder that it is unilluminating of what artists do and as remote as it is from what it is ostensibly about. No wonder, then, that it is an abyss of boredom; a desolation and, in some moods, a nightmare.

Am I then suggesting that aesthetics in this manner is impossible? I certainly am. Empirically it is impossible to talk sense about the arts at the high altitude at which a man must cruise if he is to attain the generality at which he may embrace them all. There is no such altitude and no such universal embrace.[1] The

---

[1] The point is a familiar one; it is that made in a more general way by Margaret Macdonald, for example, in the opening paragraphs of a paper 'Art and Imagination' published in the *Proceedings of the Aristotelian Society* (N.S. vol. LIII, 1952–3). She comments that aesthetic theories 'tend to begin in paradox and end in tautology or verbal legislation. They seek a completely *general* answer to the question "What is Art?" or a simple definition of "Art" which will apply to all works of art without exception. The procedure, as for other problems, is to formulate such a definition from characteristics of some of the objects ordinarily covered by the term to be defined, and then either to extend the defining expression by analogy to other members of the group which yet have such different characteristics that its meaning evaporates, or to exclude from the original field those objects to which it cannot significantly be applied. The result is a well-known series of formulae or slogans:

20

more closely one looks, really looks, at painting, for example, the more is borne in on one the impossibility of constructing any comprehensive theory. As for the common essences that have in fact been alleged, not only have they been extracted by a process of abstraction that quite simply leaves out too much that is ingredient into our experience of works of art; but, as we have seen in the case of the allegation that the common essence of these works is that they are 'expressive of emotion' or 'productive of pleasure', these essences also explode under scrutiny.

This does not, of course, imply that one cannot make general statements of any kind, or that hypotheses and theories in regard to the arts are all useless. They are not useless if they contribute to our understanding of what it is that paintings, to stick to this branch of the arts, do to us; they are useless if they bludgeon us into thinking that all paintings do or should do the same sort of thing. In any case the urge to reflect on our experience is an inveterate endowment that does no harm so long as it does not get in the way of our experiencing or does not distort or blur our experiencing; and there is no reason in the nature of things why it should not clarify it and by clarifying enhance. There is no reason why this should not be so; it does, however, happen to be the case that usually in fact it is not so, and that most theories serve neither utility nor delight.

Demolition jobs will always be necessary as long as aestheticians think in the thought-forms evolved by their idealist begetters. The monstrous damage done by metaphysical idealists in political thinking is sufficiently acknowledged; they have had a hand in the brutality and blood-letting of our times. The damage they have done to the arts is not recognized at all; yet in

"Art is Imitation", "Art is Significant Form", "Art is Expression", "Art is Imagination" and many others. These have been hurled at each other by rival theorists throughout the history of aesthetics and criticism with no clear realization of their linguistic function. Tautologies have been reverenced as profound truths: verbal legislation as major discovery. By their partial light not only individual works but whole arts have been sacrificed.' Miss Macdonald assigned the unsatisfactoriness of aesthetics to the ignoring of 'the complexities of discourse about art and the logic of language'; but if I am right there is much more to it than this alone.

the art world the aesthetician, and with him the art critic, has become a kind of medicine man (to borrow a simile from Professor Wittkower) who canalizes the emotions of the modern tribe and often enough creates the symbols of its emotivity. Quite obviously the philosophical idealists have had a hand in the monstrous inflation of all contemporary talk about the visual arts; and the corruptions of this talk are pervasive. Art is not indeed, as they held, a collaboration between artist and public; it is, however, except for the rare major endowment or the toughest spirit, a business of constant and subtle interplay and chain reaction between artist and aesthetician and critic and public. The critic is not unaffected by aesthetical assumptions, nor therefore is the public. That the public should be told fairy stories that obstruct vision is bad enough; it is worse when artists swallow them. Echoing these stories, their accounts of themselves and their work—and painters and sculptors have grown immensely articulate since the end of the Second World War—come to confirm what the aestheticians say; and the interplay begins all over again. For is not what an artist says himself of decisive importance? It is always relevant; but it is not always decisive. It all depends on the artist. It is not his business to talk about what he does but to do it, and he may not have the equipment to talk. Oddly enough, sculptors appear to be better off in this respect than painters; to select examples from celebrated names, it is instructive to compare what Mr. Henry Moore says about his work with what Mr. Ben Nicholson and Mr. Graham Sutherland say about theirs. Worst of all is the effect on the artists themselves, but of this it would be invidious and perhaps libellous to give illustrations.

There will be those who are disappointed and who feel that the legitimate claims of mind are cheated by any argument that there can be no panoramic philosophy of the whole of human activity in which everything falls into its allotted place on the unfolding map of the spirit. It is odd that many Christians should feel thus cheated, for it is the old idealist dream. And as for the arts, the arts need no such justification. The arts are their own justification; and so are their satisfactions.

22. *Aesthetics and Metaphysics*

DOM ILLTYD TRETHOWAN

Dom Illtyd Trethowan, monk of Downside Abbey, was the first speaker to attempt a positive theory of art and the aesthetic experience.

AESTHETICS is emerging from a period of comparative neglect among English-speaking philosophers. And there are signs that the same may be true of metaphysics. Nevertheless, any attempt to relate aesthetics to metaphysics is unlikely to win much sympathy except in Thomist circles, and in that case the metaphysics would have to be of a certain kind. The attempts which have been so far made to evolve a Thomist aesthetic leave me puzzled. This statement should be taken as meaning precisely what it says. It is possible that the view expressed by M. Maritain, for example, may be to some extent the same as that which I shall put forward: I do not know, because I cannot be sure what M. Maritain means, and I am quite prepared to believe that this is my own fault. In the same way the more Platonic position of the late Mr. Ananda Coomaraswamy, although I can see in a general way what it means, seems to throw no light on what happens when I appreciate works of art. I do not find that in appreciating works of art I penetrate to the 'essences' of things. All I can do, in answering the request to write a paper on this subject, is to put before you the only explanation of the value commonly ascribed to works of art which (so far as I can see) fits in with what the appreciation of works of art appears to be in my own very limited experience. The outlook, then, is rather black.

It is, however, a consolation to discover that in my account of what a work of art essentially is (and I shall have to devote nearly all my space to that) I have the agreement of Mr. Harold Osborne. With the implications of this account for the theist, which I shall suggest in conclusion, Mr. Osborne, as at present advised, would have no concern. My hope is that if, with Mr. Osborne's help, I can persuade a theist to accept the account, I may be able to persuade him also that it fits in, not with any elaborate metaphysical system, but with a metaphysical conclusion, with a certain view of our knowledge of God.

Mr. Osborne has developed, in two recent books, with much learning and penetration, a thesis about works of art which commended itself to me, in a very crude form, more than twenty years ago.[1] In the crude form there is nothing original about it. It is simply the ancient thesis that a work of art must be a complete unity. I have never been able to understand what is supposed to be wrong with it. Admittedly it does not take us far. But it does seem to be a perfectly sensible and satisfactory answer, so far as it goes, to the question: 'What is the property possessed by all genuine works of art in virtue of which we call them genuine works of art instead of just artefacts?' The difficulty, in the present climate of philosophical opinion, is that this sort of question is generally ruled out as unnecessary or even improper. Mr. P. F. Strawson, for example, reviewing Mr. Osborne's *Theory of Beauty* (1952) asks: 'Why does Mr. Osborne think it so important that there should be just one objective property in virtue of which works of art are judged to be good?'[2] I should have thought it a fair enough answer that we find a certain sameness in the effects which such works of art have upon us. 'And then,' Mr. Strawson continues, 'works of art are so diverse. There is, I think, no more specific word of praise which we should be prepared to apply to all works of art which we admire than the word "good". It is hopeless to look for a common element in

---

[1] For example, 'The Beautiful in Art', *The Downside Review*, October 1933. I should confess here that this essay, though containing Mr. Osborne's central doctrines, seems to me now cluttered up with a good deal of metaphysical nonsense.

[2] *Mind*, July 1954, p. 415.

all the things we go on to say in amplification of this.' That seems to me a piece of dogmatism. Modern philosophers are often so anxious to avoid generalizations that they make unfounded claims to have proved a negative. But I was glad to see that Mr. Strawson described *Theory of Beauty* as 'a serious and intelligent book on aesthetics, one of the best attempts to describe in general what it is to appreciate, to enjoy a work of art, that I have read'. So, too, Professor W. B. Gallie, in an article typically entitled 'Art as an Essentially Contested Concept' in *The Philosophical Quarterly* for April 1956, after praising Mr. Osborne's analyses and 'the spirit with which he sets about his task', concludes, 'Nevertheless, Mr. Osborne's programme seems open to all the familiar objections that have been raised against theories which seek to define the characteristic excellence of works of art in terms of a single essential property. Is he not indeed guilty of the extreme error of seeking for a general recipe or formula for judging works of art?' I fully agree that Mr. Osborne's claim will be a startling one for most people, and that there are apparent objections to it; I shall say something about them later. At the moment I am concerned only to suggest that such passages as the above, unsupported by any serious argument, show a certain prejudice.

Before I begin to expound Mr. Osborne's thesis it may be wise to make clear what it does not purport to do, since there has been misunderstanding on the point. The misunderstanding has not been Mr. Osborne's fault, for he has made himself perfectly clear, at least in his second book on our subject, *Aesthetics and Criticism* (1954). (Here I may perhaps be allowed a parenthesis: In this book and in *Theory of Beauty* Mr. Osborne's opening pages are, from several points of view, most discouraging. When he gets into his stride one can hardly believe that it is the same writer.) In *Aesthetics and Criticism*, then, we find the following lucid distinction:

> On the one hand a work of literature is assessed for its excellence as literature, its aesthetic value. On the other hand it is assessed for certain utility-values, the values of wisdom and moral illumination.

The former mode of assessment, and the former mode only, is literary criticism proper; the latter mode differs in no respect from similar assessments of a human being or a non-literary treatise; it is the function of the philosopher, the moralist or the preacher. There is no reason why one man should not combine the two functions, unite the two types of assessment in one piece of writing; but unless he keeps the two types of judgement reasonably distinct, what he means to say will not be apparent in his words (pp. 301–2).

It has been failure to give due weight to this distinction (on which Mr. Osborne frequently insists) that has led some of his critics to regard his aesthetic theory as narrow and arbitrary. The distinction, as Mr. Osborne observes elsewhere, is 'not a distinction very much to the taste of critics and those who appreciate literature in general' (p. 100). He notes that it is Pater's distinction between 'good art' and 'great art', although Pater did not properly understand the implications of it, and he adds usefully that the *appreciator* need not make the distinction, at any rate not explicitly. His total response may be built up of many responses of diverse elements of value 'included in the organic oneness of a living appreciation'. But the *critic* 'must anatomize his appreciation, disentangle the interwoven strands, trace the elements to their sources and justify each judgement by his aesthetic creed' (p. 101).

This conclusion will offend many who take it as established that we can never properly separate form and subject-matter in a work of art. Sometimes, of course, we cannot, because there is no subject-matter, that is to say no materials which have value as such other than the values which they have as the materials of the work of art. Music is the clearest case of this, but I cannot hope to convince anybody of it in this paper, although I hope to show in a general way the grounds on which the claim would be made out not only for music but for other arts also. In the case of literature it is often supposed that certain moral qualities or attitudes are indispensable to good writing. It is obviously true that one can sometimes divine a man's moral attributes from his style; no one, we may say, who was not profoundly conscious of whatever it is

could write like that. A writer needs something to write about,
and he may need to feel strongly about it if he is to express
himself effectively about it. Nevertheless, it is one thing to feel
strongly about it and another thing to express oneself effectively
about it; and the literary critic as such is directly concerned, in
Mr. Osborne's submission and mine, only with the latter. The
only attitude to life which is essential to the production of works
of art is an attitude to that part of life which consists in producing
works of art. This does not mean, I repeat, that the literary critic
is debarred from expressing himself about other attitudes to life.
It means only that he should distinguish what he is then doing
from what he is doing when he criticizes a work of art simply as
a work of art. It is also true that we may detect moral weaknesses
in a man from his style; no one, we may say, would produce this
broken-backed or bombastic poetry if he were honestly facing
up to life. We may, indeed, detect an insincerity in a writer's
work. But to say that good art must be sincere is only to say that
the artist must not allow his artistic powers to be warped by
weaknesses of character. It does not follow that strength of
character (apart from the integrity demanded of the artist in his
work as an artist) is an essential ingredient in a work of art. It is
true, finally, that some subject-matters lend themselves more than
others to artistic treatment. But it does not follow that the presence or absence of such subject-matters goes any part of the way
to answering the question: What *is* a work of art?

We shall be approaching an answer to this question if we spend
a little longer in considering what a work of art is not. It is not,
as such, a representation of anything. Even if we thought that
some form of representation is an ingredient in a work of art as
a *conditio sine qua non*, it would still not be the essential characteristic of works of art. This is too obvious to require discussion.
Yet, as Mr. Osborne has pointed out, again in *Aesthetics and
Criticism*, so often

> when a work is judged to be successfully realistic, 'true to life' as it
> is called, it is praised for that very reason, with the concealed

implication for theory that realism is a norm of excellence to be applied in assessing the merits of literary art (p. 69). The man who leaps on to the stage to save Desdemona from death, the man whose mouth waters at a Van Dongen or who vicariously delights in the beauties of natural scenery portrayed by Cotman or Girtin, the man who weeps for Little Dorrit, and all the many who enjoy a good cry in the cinema—these have not even begun to put themselves into the frame of mind for which artistic enjoyment is possible (p. 66).

The conclusion to which we are led is that works of art, considered precisely as such, have no meaning outside themselves. The materials of which they are composed may have meaning or symbolic function, and in the case of literary works of art must have meaning. But these meanings are taken over into the total structure of the work of art which, as a total structure, is to be appreciated simply for what it is. A picture need not be anything else than a structure of shapes and colours. I wish I had space to quote from what Mr. Osborne has to say on this aspect of his subject; he is deeply illuminating even to people (like myself) who find this field of art the most difficult. The theory does not rule out representation in a painting as improper.

But if a picture *does* represent an emotional situation, if it does symbolize figures symbolizing emotion, this fact is certainly germane to its full appreciation by the ordinary unspecialized observer. And if it represents anything at all, even though no emotion is expressed, the mere fact of representation is germane to seeing the structure of colours and shapes which is the picture. For a shape which is recognized as representative, as a natural symbol of some known object, immediately acquires additional insistence and weight in the balanced harmony of visual impressions which is the picture (p. 87).

We are now in a position to see more clearly what Mr. Osborne means by calling a work of art an 'organic whole' which has 'complex configurational unity'. He has said what I should have wished to say so much more clearly than I should have said it that I must be excused for quoting him *in extenso*.

The quality of being an organic unity may be possessed by any construct in a greater or less degree and it is this quality which constitutes the beauty or proper excellence of all works of art. Coleridge vaguely anticipated this when he said: 'The Beautiful is that in which the *many*, still seen as many, become one.' . . . Any construct which enters into awareness as an organic unity is apprehended 'synoptically' as a single complex whole of multifarious and intricately related parts. . . . Such synoptic apprehension demands a heightening and tautening of awareness—visual, aural or intellective— far beyond the normal needs of practical life. . . . This is why the experience of beauty is valued. It is valued because it makes us more vividly alive than we otherwise know how to be (pp. 228–9).

That is Mr. Osborne's summary of his view. It has been supported in his earlier book, *Theory of Beauty*, with an impressive mass of analysis and much careful argumentation. The following passage from *Aesthetics and Criticism* will shed further light on it:

In aesthetic appreciation awareness is concentrated upon the perceptual situation as it is presented, as the connoisseur savours the bouquet of a wine or the Chinese savour the qualities of jade. When you begin to attend to the sensations themselves, to see the picture which is before your eyes and to hear the sounds which your ear presents, you are making the first step in appreciation. If someone asks you what a picture by Kandinsky means, he is not looking at it in order to see it and probably lacks the capacity to see the familiar pictures of the National Gallery which he thinks he can interpret. Nor is it any otherwise with literature, which is apprehended by intellective and imaginal awareness. In ordinary life we habitually attend only to the fragmentary meanings of spoken or written sentences which have practical implications for the situations in which we find ourselves. But when language is literature and we attend to it as literature, our minds must be opened to uninhibited awareness of the full meanings of words and sentences. The man who asks what a poem means is asking a ridiculous question; for unless the poem is a bad one, the poet himself cannot say what he meant except in precisely the words of the poem (p. 249).

To complete this very hasty account I must add some of the conclusions listed by Mr. Osborne at the end of his *Theory of Beauty*:

An objective theory of beauty implies that appreciation is cognitive in character or mode of intuitional awareness. . . . A set of sensory impressions characterized by beauty is an organic whole of considerable complexity, the constituent parts of which are interpenetrating organic wholes. . . . An organic whole is a configuration which is not an additive resultant of its parts and the relations between the parts but a prior configurational unity such that the parts are what they are in virtue of the whole of which they are part. . . . It is appreciated intuitively as unique and individual, not by analysis and discursive synthesis of the theoretical reason. In aesthetic appreciation a perceptive activity functions at exceptionally high intensity, and provided that the object is adequate to sustain attention, consciousness through the activated perception is stimulated to exceptional vivacity (pp. 202–3).

Some illustration of these high-sounding generalizations by treatment of particular works of art may seem already considerably overdue, but before attempting anything of the kind I must ask patience for a few comments on some of Mr. Osborne's formulas. The insistence on a cognitive mode of awareness is particularly welcome. Accounts of beauty in terms of emotion or imagination as opposed to cognition have always seemed to me profoundly unsatisfactory. It seems to me plainly the fact that when we appreciate a work of art we *perceive* something. This activity of perception may require the use of powers to which the name 'imaginative' is properly to be applied, but the activity itself is apprehensive. In my own view our faculty of awareness is unitary, it is to be called the mind or intellect, and it is operative *in* the faculties of sensory perception. But this, for the moment, is not material to the argument. It is enough that we may speak of an act of awareness without postulating some special and mysterious aesthetic faculty. This, like most acts of awareness, I suppose, generates emotion but more powerfully than most acts of awareness. The communication of emotion is not *directly* the artist's business. This has been argued exhaustively by Mr. Osborne, and I think conclusively, although he does not perhaps sufficiently recognize that the generation of powerful emotion is in fact the indication that an act of vigorous apprehension is being exercised. But I agree with him that criticism must be conducted in terms of what is objectively apprehended, not in terms of what is subjectively felt. The emotion theory is the refuge of those who are unable or for various reasons unwilling to bring to light an objective property in virtue of which works of art may be called beautiful. But it is in any case condemned by facts. A work of art may be occasioned, and commonly is, by emotions and it may cause emotions. But what is communicated by the artist is the work of art. In the process he may or he may not provoke emotions broadly similar to his own, but that is another matter.

I must also comment on what Mr. Osborne says about the intuitive character of aesthetic awareness. If this is inspected more closely, and in the light of a philosophy less 'positivist' than Mr. Osborne's, it may become easier to understand why it is accompanied by a peculiar 'vivacity'. Mr. Osborne's approach I have described as 'positivist' because he is content, on the whole, to speak of the 'vivacity' of our sensations without considering how it is that they are *correlated* in experience. It seems to me that the unification of our sensations as an 'organic whole' leads necessarily to the conclusion that we have a power of awareness which embraces the deliverances of particular acts of sensation. This power I propose to call the mind. That aesthetic appreciation is a function of mind would be accepted in a general way, I think, by theist philosophers, although they would not all agree about the way in which the mind is related to the sensations in our knowledge of material objects. What I wish to suggest here is that the unitary power of apprehension, the mind, bears directly in aesthetic awareness upon the deliverances of the senses and *contemplates* them; it does not, in the exercise of aesthetic awareness itself, draw conclusions from them or read anything into them; it simply perceives the complex unity which they possess. A work of art, as Mr. Osborne puts it in *Theory of Beauty*, is 'an enduring possibility . . . of a specific set of sensory impressions' (p. 202). And one reason why the mind delights in it is that it has only to *attend* to a set of sensory impressions; it takes a holiday from its usual task of interpreting them as symbols for the guidance of its practical, or speculative, concerns. Another reason—and this will become important later—is that the complexity of the set of impressions gives full play to the mind's powers of attention. Its void is for the moment filled.

Now that the stage is at last set for the application of these principles to particular works of art, we have to face the disconcerting fact that Mr. Osborne seems to impose a ban of silence on the whole topic.

> There are those assuredly who will complain that this account of an organic whole is too abstract, will ask that we display an example of an organic whole concretely, take it to pieces, hold up the parts to inspection, show how they are fitted together, then assemble them again, so that everyone may see and understand 'the works'. Unfortunately this cannot be done. . . . An organic whole cannot be broken down, because in the breaking down the parts of which it is composed change their nature and become something else. The relations in which they now stand, each set of relations being displayed in isolation from the whole, have become other than the relations in which they stood within the whole. . . . You cannot know by logical reason any specific concrete organic whole, and you cannot describe it analytically. (*Aesthetics and Criticism*, pp. 247, 248.)

But this is only to say that you cannot appreciate a poem except by apprehending it as it is, and this we know already. It does not prove that we can do nothing to show somebody that it is an organic whole, and if we could do nothing the work of criticism, which Mr. Osborne is trying to establish upon a proper basis, would be clearly impossible. For instance, Mr. Osborne has laid it down that an organic whole may be itself composed of organic wholes, and it must surely be possible to indicate that this is so in particular examples. Indeed he does so himself sometimes, but in so casual and allusive a manner that I shall be compelled to attempt something of the sort on my own account. That he does not disapprove of such an undertaking in principle is clearly shown by the following passage:

An artist's technique is the manner in which he utilizes his medium in order to mould his material into an organic whole. It is the essence of his individuality and personality as an artist and is closely allied to what is known as style. Study of technique tends to focus attention upon the heart of the aesthetic object. It cannot take the place of appreciation—no criticism can do that. But more than any other mode of talking about an aesthetic object it encourages the reader to observe it as a single entity of inter-related and interacting parts . . . (p. 318).

This mode of talking I must now attempt, with great trepidation, to illustrate.

> Come, seeling night,
> Scarf up the tender eye of pitiful day,
> And with thy bloody and invisible hand
> Cancel and tear to pieces that great bond
> Which keeps me paled.

(I accept Staunton's conjecture 'paled', in the sense of 'confined', for 'pale'.)

In a play of wonderfully sustained tension these words of Macbeth's, when he has just arranged Banquo's murder, will strike most people, I think, as raising the tension further in a marked way (not that many other passages in *Macbeth* are not equally or even more remarkable in that way). The reasons for this are manifold, and I shall not attempt the impossible task of exhausting them. The one which first occurs to a critic might well be that the persistent images of night, sleep and blood are reintroduced rather suddenly with an effect of impact which adds to their already accumulated force. At once, too, we have what might be called the 'Macbeth-music',[1] the looking backward to the lost world of loyalty and wholesomeness, evoked by the cadence of the first dozen words—pitiful, indeed. Somewhere at the back of our crowded picture of the play is the contrast between these words and Lady Macbeth's earlier invocation of the powers of

---

[1] On the analogy of Wilson Knight's 'Othello music'.

darkness before Duncan's murder, the perfect appropriateness of
these passages when seen in conjunction with one another:

> Come, thick night,
> And pall thee in the dunnest smoke of hell
> That my keen knife see not the wound it makes,
> Nor heaven peep through the blanket of the dark
> To cry 'Hold, hold!'

The same images, the same appalling theme, but what an
exactly right difference in the use of language! Of course Lady
Macbeth must employ so many monosyllables ('Yet who would
have thought the old man to have had so much blood in him?');
of course her rhythms must go directly on—no looking back for
her, at least not yet. Of course there will be a horrible metallic
distinctness in her syllables ('pall thee in the dunnest smoke of
hell'). Night for her is not 'seeling night', it is simply 'thick'.
But what is it in Macbeth's words which turn them finally to gold?
Surely it is their precise placing in these particular verse-lines?
Look at the poignant effect of 'seeling', coming just where it
does. Look at the subtlety of the stresses in 'scarf up' and 'pitiful'
and the half-muted stresses in 'the tender eye'. The next line has
three tremendous stresses, varying the normal five-stress pattern
with absolute propriety, 'and with thy *bloody* and in*vi*sible *hand*'
(the last two syllables of 'invisible' suggest a ghastly hush).
CANCEL and *tear* to *pieces that great bond*—no less than six stresses,
the first beginning the explosion magnificently because it follows
the last stressed syllable of the preceding line—so that the impact
of 'hand' and 'cancel' are the very ripping and tearing across of
the bond, the parchment which is Banquo's life. And so one
might go on.

I have been trying to illustrate the truth of the contention
expressed as follows by Mr. Osborne in *Theory of Beauty*: 'the
degree of beauty manifested by any work of art will be a
resultant of two factors: (*a*) the richness, complexity or subtlety
of the configurational organization, and (*b*) the completeness or
compactness of the organization for experience' (p. 126). I

agree with him that the artistically perfect (impossible) play
would be a perfect organic whole of organic wholes, and I think
that *Macbeth* is as good an approximation to this as we are likely
to find. To say this, I had better repeat, is not to say that the
gigantic spiritual issues which are put before us in *Macbeth* are
irrelevant to a proper appreciation of it; they are a part of the
play's materials. It is to say that the play is a work of art, a thing
of beauty, in the organization of its materials, in virtue of the
relation of congruence, to use another phrase of Mr. Osborne's, in
which they stand to one another in the total construct which is
the work of art. That these spiritual issues are presented *in a
certain way*, by the adoption of *certain means*, is the fact which we
have to consider. A vision of the world is indeed shown to us in
Macbeth, and this enters properly into our total appreciation of
the play. But we are now considering a value *in* the play, not the
play itself. If you state this vision of the world in abstract
conceptual terms or in any prose terms or in any terms at all
which are not *Macbeth*, then quite obviously you are ceasing to
appreciate *Macbeth*. There is no reason why one should not
appreciate *Macbeth* and at the same time appreciate the value of
Shakespeare's 'vision of the world' (that, no doubt, is what one
should do), but it is desirable to realize that these appreciations
are not one and the same thing. Again, no doubt one should
experience, to use yet another phrase of Mr. Osborne's, 'sympathetic reverberations' when we witness the portrayal of powerful
emotions, but the emotions which the work of art, as such, are
calculated to produce in us are of a very different kind—
gaudium de veritate or, more precisely, *de congruitate*.

It is commonly thought that a work of art conveys 'a vision of
life' by the employment of some mode of communication
peculiar to itself. Thus we shall be told that Shakespeare has
communicated to us in *Macbeth* 'a vision of evil' or a 'vision of
our moral dilemma' or something of the kind with a fullness and
power which are hardly to be found elsewhere. But this is
mystagogy. The vision is there all right, pervading the play.
Without it the play could not have been written. It has acted,

presumably, as a stimulus to writing it, and the interest of it acts as a stimulus on us, and gives the play a certain sort of impressiveness which otherwise it could not have. This impressiveness becomes *confused* in our minds with the impressiveness of the play as a work of art, and we accept a muddled theory about a special communication of philosophical truths by artistic means. There are philosophical truths which cannot be directly stated but only hinted, and a certain sort of poetry (or of prose) is an appropriate medium for this hinting. Even so, the appreciation of poetry (or prose) as a work of art is different from the appreciation of the truth thus communicated. Isn't there prose (or poetry) which stirs us simply because it reproduces for us a valuable experience of the writer's, a full response to natural scenery, for example? There is, and I think it will be found, as a rule, to be also a work of art. If not, it will be a sort of photograph of the real world, and the beauty which we appreciate is then *that* beauty.

A certain difficulty is thus discovered in Mr. Osborne's theory, for according to him only works of art possess organic wholeness (beauty) in more than a rudimentary degree.[1] Mr. Strawson, in the review mentioned earlier, makes the point that a human face or a landscape may have just as much organic wholeness as a picture. But all that follows is that 'beauty' has an extension wider than Mr. Osborne supposes. It does not invalidate his theory of what beauty is, as Mr. Strawson supposes. I think that beauty has this wider extension.

In attempting to illustrate from literature the theory of the organic whole, I have exposed the theory, I think, to the utmost searching test. Mr. Osborne's critics have been ready, sometimes, to allow that it is not easy to controvert it in respect of painting, the plastic arts, and music. The alternative in painting or the plastic arts, unless we declare the question unanswerable, is to fall into some form of representationalism. The alternative in music, as Mr. Osborne points out, is the unintelligible theory of

[1] *Theory of Beauty*, p. 159.

21

'emotional language'.[1] He goes on to discuss Mrs. Langer's modification of the theory in *Philosophy in a New Key*, according to which music is the '*logical expression*' of feelings, the symbolization not of actual feelings but of 'the general forms of feeling' or, in Mr. Osborne's words, 'affective patterns'. He observes that music exercises upon people 'a very profound effect which, because it is not linked to conceptual or ideational thinking, seems to be generally affective in character',[2] and adds, quite properly, that this does not justify us in calling music a mode of symbolism. All we can say is that it is the *cause* of the affective condition.[3] And I would add that it is always fundamentally the same sort of affective condition, although it may be shot through with associations of one kind and another. Music may contain associations with human activities and emotions of various kinds, just as painting may contain an element of representation. But it seems to me more immediately obvious in the case of music than in any other case that it is the organization of sensory impressions, and this alone, which is the cause of the *special* delight which we take in it. It may be true that the musician needs something to compose *about*, just as the poet needs something to write about, but *what* he composes is just music.

So far I may seem to have been engaged in expelling metaphysics from aesthetics. And now that I come to my last section, with the limits of space already exhausted, I must be extremely brief in suggesting how it comes in again by the back door. The metaphor, though crude, is less inappropriate than it might appear. For what I have to suggest is simply that there is always in our fully conscious awareness a 'background' knowledge of God, and that any considerable intensification of our 'foreground' knowledge will provoke reactions in it. Obviously I cannot be expected to defend at this juncture the assertion of such a 'background knowledge'.[4] But a passage from P. de Lubac's *Sur les*

1 *Aesthetics and Criticism*, p. 105.
2 *Ibid.*, p. 107.
3 *Ibid.*, p. 108.
4 See Illtyd Trethowan: *An Essay in Christian Philosophy* (Longmans, 1954).

Chemins de Dieu will give some indication of what it is:

> God reveals himself constantly to man by constantly impressing his own Image upon him. It is this divine operation which constitutes man in the centre of his being. This it is that makes him rational. Thus no other revelation would have been necessary, strictly speaking, so that man might know his God, apart from all supernatural revelation. This 'natural revelation' is sufficient. Let us say, to avoid all exaggeration, that it is sufficient in principle. Sin has not altogether extinguished it. For if the human soul knows itself today with an actual and graspable knowledge only through the acts which it posits, it has nevertheless a certain 'habitual knowledge' of itself, real though obscure and enveloped, constant although always fugitive, which arises from its being always present to itself. Thanks to this presence of the soul to itself it can discover, as in a mirror, the presence of God in it.[1]

'The *value* we assign to beauty', writes Mr. Osborne, 'derives from its power to awaken and exercise our dormant capacities of awareness'[2]: if we realize the full extent of these capacities, we understand that there is after all a mystery behind beauty—the *mysterium tremendum et fascinosum*. It is that, I believe, which is the secret of the 'overtones' which are represented, often confusedly, in so much poetry:

> Meanwhile the Mind, from pleasure less
> Withdraws into its happiness;
> The Mind, that Ocean where each kind
> Does streight its own resemblance find;
> Yet it creates, transcending these,
> Far other Worlds and other Seas. . . .[3]

[1] *Ibid.*, pp. 15–16. An English translation of this work is to appear shortly.
[2] *Theory of Beauty*, p. 126.
[3] Andrew Marvell: 'The Garden'.

23. *The Still Centre*

DOM SEBASTIAN MOORE

Another Monk of Downside, Dom Sebastian Moore, was asked to give a theologian's evaluation of the arts, our practice and experience of them.

INTRODUCTION

SPEAKING as a theologian in the symposium on morality I talked of charity. In this present context, a symposium on the arts, the theologian must speak of vision.

We are travellers, and our home is truth. But we are fallen men, and are so debilitated for this journey that we can, and indeed must, put the end in question. 'What is truth?' The enormous number of answers that this question has received serves only to confirm our fallen condition. May I, for the purpose of my paper, be absurdly optimistic, and narrow them down to two? For before anything so ambitious as a definition is attempted, men divide radically in their general way of envisaging what it is they want to define. To describe this first and radical division as twofold is not, perhaps, so *simpliste* as might appear at first sight.

It consists in two sets of basic assumptions. The first set runs like this: There is the world, and here is my mind, and both are constants. In bringing my mind to bear on the world, it is an instrument that I am bringing to bear on an object. The instrument is faulty and subject to improvement, but the fault is not radical, so that its gradual lessening will not constitute a radical change. I do not, then, expect ever to see the world quite differently from the way I see it now, only very much better. The second runs like this: There is the world, and here is my mind, and neither is a constant. Indications from another quarter give me more than a suspicion that my present vision is radically defective. I have had what I must call moments of consciousness. I find that I must use these as my yardstick. And from this point of view I must say that I am not now really conscious at all. I cannot take my everyday common-sense vision as basic, a thing to be improved while remaining substantially the same. I am not at all sure of common sense, for I've caught myself out too often making things into words and then resting on the words while thinking I was still in touch with the things. So much of common sense rests on this convenient equation. So the search for truth means, for me, not the attempt to understand better what is over there but the attempt to become more conscious. And then I realize that 'attempt' is not the right word, that this process must be one in which my busy ego has but a minor rôle, that of 'getting out of my own light'—and this realization enlarges still further the gap between my approach and that of the 'objective' seeker.

May I call the first of these approaches 'the scientific' and the second 'the artistic'?

The conflict between them must not be exaggerated. In the early stages of the search, before we envisage more than this world, they are complementary. The very possibility of talking about 'this world' argues a great step forward in consciousness. It is by no means obvious that the indefinite number of widely diverse objects that come into our field of awareness form a whole that can be embraced by one word. It was the discovery of Lucretius, and it came not by observation. It is now the basic scientific assumption. We have made it a part of common sense, which means that we do not think about it any more, and so forget that it depends, as a real notion, on a degree of personal unity or wholeness such as the artist seeks. Scientists are becoming increasingly aware that great discoveries are made through an interior illumination rather than through the patient collation of observed detail, however important that may be by way of preparation. In general, Aldous Huxley is representative of much of what is most promising in modern currents of thought when he says education should be addressed primarily to 'the not-self': when harmony has been established with this massive silent partner, the powers of the self are quickened in an amazing way. In all that concerns our activity, whether of knowledge or technique, whether of mathematics or music, the 'science-type' can accept the artist as partner with the greatest profit and without sacrificing his basic assumptions. 'There is the world', he can still say, 'and here am I. My goal is to understand and use the world within these terms of reference. I relax, with the artist as guide, in order to increase the efficiency of this understanding and use.'

The artist may feel slightly affronted by this way of putting it. He will probably feel that his part is by far the more important— but he'll probably let it go. Let the scientist keep his vanity— after all, he cannot acquit himself on that score. But when the matter under consideration is no longer piano-playing or physical experiment but metaphysics, the protest of the artist-type will become thoroughly obstinate. 'This is really too much,' he will say. 'I'll keep my ideas up my sleeve and let you keep your line of talk as long as we are dealing with secondary realities, but when we come to the primary reality, then my ideas are the only ones, and yours are simply invalid. I have improved you in your own sphere by persuading you to let in a force from beyond your ordinary experience. Well, you are now talking *ex professo* of what lies beyond experience. If your ordinary common-sense ideas got in the way of your piano technique, how much more will they be out of place in metaphysics.' But the other is now just as belligerent. 'If I give you your head here,' he says, 'you will reduce everything to consciousness, a pure *state* in which the distinction of subject and object will have no place. I take it you wish to remain a Christian. Well, where is Christianity without this distinction? God is not just pure consciousness, he must always remain the object, if we are not to be lost in oriental mists. I noticed that you were rather sulky when I said your ideas were merely ancillary to my technique, but I did not take you up.

After all, we all have our vanities. But now you have come out into the open I must come too.'

I believe that this conflict is fundamental, and that we shall see it intensified in the next few decades. What our scientist called 'oriental' ideas are destined, I believe, to have an impact on our society comparable to that of Freud. This impact is something much more serious than the mystical appeal represented by a movement such as theosophy. It is a conflux, such as history provides from time to time, of new discoveries in our western life and a way of life that is immemorial.

I

'I am contributing to a symposium on the arts,' I said. 'What's your subject?' he asked. 'Well, consciousness really.' 'Consciousness of what?' 'Nothing'—raising of my interlocutor's eyebrows —'Oh, well, I suppose, God.' This exchange showed me what I wanted to try to say to you. It isn't easy, because it is so obvious, in fact the most obvious thing in the world, and how right Aristotle was when he said that the human mind contemplates self-evident truth with difficulty. We look at things in the light, not at the light; common sense, that fruitful source of philosophy and of gross error, comes to assume that the light is for seeing by and therefore a means to an end. In physical vision it is, I suppose, a means, though Turner got to the stage of painting pretty well pure light. In the late pictures, the things are for the light, not the light for the things. This inversion should not surprise us, for physical vision provides an incomparably closer analogy for spiritual understanding than does the life of the other senses. One has only to read Christian literature—whether it be the Nicene Creed, with its *lumen de lumine*, or Dante, or St. John of the Cross—to realize that the language of light has a privileged position in the world of analogy. But this is only an introductory ramble before taking the plunge, a toe dipped nervously in the freezing water, a situation which it is bad for us to prolong.

What do we mean by consciousness? Common sense plunges into the fray—into the fray, mark you, not into the water—with the ready answer: consciousness of things and people, of course. Typical, if I may say so, my friend common sense; you have used in your definition the very word you think you are defining. And no other word, such as awareness, will get you anywhere, because it will only be a synonym. Well, retorts common sense balefully, you can't define these basic notions, they are things to get along with, not to define. In fact—warming to the attack—if you try to define consciousness you will be making it into something, *of* which you are conscious, so you will get a *regressus ad infinitum*, with consciousness always slipping away from you. And now common sense has put on his philosophical clothes and I respect him. He has given, in fact, a very salutary warning. What I am trying to talk about is seen only out of the corner of my eye, and if I try to drag it into the main field of vision I shall start talking nonsense about it, while it continues to mock me from its hiding place, still at the corner of my eye. I shall agree, then, with common sense, that there can be no definition, in the ordinary way, of consciousness; but I shan't accept the pseudo-definition with which he started—he was still rubbing his eyes—whose only purpose was to shut me up. I shan't stop talking.

I shall try another approach. One may, it seems, be more or less conscious. If we cannot look at consciousness itself, we can perhaps look at the more and less, and so get an indirect line on what there is more and less of. You are more conscious now than you were in the small hours of this morning. The world has come back, as it comes back every morning. In this case the return of consciousness is the return of the world: but there is another kind of increase in consciousness which is not a return of something that was here yesterday, of the all too familiar, but has something new about it. You are a more conscious person than you were four years ago. You notice that I say, in this context, 'conscious *person*', whereas in the other case I mentioned, I just said 'conscious'. It seemed natural to talk like that. In its deeper sense, consciousness implies not a light switched every twenty-four hours on to the objects around us but a radical personal quality: in other words, it has to do not with objects but with the subject. I always think in this connexion of an incident in Eliot's play *The Family Reunion*. John, the ineffably dull elder brother, has been concussed in a motor accident, and Harry, his brother, has just outraged the family by failing to show 'the proper concern'. In defence of his attitude he says:

> A brief vacation from the kind of consciousness
> That John enjoys, can't make very much difference
> To him or to anyone else. If he was ever really conscious,
> I should be glad for him to have a breathing spell:
> But John's ordinary day isn't much more than breathing.

Philosophers, and, I imagine, especially contemporary Oxford philosophers, tear their hair out over the language used by psycho-analysts. Can't you see, they say, that to talk of making the unconscious conscious is a contradiction in terms? If you merely mean becoming aware of something you weren't aware of before, why talk of 'the unconscious' as though it were *something*. There is no such thing as 'the unconscious' mysteriously transmuted into consciousness; there are only things that have been forgotten and that can be remembered. But for the psychologist, those things haven't just been forgotten: they are doing things to the person, making his life miserable, filling it with imaginary fears. He is not merely unconscious of them, as I am unconscious of the egg I had for breakfast until you remind me of it; he is, *because* of them, a relatively unconscious person, which is to say an unhappy person. You see the point? The philosopher is thinking of consciousness simply as light on things around us, the light that comes on every morning; the psychologist is thinking of it as a personal quality, as spiritual health, as freedom. Let us take an example. Let us say that many years ago, standing at the edge of a cliff with my sister, I conceived a violent desire to push her over. This horrified me so much that I suppressed it: I mean, not only did I resist the temptation, a laudable thing to do, but I persuaded myself that I hadn't had it. How could I have thought of such a terrible thing. But now, many years later, I am distressed to find that I get giddy whenever I go upstairs—to mention only the more mentionable of my symptoms. At enormous cost of time and money, I have that ugly moment on the cliff restored to my memory by a psychologist. I accept it, relive it. It is restored to consciousness, which really means that I am restored to conscious-ness: which means, not that I now have that moment continually in my mind, but that I bound up the stairs two at a time singing a psalm. I am not conscious of more, but more conscious. Con-sciousness, in other words, has no object, it is simply the delight and strength of self-hood. It has objects—I am conscious of you now—but no proper object in the sense that colour and shape form the proper object of physical vision. Yet this does not make it private and unreal—it is supremely the opposite of this.

You may say that I am using the word in a special sense, con-verting it from language into jargon, and that the philosopher and theologian must understand words in their ordinary sense. Yet I don't think it has yet been suggested that Henry James was influenced by Freud, other than in the way that we are all influenced by him, and when a thinker's ideas become part of everyone's basic assumptions they enter the language not as jargon but as ordinary language. The idea of consciousness as the state of a person rather than the particular awareness of objects is the key to James and to the writers he has influenced.

Unconscious people are difficult to live with. They love you one moment and hate you the next. They create chaos all around them. They don't know what they're doing, but, by God, they're doing it all right!

Consciousness has no object, but it has an end. I mean, that the process of becoming more conscious is going somewhere. Not towards an object that I shall one day discover, but towards a completeness of itself. In other words, it is not so much some-thing I can always have more of, as something I always have less of than I might have, therefore something I am destined eventually to have all of. Am I stretching the word now out of all recogni-tion? A highly conscious moment is a moment relatively free of the particular objects around us, a moment when we can breathe, and actually, if we observe ourselves, do breathe more deeply, a relaxed moment. We are not then, in Arnold's telling phrase, 'immured in the hot prison of the present'. Which is exceedingly odd, because although we call it a moment it seems to be trying to get outside time. The poet or mystic who has known such a moment—and I think they are more ordinary than we imagine, like M. Jourdain's prose—finds that his memory has recorded only part of it, the part that is in time. So you get those haunting lines in an Eliot poem:

> To be conscious is not to be in time
> But only in time can the moment in the rose-garden,
> The moment in the arbour where the rain beat,
> The moment in the draughty church at smokefall
> Be remembered, involved with past and future.[1]

There's nothing particularly modern about this. Dante says the same thing about the vision of God, at the end of the *Paradiso*. The universal form of that great whole I *think* I saw *since*, as I say this, I feel that I rejoice.

The word, is now stretched to its limits where it verges on self-contradiction. For that of which I cannot now become conscious in the moment of consciousness is precisely the conscious part of it. Consciousness escapes from the time-track of memory, recording there only an excitement, a longing.

Another striking thing—it is the same thing really—about the conscious moment is that what is known there is not new. This is not surprising, as it is only in the world of objects that we can encounter something simply new. Paradox again: although we come newly to it, it is not new. When Augustine says, 'in a trembling thrust of the mind I came on that which is', how could he know it as that which is and had been always, if he was really finding it for the first time. No, he is knowing what he has always known, what he has always been. This gives the final stretch, or twist if you like, to the meaning of the word 'consciousness'. It is not something that comes to us, but something we come to. Things happen to us, but we happen on consciousness. This is not a playing with words, but an attempt to do justice to the witness of the mystic who knows, obscurely, in the moment of realization, 'here I have always been'. This co-presence of the new and the always is found in experiences less than mystic, in fact in any new understanding, whether in mathematics or in history: when an idea is born in our mind, not pushed into it with a view to impending examinations: something new, yet something we have always known in a way. God, the *pulchritudo tam antiqua quam nova*, speaks in us in every such experience, and it is the object of any education worth the name to multiply them. God speaks in us—that is why theology sets the first great mystery, the generation of the Logos or Son, in the birth of the idea in us. An education directed primarily to examinations is in a very real sense, indeed in the worst sense, atheistic. To have no care for the mind is to have no care for God. This is not really a digression from the supreme mystic experience, the plenitude of consciousness, which throws its roots down into every intellectual awakening, be it rational or imaginative. Here is a fine description of a moment of consciousness, in the *Confessions*.

And I marvelled to find that at last I loved You and not some phantom instead of You; yet I did not stably enjoy my God, but was ravished by You, by Your beauty, yet soon was torn away from You again by my own weight, and fell again with torment to lower things. Carnal habit was that weight. Yet the memory of You remained with me and I knew without doubt that it was You to whom I should cleave, though I was not yet such as could cleave to You: for the corruptible body is a load upon the soul, and the earthly habitation presses down the mind that muses upon many things. I was altogether certain that Your invisible things are clearly seen from the creation of the world, being understood by the things that are made: so too are Your everlasting power and Your Godhead. I was now studying the ground of my admiration for the beauty of bodies, whether celestial or of earth, and on what authority I might rightly judge of things mutable and say: 'This ought to be so, and that not so.' Enquiring then what was the source of my judgement, when I did so judge, I had discovered the immutable and true eternity of truth above my changing mind. Thus by stages I passed from bodies to the soul which uses the body for its perceiving, and from this to the soul's inner power, to which the body's senses present external things, as indeed the beasts are able; and from there I passed on to the reasoning power, to which is referred for judgement what is received from the body's senses. This too realized that it was mutable in me, and rose to its own understanding. It withdrew my thought from its habitual way, abstracting from the confused crowds of phantasms that it might find what light suffused it, when with utter certainty it cried aloud that the immutable was to be preferred to the mutable, and how it had come to know the immutable itself; for if it had not come to some knowledge of the immutable, it could not have known it as certainly preferable to the mutable. Thus in the thrust of a trembling glance my mind arrived at That Which Is. Then indeed I saw clearly Your invisible things which are understood by the things that are made; but I lacked the strength to hold my gaze fixed, and my weakness was beaten back again so that I returned to my old habits, bearing nothing with me but a memory of delight and a desire as for something of which I had caught the fragrance but which I had not yet the strength to eat.[1]

Notice the conviction he obtains, of a certainty 'that truth is', that is firmer even than the certainty of his own existence. Of what can a man be more certain than of himself; are not self and certainty almost synonymous? Indeed they are. St. Augustine's greater certainty is born of the contact with a firmer self than that of everyday experience. The implication is 'here I am, in eternity and from eternity and for eternity'. He doesn't bring out this implication, perhaps for fear of being misunderstood, although he dares to say, in another place, *Deus meus, forma mea*.

I'm afraid that anyone who is being trained in linguistic analysis will by now have stepped off my band-wagon. May I just say, in my own defence, that I have managed by this line of talk to convert a logical analyst—not to Catholicism, for he was a pious Catholic already—but to the beginnings of a possibility of an intellectual as well as a purely pietistic approach to God. He couldn't see God as an object of consciousness, but he could

---

[1] *The Confessions of St. Augustine*, translated by F. J. Sheed, p. 117.

begin to think of him as the wholeness of consciousness. This
confirmed a suspicion that I already harboured: that there is
a clean jump from logical analysis to 'the mystical'—the expression, significantly, is Wittgenstein's, not mine. Logical analysis
has in fact cleaned up a lot of muddled talk about God, the muddle
being due to a failure to attend to consciousness, to that which
escapes us and yet pervades us. This muddled talk makes God real
in the wrong sort of way; I heard it said of a certain scholastic
lecturer that he presented the proof of God's existence with such
dexterity that one expected the door to open at any minute and
God to come in. He tried to make God real instead of letting
God declare his own reality. He did what so many writers on
religious subjects do: dragged the elusive reality from its position
at the corner of the eye to the forefront of vision. And that is
where nonsense is talked about it, because it doesn't belong
there.

2

The Catholic artist finds himself inhabiting two different
worlds. The one is simple. Of course his art poses problems, but
there is an underlying simplicity, and the existence of problems
only indicates that this has not yet been attained. The other is
complex. And what puzzles him rather is the fact that it is in the
complex world, not the simple one, that he is supposed to be in
touch with supreme reality. He must somehow believe that the
simple state of self-realization that he knows, in blessed moments,
in his art, is—well, it is not the one thing that matters, and that
the one thing that matters doesn't take the form of a state of self-
realization. At its simplest, this one thing that matters is an
affaire à deux between him and God, and then there's the whole
gamut of sacraments and dogma. And even the *affaire à deux* is less
simple than what he knows, sometimes, in his art. There, there
is only one, a reality that he sometimes just *is*, and he must
sometimes be tempted, just a little tempted, to wonder why
religion isn't like that. You can't help believing in what is simplest,
provided of course you are completely absorbed in it. You

remember (one of you created her) Nanda Grey in *Frost in May*, repeating like a charm Augustine's 'Late have I loved thee, beauty ancient and new', not knowing quite who or what she was addressing but knowing it wasn't God, God who claimed her allegiance as a person to whom one must be faithful and who is offended by her moral faults, the very personal but not very intimate God of Confession, chapel, and sermons in chapel. If he reads a little outside the normal religious curriculum, he may find a guilty delight in Eckhart's saying 'God is not good. I am good'; he may sense a blessed repose beyond the God of religion and morals—but that's not orthodox, of course, and so he continues to plod the weary road of religious practice. The well-meant assurances of priests, that 'feelings don't matter', doesn't quite meet his case, because he knows a world where feelings do matter and are integrated into a simple state of self-realization. In that world he is spiritually mature, he has tasted the real thing; it is this, and not the fact that prayer is difficult for the person who is not an artist, it is this that makes him wonder about the religious 'real thing'.

The artist seeks a 'condition of complete simplicity', but religion seems to offer a mechanism of salvation. For the artist, every trembling leaf has God in it. Religion tells him that God is in the Host in a unique way. It admits the immanence of God in everything, but that is another matter; and so complication gets in at once. The artist can't see how God can be more in one thing than in another. Yet his simplicity is not the simplicity of pantheism, which is a philosophical short-cut, but is the fruit of an intense and prolonged discipline of contemplation and submission.

But religion has more in it than religious people generally suspect. What I want to do now is to take two doctrines which are quite crucial, as a navigator takes two bearings: I want then to suggest where they cut. And then I just want to talk. Two doctrines, then, a suggested point of intersection, then a Upanishad.

The first doctrine is creation in the Word. All things were

made through him, and without him was nothing made. That which was made was life in him. This doctrine asserts, or at least implies, that the question how the Infinite could produce the finite, the question that bothered Prendergast the parson in Evelyn Waugh's *Decline and Fall*, is one of those bothers laid by God upon the sons of men, as Ecclesiastes wrily puts it, but that it does not bother God. *There* certainly is a state of simplicity. God is not confronted with a finite world. He has only his Word, in whom he sees all that is, sees it as himself, his self-affirmation. There indeed is the vision for which the artist craves, a point of view in which 'reality' is synonymous with self-realization.

Now if you try, as a philosopher, to 'add up' the generation of the Word and the creation, making the former a kind of pre-creation, a stage between God and the world, you get the primordial heresy, some sort of emanationism. That is because you are using the doctrine wrongly. It is not the answer to the question 'How does God create?' It indicates a point of view, God's, which is not qualified by creation, yet in which creation is contained. Understand it from your point of view, as a thinker, and you get it wrong. The doctrine of creation in the Word is the great doctrine of God's point of view.

But now look at my second doctrine. It says that by the grace of God we share the sonship of Christ. The sonship of Christ is his eternal generation as the Word of God. By grace *we* are born of God, we are enclosed within the eternal birth of the Word. In grace, then (and here is my cut), we are the wisdom of God, in which all reality is seen in God. We are in the point of view in which there is only self-realization, in which the problem of creation does not arise, in which the finite is seen in the infinite; *as* the infinite, St. Thomas will say, commenting the words 'that which was made was life in him'. It would be nonsense to say we only have the Word's point of view, not the Father's, because they are the same: the Word *is* the Father's point of view.

I have made my fix, and now I step out of the chartroom and stand on deck. I now know where I am—on the chart. But now, here I am, at sea. The night sky, whose irregular pattern of stars holds the eye and the mind through the eye; the feel of the inaudible seawind; the scent of the sea; the sound of the water, immemorial sound of sea-travel—all this is one, it is simply 'this'. Then, as surely as 'this', I know 'not this'. As surely, because it is the very ground of my knowing 'this', the very meaning of 'this'. It is not that I know something else than this, for that would be distracting me from this. 'Not-this' is not something other than this, but is the meaning of 'this'.

The night has given a new direction to my senses, I am passive to it, it moulds me. But what is it that receives the shape of the night? Doubtless it is something that can receive any shape, and is therefore in itself shapeless, but this shapelessness is the very opposite of indefinite. It is not unthinkable in the way that pure vagueness is unthinkable. It is not nothing, turned by the night into 'this'. It *makes* 'this'. Its formlessness is not indefiniteness but infinity.

This truth, that is so difficult to express in its naked reality, is very easily expressed symbolically. In its gentle way, all nature teaches it. Thus light is the negation of colour, yet its condition. It is not something vague, waiting for some colour to give it precision. Its lack of colour is its power to take colour, nay to give it, for without it coloured objects have no colour. Silence, for the musician, takes a curious and agonizing precedence over music. It is a trembling infinity, in which he tries to realize wholly the melody. The melody will be perfect if, in a sense, it never leaves the silence, as the Word never leaves the silent bosom of the Father. Coming down to the point of rhythm, the beat as audible in its mesh of melody and tone-colour, the beat that can be put on to the metronome, is not the true beat, and a musician for whom it is has no sense of rhythm. Witness traditional jazz, which has a wholly unprofitable sadness about it. For the dancer,

> except for the point, the still point,
> There would be no dance, and there is only the dance.

22+

Yes, it is easy to express in this symbolic way, the way of the artist. But that of which it is the symbol, that which is the pure meaning of the mysterious precedence of negation over affirmation that I find everywhere is not so easy to express thus. Yet much simpler. For if it is negation that gives meaning, here is pure negation: not just no-colour, or silence, but 'not-this'. And if the silence always loses something in becoming sound, fails to embrace sound completely, 'not-this' does embrace 'this', and, not so embraced, 'this' is nothing at all.

Inside, the mess-room piano is banging out one of 'the top twenty'. An unprofitable sadness? Not entirely, on second thoughts. This completely unsubtle rhythm burlesques for me the captive notion of human life, the notion that the only reality is 'this' without not-this, sound without silence, colour without light. There, in the background of the night, is one version of the human condition, manifestly and innocently absurd. As such it fits very well into the night, which is a night of manifestation, *avertissement*, not romance. I bless them for the noise they are making. It comes into the meaning.

The point is that 'this' is not the starting point. But in ceasing to be the starting point it becomes, for the first time, completely significant. Everything is made anew, 'the sea explodes on the rocks in a different language'. 'In the soul of the believer', says Eckhart, 'all things pass from their existence into their being.'

'This is not the starting point' does not mean that something else is. It means that 'not-this is the starting point'. I seem to have got into an inverted logic, according to which non-being is the heart of being.

Theology talks of God by negations. It takes 'this' as the starting point, and *then* denies 'this' of God. It takes the mind on to an end in which it is lost. But tonight the mind seems to be lost in its beginning. The denial does not follow the affirmation of objects around me: it precedes it, gives it meaning, and what is affirmed as 'this' is no longer objects, any more than the hazel nut that our Lord showed to Julian of Norwich, lying in the palm of her hand, was an object. The artist, too, embarks on this kind of *via negativa*. For him the silence precedes and 'makes' the sound, makes its reality as opposed to its sheer meaningless impact.

In the beginning was the Word, the Word wholly meaningful, wholly within silence. This is true *now*. It means 'this is not the starting point'. How much of our lives is based on the opposite assumption, that 'in the beginning was the situation'. This comes about naturally. Things seem to stand *over against* nothing, to be a triumph over nothingness. They assault our mind with their solid being. They get into the one position where they will not let us see.

In realizing 'not-this', I have stepped back from being thus filled with things, from 'this'. But where have I stepped back to? Not into a private self, a private history for which 'this' is but an episode, but into the self, or place, of meaning, the point whence the world is transfigured with meaning.

If I am a romantic, 'the infinite', tonight, means a womb of reverie into which I can plunge by exploiting to the full the imprecision of the objects around me. But there is a quite other way in which objects can cease to be objects: when the infinite is within. Then 'this' receives the precision of meaning, *la pointe acérée de l'infinie*.

Theology normally takes two complementary ways. It says that God is expressed in the world, that the world bears his impress, but inadequately. It says, in the other way, that God is infinitely other, that we can only say what he is not, not what he is. Expression in the world, denial of the world. But at the starting point both ways meet and are changed. For there, denial is the very meaning of what we see and sense. There the senses are crucified not by an imposed ascesis but by the denial that is their meaning. There the Cross is not an imposed ascesis but what it originally is: the horizontal bar of experience cut by the vertical tree of meaning and so made all-embracing.

In thought we must affirm before we deny. Yet when meaning begins to declare itself, when the composer begins to sense the silence as that out of which music will come, all things cry out in the opposite sense: denial is the source of affirmation.

The yew hedge in the bright sunlight. As long as you scrutinize it you will never see its meaning. You must change your position, not to another bearing, another position relative to it, but to that which, relative to it, is no position: that is the starting point.

Colour without light is no colour, and the colour is not the light. Experience without meaning is no experience, and the experience is not the meaning. When the experience comes into the meaning, you are no longer 'the experiencer', you are not the shifting subject of experience, you are at the starting point.

Simplicity is not the denial of the complex but its meaning. Unity is not the denial of multiplicity but its meaning. It looks as though we shall have to discard the language of denial, in our attempt to articulate the starting point. For 'not-this' implies, by a necessity of language, that 'this' does come first. Can we think of a denial that does not bear *on* anything but that bears all things, carries them in the womb of meaning? Perhaps we can't, but that is where we start.

All, absolutely all experience, even the highest mystical experience, is coloured. The vision at Ostia is coloured with Augustine. The reality is uncoloured and universal, the reality of all things, known in God not from the standpoint of experience. Augustine knew this, but he could not write it down, for the *Confessions* are a document of experience. The vision that embraces the vision at Ostia embraces likewise the sands of Ostia. Only the mystic sees the vision, but the mystic knows that the vision is not for him. That is why he sees the vision. He sees in the medium of God, not of himself. In that medium, things are not what they do to us: they are life in the Word, as St. John says. They pass from their existence into their being, their original place, as Eckhart says. And as they are carried away from the ego, so the seer is carried away. So Eckhart will say 'he who contemplates, and does not realize that God alone contemplates, makes himself to be God'. This lifting, of the soul and of the sands, is all one: it is God speaking his original Word: it is reality, the true starting point, declaring itself. *Ego principium qui et loquor vobis.*

What is it, this starting point, this silence that is meaning? The silence is not *broken* by the music but *makes* the music. We must think of the original silence that is not broken by the Word but speaks the Word: to which the Word is not the opposite but connatural. We are beyond the opposition of word and silence, of form and infinity. From every other standpoint they are opposed. Form means limitation. Here it is the face of the infinite. Here form does not mean limitation, any more than infinity means indefiniteness. Here the Word does not break the silence, any more than silence is the absence of the Word. We are at the heart of things, where words are reversed. Here we deny before we affirm, and the affirmation is the form of the denial. Here, 'not-this' is not the opposite of 'this' but its heart. Everywhere else 'nothing will come of nothing', and what comes stands over against nothing. Here there is no opposition. It is only here that things ultimately make sense, in the Word that is the form of silence. We live everywhere else, but we are here, and everywhere else sends us back here.

The poet breaks into song, but the silence makes the song. The poet breaks the silence, but the silence makes the poem. The artist forms the indefinite, but the infinitive gives the form. The artist puts something in the place of what is not: but that is only a point, under which 'what is not' gives form.

It is extraordinary, this meeting, in which what seems to come first, experience, gives way to what is really first and all-embracing. The point of intersection, the place of meeting, even the meeting itself pre-exists our meeting. The point of intersection of the Cross is prior to the tree and cross-beam. This is the logic of the Cross, which sets the whole world in reverse. For the geometrician, the point is merely the resultant of the meeting. From the other point of view, the point is the origin out of which the meeting grows, so that the latter is more than meeting, is the still point become the meaningful dance. From the ordinary point of view it is an inverted logic. But there is nothing of permanent value in the way of poetry, in what poets have to say about their art, in the techniques of music and the dance, that does not endorse it and urge it on the pupil. There may be no

22*

general theory of aesthetics, but there is one golden rule: what you are aiming at is already; what you think you are trying to say will either say itself or it will not be said.

We return, from the moment of consciousness, to our habitual way of seeing the world, and we continue to stake our lives on this incomplete vision. The prophet and the sage make us more aware of this dialectic, but Christ brings it to a crisis. His impact in the gospel differs from that of the sage by its violent and crucial character. The sage shows us the vision where the world is upside-down. Christ, we might almost say, turns it physically upside-down. The sage opens a perspective beyond this world. Christ opens this perspective under our feet. This brings him to the Cross. The Cross is the symbol of reality, if we will understand it. But with God nailed to it, God the victim of his own reality, it becomes a challenge, ignoring which we do not live at all. We stake our lives on this world as we see it: God stakes his life on the Cross. The dialectic becomes an either-or. The Christian is not only in the Word, in vision: he is in Christ, in life. The world is not only transfigured, but transformed. That is the sacrament, the *mysterium*, of the body and blood. And yet there remains only the vision. The vision is not supplemented but implemented. When St. Paul sees Christ reconciling by the blood of the Cross all things whether in heaven or on earth, that is the simple vision, with a tragic density, a dark side where it is grappling with our flesh and blood. Thus the task of the artist becomes more serious. In so far as he enjoys the vision he is in touch with the pains of Calvary. He may not enjoy it otherwise. He may not enjoy, have joy in, less than the vision, which is, until this world ends, an affair of blood.

So ends the Upanishad. *Shantih shantih shantih.*

3

Are we any farther now with the problem with which we started, the relation between consciousness and theology? Objective theology, we can now say, gives the bearings and suggests the fix: but then I have to start again and make my

Upanishad, wherein the meaning of theology may show. The conflict between theology and consciousness arises when the former fails to realize that its meaning lies beyond its terms, beyond the world of objects: is in fact the divine vision, the *deificum lumen*, in which there are no objects. What so often happens is that theology, in the attempt to meet our spiritual needs, becomes prematurely mystical and offers, as its heart, an existential relation between the soul and God, a relation conceived in the language of objects, animated with existentialist rhetoric. Thus the real centre, which is beyond the idea of relation, is cut off. Historically it was in the high period of scholasticism, when theology was limited to its objective sphere and accepted the complexities imposed by this limitation, that the great mystics of simplicity, the metaphysical mystics, flourished. The artist, whose aim is simplicity, is at issue with an ill-conceived, encroaching theology, not with the traditional scholastic theology, so much duller, so much more complicated, and adding up, blessedly, to nothing. And when it has taught us to be nothing, then begins the vision. The keyword for this is consciousness. That word, as it is often used today, stands for an idea that I find quite fascinating—and this leads me to say what I want to do in this paper. It might have been expected that, having stated the artist's problems, I should propose the theological solution of those problems. I'm afraid I shall not. I have a huge problem of my own as a theologian, which I suspect is analogous to the problems of the Christian artist. My problem is to wed successfully my theological knowledge and the idea of consciousness. The problem touches the artist's in so far as the idea of consciousness is congenial to him as an expression of the *summum bonum*. So I may hope that as I wrestle with my problem he may get some light on his. First, then, I shall describe the idea of consciousness as I see it. Then I shall bring in theology, and see how the two get on together. Then we may proceed, tentatively, to the espousals.

Have I got it right, then, this problem of the artist who is a Catholic? As an artist, he desires, and sometimes blessedly enjoys, a vision that is, from the ordinary point of view, impersonal. But his Christianity reminds him that he has a soul to save. Hence arises a tension, a sense of guilt. What I have been trying to show is that theology can alter completely the sense of this tension by indicating its deepest treasure, the vision of God, in which we see with God's eyes. The artist may then come to see that his impersonal vision is not taking him *away* from the primary Christian concern, but is not taking him *far enough*. He may learn, not to retreat from the impersonal viewpoint to a point where love can more easily have place and meaning, but to let that very different thing, the love of God, come to birth where no purely human love can be born. That is the Holy Spirit who, proceeding from the Father and the Son, completes the divine movement, brings the dance into the stillness it has never lost. It is the circle which embraces the Cross, the circle whose law is at once the point and the Cross. The Irish Cross is the most wonderful symbol of the Trinity. Can it be like this, he wonders when, in moments of vision, there is no ego. Does he, in this state, feel the slightest desire to do good? But the disappearance of egoism may feel like the disappearance of morality. Christ does not tell us to transpose our egoism to a higher plane, but to break with it. The beginning to be good may feel like an unconcern to do good. Of course this is absurdly oversimplified. I am not saying that the artist's transcendence of egoism is the Christian transcendence. It is not a question of what his art does for him, but of what it may show him. And what it shows, theology declares in its fullness, and with the authority of Christ, the divine viewpoint made flesh. What his art shows, seen in this fuller light, may very well dictate for a time—self-denial as an art is far more radical than that dictated by a Christianized egoism. May I conclude by interpreting, in the sense of the foregoing, some lines of Eliot?

> We had the experience, but missed the meaning,
> And approach to the meaning restores the experience
> In a different form, beyond any meaning
> We can assign to happiness.

When you are *there*, when experience has been transfigured with meaning, you who experienced are no more. There is happiness without anyone to be happy. Yet to live there is to be happy beyond any conception of happiness. When St. Paul says that eye hath not seen nor ear heard nor hath it entered into the heart of man, what God has prepared for those that love him, he is saying far more than 'it's even better than you think'. He is pointing to the vision, in which we see in God, not from ourselves. That is the end. For the Christian, born of God, it is the starting point.